# The SIOP® Model for Teaching History-Social Studies to English Learners

**Deborah J. Short**
*Center for Applied Linguistics, Washington, DC*
*Academic Language Research & Training, Arlington, VA*

**MaryEllen Vogt**
*California State University, Long Beach*

**Jana Echevarría**
*California State University, Long Beach*

**With contributions by**
**Robin Liten-Tejada**
*Arlington, VA Public Schools*
**John Seidlitz**
*Seidlitz Education*

Boston   Columbus   Indianapolis   New York   San Francisco   Upper Saddle River
Amsterdam   Cape Town   Dubai   London   Madrid   Milan   Munich   Paris   Montreal   Toronto
Delhi   Mexico City   Sao Paulo   Sydney   Hong Kong   Seoul   Singapore   Taipei   Tokyo

## Dedication

*This book is dedicated to all the teachers who are committed to teaching English learners the content and language of the social sciences using the SIOP® Model. May you discover new learnings for yourself within. This book is for YOU!*

Vice President, Editor-in-Chief:   *Aurora Martinez Ramos*
Editorial Assistant:   *Meagan French*
Marketing Manager:   *Amanda Stedke*
Marketing Manager:   *Danae April*
Production Editor:   *Gregory Erb*
Editorial Production Service:   *Nesbitt Graphics, Inc.*
Manufacturing Buyer:   *Megan Cochran*
Electronic Composition:   *Nesbitt Graphics, Inc.*
Interior Design:   *Nesbitt Graphics, Inc.*
Photo Researcher:   *Annie Pickert*
Cover Designer:   *Linda Knowles*

For Professional Development resources visit www.pearsonpd.com.

Credits and acknowledgments borrowed from other sources and reproduced, with permission, in this textbook appear on appropriate page within text or on page 228.

Library of Congress Cataloging-in-Publication Data

Short, Deborah.
 The SIOP model for teaching history-social studies to English learners /
Deborah J. Short, MaryEllen Vogt, Jana Echevarria ; with contributions by
Robin Liten-Tejada, John Seidlitz.
    p. cm.
 Includes bibliographical references and index.
 ISBN 978-0-205-62761-5
 1.  English language--Study and teaching--Foreign speakers. 2.
History--Study and teaching--English-speaking countries. 3.  Social
studies--Study and teaching--English-speaking countries. 4.  Lesson
planning.  I. Vogt, MaryEllen. II. Echevarria, Jana, 1956- III. Title.

 PE1128.A2S52 2011
 428.0071--dc22

                                                    2010022903


10 9 8 7 6 5 4        EBM 14 13 12

www.pearsonhighered.com        ISBN-10: 0-205-62761-7
                               ISBN-13: 978-0-205-62761-5

**Deborah J. Short** is a professional development consultant and a senior research associate at the Center for Applied Linguistics in Washington, DC. She co-developed the SIOP® Model for sheltered instruction and has directed national research studies on English language learners funded by the Carnegie Corporation, the Rockefeller Foundation, and the U.S. Dept. of Education. She recently chaired an expert panel on adolescent ELL literacy. As the director of Academic Language Research & Training, Dr. Short provides professional development on sheltered instruction and academic literacy around the U.S. and abroad. She has numerous publications, including the SIOP® book series and five ESL textbook series for National Geographic/Hampton-Brown. She has taught English as a second/foreign language in New York, California, Virginia, and the Democratic Republic of Congo.

**MaryEllen Vogt** is Professor Emerita of Education at California State University, Long Beach. Dr. Vogt has been a classroom teacher, reading specialist, special education specialist, curriculum coordinator, and university teacher educator. She received her doctorate from the University of California, Berkeley, and is a co-author of fifteen books, including *Reading Specialists and Literacy Coaches in the* Real *World* (3rd ed., 2011) and the SIOP® book series. Her research interests include improving comprehension in the content areas, teacher change and development, and content literacy and language acquisition for English learners. Dr. Vogt was inducted into the California Reading Hall of Fame, received her university's Distinguished Faculty Teaching Award, and served as President of the International Reading Association in 2004–2005.

**Jana Echevarría** is a Professor Emerita at California State University, Long Beach. She has taught in elementary, middle, and high schools in general education, special education, ESL, and bilingual programs. She has lived in Taiwan, Spain, and Mexico. An internationally known expert on second language learners, Dr. Echevarría is a Fulbright Specialist. Her research and publications focus on effective instruction for English learners, including those with learning disabilities. Currently, she is Co-Principal Investigator with the Center for Research on the Educational Achievement and Teaching of English Language Learners (CREATE) funded by the U.S. Department of Education, Institute of Education Sciences (IES). In 2005, Dr. Echevarría was selected as Outstanding Professor at CSULB.

**Robin Liten-Tejada** has taught ESOL in Arlington (VA) Public Schools since 1986. She received National Board Certification in 2001, and was the 2002 Arlington Teacher of the Year and the 2003 Virginia Region IV Teacher of the Year. She is currently the Secondary ESOL Specialist in Arlington. She writes curriculum and conducts numerous workshops for teachers in Grades K–12 on effective strategies for teaching language learners, including training in the SIOP® Model. Ms. Liten-Tejada was one of the original teacher-researchers in the first project that developed and field-tested the SIOP® Model for the National Center for Research on Education, Diversity & Excellence. Prior to that, she participated in another national study, "Integrating Language and Culture in the Social Studies," for the National Center for Research on Cultural Diversity and Second Language Learning. Both of these studies were funded by the U.S. Department of Education.

**John Seidlitz** is an independent consultant and author of *Sheltered Instruction Plus: A Guide for Texas Teachers of English Learners* and of *Navigating the ELPS: Using New Standards to Improve Instruction for English Learners.* As co-developer with Bill Perryman of Perspective-based Learning™ he works with teachers throughout the country implementing strategies that promote academic language development for all students and the use of perspective in the classroom. For several years, John served as a SIOP® National Faculty member. He is a former social studies and ESL teacher and secondary ESL program coordinator. He also worked as an educational specialist for ESC Region 20 in San Antonio and South Texas.

**Pisethkoma Phat** illustrated the activities for the K–2 unit in Chapter 5. Piseth came to the United States from his native Cambodia in February 2009 at age 17. He is currently a student at Arlington Mill High School Continuation Program in Arlington, VA, and he is learning English. He started drawing at age 7 and hopes to become a pharmacist.

# contents

*Preface*    ix

## 1 The Academic Language of History and Social Studies    1

What Is Academic Language?    3

How Is Academic Language Manifested in the Classroom?    5

What Is the Academic Language of Social Studies and History?    8

Why Do English Learners Have Difficulty with Academic Language?    12

How Can We Effectively Teach Academic Language with the SIOP® Model?    15

   Academic Vocabulary    16

   Oral Discourse    17

Concluding Thoughts    22

## 2 Activities and Techniques for SIOP® History-Social Studies Lessons: Lesson Preparation, Building Background, Comprehensible Input, & Strategies    24

Mr. Michaels's Vignette    24

Introduction    25

History and Social Studies Techniques and Activities    26

Lesson Preparation    27

   Building Language Objectives from Content Objectives    28

   Differentiating Sentence Starters    30

Building Background    31

   Concrete Personal Experiences    31

   Post a Connection    34

   Oh Yesterday + Year!    35

   Predict Definitions    36

   Vocabulary Scan    38

Comprehensible Input    40

   Prop Box Improv    40

   Listen for Information    42

   Move It!    44

Strategies    45

   Highlight Key Information in Text    46

   Cut and Match Answers    47

   Expert/Novice    49

Concluding Thoughts    51

**3** **Activities and Techniques for SIOP® History-Social Studies Lessons: Interaction, Practice & Application, Lesson Delivery, Review & Assessment** 52

  **Introduction** 52

  **Interaction** 53

    Structured Conversations 53

    Learning Styles Debate 55

    You Are There 56

  **Practice & Application** 58

    Reader's Theater 58

    Living Diorama 60

    Partner Listening Dictation 62

    Go Graphic – One Step Further 63

  **Lesson Delivery** 64

    Group Response with a White Board 65

    Chunk and Chew Review 66

    Stand Up/Sit Down 68

  **Review & Assessment** 70

    Oral Number 1–3 for Self-Assessment 71

    Self-Assessment Rubrics 72

    Number Wheels 73

    Whip Around, Pass Option 76

    Numbered Heads Together with Movement 77

    Differentiated Tickets Out 79

  **Concluding Thoughts** 80

  **Revisiting Mr. Michaels** 80

**4** **SIOP® History and Social Studies Unit Design and Lesson Planning** 82

  **Ms. Parry's Vignette** 82

  **Introduction** 84

  **SIOP® Unit Design** 85

    SIOP® Unit Planner 1 85

    SIOP® Unit Planner 2 87

  **SIOP® Lesson Planning** 87

    Technology in SIOP® Lessons 91

    SIOP® History-Social Studies Lesson Formats 93

  **Concluding Thoughts** 95

**5** **SIOP® Social Studies Unit, Grades K–2** 97

  **Introduction** 97

  **Past and Present** 98

Unit Overview, Grades K–2    98

SIOP® Lesson Plan 1: My Personal Timeline    101

SIOP® Lesson Plan 2: My Life in Past and Present    103

SIOP® Lesson Plan 3: Comparing the Past to the Present    104

SIOP® Lesson Plan 4: How Do You Know It's from the Past?    107

SIOP® Lesson Plan 5: Living in the Past and Present    108

SIOP® Lesson Plan 6: Flipping from the Past to Present    110

**Concluding Thoughts**    111

## 6 SIOP® Social Studies Unit, Grades 3–5    112

**Introduction**    112

*Where in the World Are You?*    113

Unit Overview, Grades 3–5    113

SIOP® Lesson Plan 1: What's the Location?    116

SIOP® Lesson Plan 2: What's My Hemisphere?    118

SIOP® Lesson Plan 3: Maps and Globes Reader's Theater    120

SIOP® Lesson Plan 4: Maps and Globes: Student-Generated Writing    122

SIOP® Lesson Plan 5: Latitude and Longitude    123

SIOP® Lesson Plan 6: Map and Globe Terms Review    126

**Concluding Thoughts**    127

## 7 SIOP® U.S. History Unit, Grades 6–8    128

**Introduction**    128

*Causes of the American Revolution*    **129**

Unit Overview, Grades 6–8    129

**Grades 6–8 Unit**    131

SIOP® Lesson Plan 1: Mercantilism    131

SIOP® Lesson Plan 2: The Effects of the French and Indian War    133

SIOP® Lesson Plan 3: Controversial Acts of Parliament    135

SIOP® Lesson Plan 4: Boston Massacre    138

**Concluding Thoughts**    140

## 8 SIOP® Global History Unit, Grades 9–12    141

**Introduction**    141

*Containing Communism After World War II*    142

Unit Overview, Grades 9–12    142

**Lesson Topics**    144

SIOP® Lesson Plan 1: Red Scare    147

SIOP® Lesson Plan 2: The Marshall Plan    150

SIOP® Lesson Plan 3: The Truman Doctrine    152

SIOP® Lesson Plan 4: The Formation of NATO    154

SIOP® Lesson Plan 5: The Berlin Airlift    157

**Concluding Thoughts**    159

**9 Pulling It All Together** 161
    What We Have Learned   161
    What Our SIOP® History and Social Studies Contributors Have Learned   163
    Final Thoughts   164

*Appendix A: SIOP® Protocol and Component Overview*   165

*Appendix B: Academic Social Studies and History Vocabulary Based on Sample State Standards*   171
    Grades K–2   171
    Grades 3–5   173
    Grades 6–8   177
    Grades 9–12   181

*Appendix C: List of Activities and Techniques by Social Science Subject Area and Grade Level*   185

*Appendix D: Blackline Masters*   187
    BLM 1   **My Personal Timeline**   188
    BLM 2   **My Personal Timeline Sentences**   189
    BLM 3   **My Life in the Past and Present (Venn Diagram)**   190
    BLM 4   **My Life in the Past and Present Activity Sheet**   191
    BLM 5   **How Can We Tell That This Is from the Past?**   192
    BLM 6   **Is It Past or Present? (images)**   193
    BLM 7   **Is It Past or Present? (chart)**   195
    BLM 8   **Is It Past or Present? Bingo**   198
    BLM 9   **Instructions for Making a Flipbook**   199
    BLM 10   **Can You Label the World Map?**   200
    BLM 11   **What's My Hemisphere? (short answer)**   201
    BLM 12   **What's My Hemisphere? (multiple choice)**   202
    BLM 13   **Reader's Theater Script: Maps and Globes**   203
    BLM 14   **Reader's Theater Rubric: Maps and Globes**   204
    BLM 15   **Understanding Maps and Globes (paragraph)**   205
    BLM 16   **Understanding Maps and Globes (word bank)**   206
    BLM 17   **Vocabulary Word and Definition Cards**   207
    BLM 18   **Anticipation/Reaction Guide: The Effects of the French and Indian War**   211
    BLM 19   **British versus Colonist Points of View**   212
    BLM 20   **Truman Doctrine Speech—Adapted Text**   213
    BLM 21   **Truman Doctrine Speech—Original Text**   214
    BLM 22   **Argumentation Chart for Truman Doctrine**   218
    BLM 23   **NATO Pro–Con Chart**   219

*References*   220

*Index*   224

We have written this book in response to the many requests from teachers of social studies and history for specific application of the SIOP® Model to the social sciences. During our nearly fifteen years of working with the Model, we have learned that the subject you teach and for whom you teach it is a major consideration. Showing a SIOP® algebra lesson plan to a U.S. History teacher, along with the advice to "adapt it," has sometimes resulted in rolled eyes and under-the-breath comments like, "You've got to be kidding." A similar reaction has occurred when we have shown a physical science lesson video clip to elementary reading teachers and asked them to modify the techniques in their classes. Many teachers, whatever the subject area, prefer to see examples specific to their content and grade level.

So, this book is intended specifically for teachers of social studies, history, geography, civics, government, and economics, including elementary classroom teachers, secondary content teachers, ESL specialists, and SIOP® coaches. If you teach in grades K–2, 3–5 (or 6), 6–8, or 9–12, you'll find information about teaching the social sciences written specifically for your grade-level cluster. If you are an elementary teacher, an ESL specialist, SIOP® coach, or teacher educator, you may teach or support multiple subjects and so you may want to check out our companion books for teaching mathematics, science, and English-language arts within the SIOP® Model.

We offer an important caveat. This book has been written for teachers who have familiarity with the SIOP® Model. Our expectation is that you have read one of the core texts: *Making Content Comprehensible for English Learners: The SIOP® Model* (Echevarria, Vogt, & Short, 2008); or either *Making Content Comprehensible for Elementary English Learners: The SIOP® Model* (Echevarria, Vogt, & Short, 2010a) or *Making Content Comprehensible for Secondary English Learners: The SIOP® Model* (Echevarria, Vogt, & Short, 2010b). If you have not read one of these books or had substantial and effective professional development in the SIOP® Model, we ask that you save this book for later. We want this book to be just what you've been looking for, a resource that will enable you to more effectively teach your subject to your English learners and other students. Therefore, the more familiar you are with the philosophy, terminology, concepts, and teaching techniques associated with the SIOP® Model, the better you will be able to use this book. If you would like a brief refresher on the SIOP® Model, please read Appendix A, SIOP® Protocol and Component Overview.

The SIOP® Model is the only empirically validated model of sheltered instruction at present. Sheltered instruction or SDAIE (Specially Designed Academic Instruction in English), in general, is a means for making content comprehensible for English learners (ELs) while they are developing English proficiency. The SIOP® Model distinctively calls for teachers to promote academic language development along with comprehensible content. SIOP® classrooms may include a mix of native-English speaking students and English learners, or the classrooms may include only English learners. This depends on your school and district, the number of ELs you have in your school, and the availability of SIOP®-trained teachers. Whatever your context, what characterizes a sheltered SIOP® classroom is the systematic, consistent, and concurrent focus on teaching both academic content and academic language to English learners.

This book is intended to deepen your understanding of the SIOP® Model and provide more specific teaching ideas, lesson plans, and comprehensive unit plans for teaching history, social studies, and related subjects to English learners. Our overall goal is to help you master SIOP® lesson and unit planning, enabling you to incorporate the components and features of the SIOP® Model consistently in your classroom.

# *Organization and Purpose of This Book*

We have specifically written this book for you, elementary and secondary social studies educators who have already studied the SIOP® Model, read *Making Content Comprehensible for English Learners: The SIOP® Model* (Echevarria, Vogt, & Short, 2008), and are ready to enhance your SIOP® lessons with specific techniques that target your content area. In the book, you will read about a wide variety of instructional activities, many of which are effective for any grade level or social studies course. The readability of the textbooks, the depth and complexity of the concepts, and the language demands of the assignments change, of course, as the grade levels rise, but nearly all of the meaningful activities showcased here will work well with all students, including ELs, in grades K–12, enabling them to explore, practice, and apply key concepts and academic language. Therefore, we encourage you to review the lessons and units from grade-level clusters other than the one in which you teach. Throughout all of the techniques in Chapters 2 and 3 and the units and lesson plans in Chapters 5–8, you will find many teaching ideas and activities that truly span all grade levels and content areas, so please don't overlook them.

## Chapter 1: The Academic Language of History and Social Studies

Chapter 1 focuses on the academic language that students need to be successful in school. While it is true that ELs benefit from similar vocabulary learning strategies as other students, they generally need more explicit support in vocabulary development (more techniques, for example, that use realia and demonstrations, highlight cognates, identify words with multiple meanings, and focus on idiomatic speech). They need direct instruction in other aspects of academic language as well, namely the academic reading, writing, and oral discourse skills that characterize a history or social studies class. These aspects may be broad-based uses of language, such as how to record observations from a video clip, take notes from a lecture or reference material, compare different points of view, or construct an argument in a debate setting. Other aspects of academic language are more narrow and related to English grammar and usage, such as using transitions and cause-effect language properly, writing conditional sentences, and making sense of the passive voice. In this chapter, we also extract examples of how academic English is used in the various social sciences, so you can be more aware of potential pitfalls for ELs as well as language teaching opportunities.

## Chapters 2 and 3: Activities and Techniques for SIOP® History-Social Studies Lessons

Chapters 2 and 3 describe effective techniques that teachers may use in SIOP® history, social studies, geography, civics, government, and economics lessons and apply them to representative classrooms. Some of these techniques have been drawn from the *99 Ideas and Activities for Teaching with the SIOP® Model* (Vogt & Echevarria, 2007) and others were suggested or created by our contributors, SIOP®-trained history-social studies educators Robin Liten-Tejada and John Seidlitz. Many are not new techniques, but we have specialized them for social science topics and included scenarios that demonstrate their application at particular grade levels in subjects different from those in the later social studies and history units. As you read through the lesson applications in these chapters, pay close attention to how language is embedded into, for example, the contributions of ancient Chinese civilizations or the influence of human actions on the environment. You may be surprised how much language is involved in teaching historical concepts once you focus on it.

## Chapter 4: SIOP® History and Social Studies Unit Design and Lesson Planning

Chapter 4 focuses on SIOP® history and social studies unit design and lesson planning. We discuss guidelines for planning SIOP® lessons and offer two model unit planners to show how teachers can build a week-long unit that not only covers the regular curriculum but also enables students to make progress with their language development in all four domains over the course of several days. We describe two different lesson plan formats used in this book and explain how to incorporate the techniques and activities from Chapters 2 and 3 into lessons.

## Chapters 5–8: Sample SIOP® Social Studies and History Lessons and Units

In these chapters, four units are illustrated, one each for Grades K–2 (Chapter 5), 3–5 (Chapter 6), 6–8 (Chapter 7), and 9–12 (Chapter 8). Many social studies and history topics are taught in different grades across the United States so we felt the cluster approach would be most useful. Our contributors describe their planning process for each unit presented, discussing the objectives they highlighted and the standards they derived lessons from, the SIOP® techniques and activities they have chosen and placed within the five lessons, their selection of materials, and other goals they have.

You will find several "Think-Alouds" and "Planning Points" throughout these lesson plans through which the writers convey their decision-making process, such as when to teach key vocabulary terms and how to elicit more academic language from the ELs when they are working in groups. For those of you unfamiliar with "Think-Alouds," they are structured models of how successful readers, writers, and learners think about language and learning tasks (Baumann, Jones, & Seifer-Kessel, 1993; Oczkus, 2009). The "Planning Points" comments clarify and provide additional information, including lesson preparation tips. The lesson plans also include handouts the teachers might use with students, such as specific graphic organizers and charts.

## Chapter 9: Pulling It All Together

In Chapter 9, we conclude the book with some of our own thoughts, insights, and recommendations, as well as those from the content specialists and SIOP® experts who served as contributors to this book. We hope this chapter will help you pull it together as you continue your journey to effective SIOP® instruction.

## Appendixes

Several resources are available in the appendixes. Appendix A provides an overview of the SIOP® Model. Appendix B offers a sample of the academic history and social studies words found in state standards. Appendix C offers a list of the activities and techniques described in Chapters 2 and 3 by social science subject area (e.g., U.S. history, geography) and grade-level examples. Appendix D contains blackline masters of student handouts for the lessons found in Chapters 5–8.

To further assist you in creating a successful SIOP® classroom, remember that several other resources are also available. These include (in addition to the core texts mentioned previously): *99 Ideas and Activities for Teaching English Learners with the SIOP® Model* (Vogt & Echevarria, 2008); *Implementing the SIOP® Model through Effective Coaching and Professional Development* (Echevarria, Short, & Vogt, 2008); and *The SIOP® Model for Administrators* (Short, Vogt, & Echevarria, 2008).

## Acknowledgments

We acknowledge and appreciate the suggestions offered by the educators who reviewed this book. They include Maggie Beddow, CSU Sacramento; Peggy Brummett; Robin L. Gordon, Mount St. Mary's College; and Judith O'Loughlin, New Jersey City University.

To our Allyn & Bacon team, we express our gratitude for keeping us focused and on task and for its dedication to sharing information about the SIOP® Model. To Aurora Martínez, our incredible editor who never sleeps, we know that it has been through your understanding of the academic and language needs of the English learners in our schools that this series of books has been written on the SIOP® Model. Thank you, Aurora.

We have been most fortunate to have as our contributors to these content area books eight content specialists and SIOP® experts. Their insights, ideas, lesson plans, and unit designs across the grade-level clusters clearly demonstrate their expertise not only in their content areas, but also in the SIOP® Model. With deep gratitude we acknowledge the significant contributions of our colleagues: Robin Liten-Tejada and John Seidlitz (History-Social Studies); Hope Austin-Phillips and Amy Ditton (Science); Aracelli Avila and Melissa Castillo (Mathematics); and Karlin LaPorta and Lisa Mitchener (English-Language Arts). Their deep understanding of the SIOP® Model shines through in their teaching techniques, lesson plans, and units, and we thank them for their belief in and commitment to English learners and the SIOP® Model. We also heartily thank Pisethkoma Phat, our student illustrator for this SIOP® History and Social Studies book.

Finally, we acknowledge and express great appreciation to our families and the families of our contributors. The SIOP® Model would not exist if it hadn't been for their support and encouragement over all these years.

djs

mev

je

# The Academic Language of History and Social Studies

For the past decade, social studies, history, government, geography, and civics have been relatively neglected subjects in our school systems. Because they are not required to be tested through the No Child Left Behind legislation, these subjects have appeared less important than reading and math. Even science is tested now and thus has a more elevated status than in the past. Time for social studies instruction has been cut in elementary schools to make way for more time for reading and language arts and/or mathematics. Social studies has also been considered a less rigorous subject: the telling of stories, the revisiting of familiar things like your neighborhood and community workers, the sharing of information of cultures and traditions around the world. History has been the story of war and victors, geography, map reading. And we know how successful that has been with the ever-increasing sales of global positioning devices for vehicles!

Yet, take a good look around us. All major news stories revolve around the social sciences. Economics has been discussed in front page news articles since the U.S. economy failed in 2008. The government bailout of investment banks and U.S. corporations has made the roles and actions of various governmental institutions highly relevant. The presidential election of 2008 gave rise to widespread civic activism not seen in many years. Global terrorism, international wars in Iraq and Afghanistan, civil wars in Sudan, and the interplay of religion and territorial possession all have their origins in world history. Natural disasters from tsunamis, hurricanes, and earthquakes around the world have people poring over maps, learning names of cities in small countries and large.

When we read news stories, we need the background knowledge from our social studies courses in school to interpret them. We also need high levels of academic literacy because there are often nuances in the writing; perspectives and biases to parse. But how much do we remember and how well can we apply that knowledge? Consider the following from an article in the *Washington Post* (January 26, 2010, p. A-2):

> The federal debt exploded to an incomprehensible $12.1 trillion, and the nation continues on its path to becoming a wholly owned subsidiary of the People's Republic of China. Yet lawmakers can't even agree on a modest proposal to form an independent debt commission and then vote on its recommendations.
>
> The debt commission is expected to be voted down Tuesday morning, as foes on the far left and the far right unite to form a status quo supermajority. Prospects have become so bleak that a couple of retired congressional leaders got together Monday morning in hopes of shaming their former colleagues into action.

To understand these lines, we need to know the meanings of many terms. *Federal debt, wholly owned subsidiary,* and *debt commission* reflect economics. *Lawmakers, vote, far left, far right, status quo supermajority,* and *congressional leaders* refer to government. *People's Republic of China* calls to mind geography. Thus, to comprehend these two paragraphs, one needs to draw on knowledge of three of the social sciences, at least. In addition, we have polysemous words like *exploded* (was there an explosion in Washington recently?) and *path* (are we walking along a path?), and low frequency words like *modest, foes, bleak,* and *shaming* to define. There are inferences to make about these concepts and background knowledge to utilize. One needs to know, for example, that China holds much of our national debt; that a supermajority in Congress means legislation won't pass so things will stay the same (status quo); that retired congressional leaders might have some clout over the current members of Congress, and that the far left and the far right rarely unite.

Clearly to be well informed and active participants in our society, we need knowledge of the social sciences. Given that, how well are our students learning history, social studies, and related subjects? Although federal legislation does not require testing for these subjects the way it does for math, reading, and science, we do have occasional national assessments. The latest National Assessment of Educational Progress (NAEP) exams were in 2006 when a representative sample of students in grades 4, 8, and 12 were tested in history and civics. Also in 2006, the first economics assessment was given, although only to twelfth graders. The results are not outstanding for any of these three subjects. NAEP's performance levels are labeled Basic, Proficient, and Advanced. For no subject did the majority of the students at any grade level score Proficient or better (Lee & Weiss, 2007; Lutkus & Weiss, 2007; Mead & Sandene, 2007) as shown in Figure 1.1. Further, Hispanic students did worse than White and Asian/Pacific Islander students.

FIGURE 1.1   *Percentage of Students at "Proficient" or "Advanced" Levels on the NAEP Exams in 2006*

|  | *Fourth Graders* | *Eighth Graders* | *Twelfth Graders* |
|---|---|---|---|
| History | 20 | 18 | 14 |
| Civics | 25 | 24 | 32 |
| Economics | N/A | N/A | 45 |

Why don't more students reach the Proficient level in history, civics, or economics? One factor may be the reduced time available for instruction. Other factors may be the abstract concepts embedded in the curriculum, the heavy emphasis on reading textbooks and source materials, the high levels of required background knowledge, and the plethora of facts that are replete in standards and curricula. Education in the social sciences involves technical terms and associated concepts, explanations, comparative and cause-effect relationships, problems and solutions. Although history can be framed in a story-like context, students won't understand the stories if they don't know the words and they can't make connections to themselves, to other texts, or to their world. Language plays a large and important role in learning social studies, history, civics, government, and economics.

Despite being well read and well educated, we have all had experiences where we became lost when listening to or reading about a new topic we know little about. We're tripped up by the terminology, phrases, and concepts that are unique to the subject matter. When this happens, we may become frustrated and sometimes disinterested. However, we do not necessarily give up. Rather, we use our skills, we access additional resources, and we reach out to knowledgeable experts for the information or advice we need.

However, every day many English learners (ELs) sit in classrooms where the topic, the related words, and concepts are totally unfamiliar to them. Even immigrant students with strong educational backgrounds may never have studied U.S. History or the history of their new state. Other ELs may have familiarity with the topic, perhaps even some expertise, but because they don't know the English words and phrases, that is, the content-specific academic language, they are also unable to understand what is being taught. Comprehension can be compromised as well when they don't understand cause-effect sentence structures or the usage of such prepositions and conjunctions as *except, unless, but, despite,* or *however*. Moreover, they have not yet mastered how to use language and content resources to help them understand.

# What Is Academic Language?

Although definitions in the research literature differ somewhat, there is general agreement that academic language is both general and content specific. That is, many academic words are used across all content areas (such as *interpret, conflict, analyze, source*), whereas others pertain to specific subject areas (*constitution, revolutionary, medieval* for history; *investment, recovery,* and *income* for economics; *photosynthesis, mitosis, density,* and *inertia* for science). It is important to remember that academic language is more than specific content vocabulary words related to particular topics. Rather, academic language represents the entire range of language used in academic settings, including elementary and secondary schools. Consider the following definitions offered by several educational researchers:

- Academic language is "the language that is used by teachers and students for the purpose of acquiring new knowledge and skills . . . imparting new information, describing abstract ideas, and developing students' conceptual understandings" (Chamot & O'Malley, 1994, p. 40).

- Academic language refers to "word knowledge that makes it possible for students to engage with, produce, and talk about texts that are valued in school" (Flynt & Brozo, 2008, p. 500).

- "Academic English is the language of the classroom, of academic disciplines (science, history, literary analysis) of texts and literature, and of extended, reasoned discourse. It is more abstract and decontextualized than conversational English" (Gersten, Baker, Shanahan, Linan-Thompson, Collins, & Scarcella, 2007, p. 16).

- Academic English "refers to more abstract, complex, and challenging language that will eventually permit you to participate successfully in mainstream classroom instruction. Academic English involves such things as relating an event or a series of events to someone who was not present, being able to make comparisons between alternatives and justify a choice, knowing different forms, and inflections of words and their appropriate use, and possessing and using content-specific vocabulary and modes of expression in different academic disciplines such as mathematics and social studies" (Goldenberg, 2008, p. 9).

- "Academic language is the set of words, grammar, and organizational strategies used to describe complex ideas, higher-order thinking processes, and abstract concepts" (Zwiers, 2008, p. 20).

When you reflect on the above examples for history, economics, and science, you can see that academic language in English differs considerably from the social, conversational language which is used on the playground, at home, or at cocktail parties (see Figure 1.2). Social or conversational language is generally more concrete than abstract,

**FIGURE 1.2**  *The Spectrum of Academic Language*

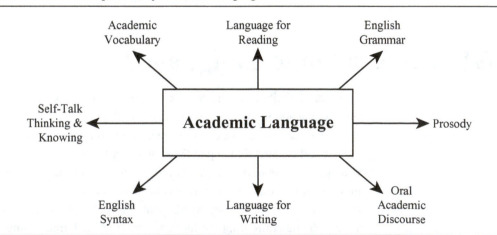

and it is usually supported by contextual clues, such as gestures, facial expressions, and body language (Cummins, 1979; 2000; Echevarria & Graves, 2007). Some educators suggest that the distinction between conversational and academic language is somewhat arbitrary and that it is the *situation, community,* or *context* that is either predominantly social or academic (Aukerman, 2007; Bailey, 2007).

For purposes of this book, we maintain that academic language is essential for success in school and that it is more challenging to learn than conversational English, especially for students who are acquiring English as a new language. Although knowing conversational language assists students in learning academic language, we must explicitly teach English learners (and other students, including native speakers) the "vocabulary, more complex sentence structures, and rhetorical forms not typically encountered in nonacademic settings" (Goldenberg, 2008, p. 13).

A focus on words, grammar, and oral and written discourse as applied in school settings is likely to increase student performance levels. Analyses of language used in assessments by Bailey and Butler (2007) found two types of academic language: content-specific language (e.g., technical terms such as *latitude* and *longitude*, and phrases such as "*The evidence points to . . .*") and general, or common core, academic language (e.g., persuasive terms, comparative phrases) that is useful across curricular areas. Similarly, there are general academic tasks that one needs to know how to do in order to be academically proficient (e.g., create a timeline, take notes) and more specific tasks (e.g., debate the pros and cons of seeking independence from England). They argue that teachers and curricula should pay attention to this full range of academic language. As a result, the enhancement of ELs' academic language skills should enable them to perform better on assessments. This conclusion is bolstered by Snow, et al. (1991) who found that performance on highly decontextualized (i.e., school-like) tasks, such as providing a formal definition of words, predicted academic performance whereas performance on highly contextualized tasks, such as face-to-face communication, did not.

# How Is Academic Language Manifested in the Classroom?

> Our teachers come to class,
> And they talk and they talk,
> Til their faces are like peaches,
> We don't;
> We just sit like cornstalks.
> (Cazden, 1976, p. 74)

These poignant words come from a Navajo child who describes a classroom as she sees it. Teachers like to talk. Just observe any classroom and you'll find that the teacher does the vast majority of the speaking. That might be expected because the teacher, after all, is the most expert person in the history or social studies classroom. However, for students to develop proficiency in language, interpret what they read and view, express themselves orally and in writing, participate during whole-group instruction and small-group interaction, and explain and defend their answers, they need opportunities to learn and use academic language.

Many of the visible manifestations of academic language use in the classroom come from the conversations between teacher and students, and on occasion among students. Most instructional patterns involve the teacher initiating a topic (I) usually by asking a question, a student responding (R), the teacher evaluating (E) the response or providing feedback (F), followed by another teacher-generated question (Cazden, 1986; 2001; Mehan, 1979; Watson & Young, 1986). A typical interaction between a teacher and students during a U.S. government lesson is illustrated in the following example:

T:    What are the three branches of government?

S1:   President and . . .

T:    No, the President is part of a branch. Who knows what it's called?

S2:   Executive.

T:    That's right. The executive branch includes the president and his staff, the vice president and staff, and the Cabinet agencies. Okay, who knows another branch?

And so it goes, often for a good portion of the lesson. Notice that the teacher asked questions that had a correct answer with no reasoning or higher level thinking required. The teacher controlled the interchange, and she evaluated student responses. Also note that the only person in the interchange to orally produce elaborated academic language (in this case, a brief explanation of the executive branch) was the teacher. The students didn't need to use more than one or two words in response to the teacher's questions in order to participate appropriately. But it is the students who need to practice using academic language, not the teacher! Further, only two students were involved; the others were quiet.

The Initiation-Response-Evaluation/Feedback (IRE/F) pattern is quite typical and it has been found to be one of the least effective interactional patterns for the classroom (Cazden, 1986; 2001; Mehan, 1979; Watson & Young, 1986). More similar to an interrogation than to a discussion, this type of teacher–student interaction stifles academic language development and does not encourage higher level thinking because most of the questions have a straightforward, known answer. Further, we have observed from kindergarten through high school that most students become conditioned to wait for someone else to answer. Often it is the teacher who ultimately answers his or her own question, if no students volunteer. And the teacher elaborates, as in the third and fifth lines above.

In a classrooms where the IRE/F pattern dominates, the teacher's feedback may inhibit learning when he or she changes students' responses by adding to or deleting from their statements or by completely changing students' intent and meaning. Because the teacher is searching for a preconceived answer and often "fishes" until it is found, the cognitive work of the lesson is often carried out by the teacher rather than the students. In these classrooms, students are seldom given the opportunity to elaborate on their answers; rather, the teacher does the analyzing, synthesizing, generalizing, and evaluating.

Changing ineffective classroom discourse patterns by creating authentic opportunities for students to develop academic language is critically important because as one acquires language, new concepts are also developed. Think about experiences you have had recently trying to follow economic failures and interventions related to the 2008–09 recession. Each new vocabulary term you learned and understood (e.g., *stagnation, entitlement benefits, deficit spending*) is attached to a concept that in turn expands your ability to think about economic downturns and evaluate potential courses of action that the government or corporations might take. As your own system of word-meaning grows in complexity, you are more capable of thinking about (self-directed speech) and discussing (talk with another) the associated concepts.

Academic English also involves reading and writing. As you most likely know, the National Reading Panel (National Institute of Child Health and Human Development, 2000) defined the major components of reading as phonics, phonemic awareness, fluency, vocabulary, and reading comprehension. Research suggests that high-quality instruction in these five components generally works for English learners as well, although additional focus on oral language development and background building are called for to enhance comprehension (August & Shanahan, 2006; Goldenberg, 2008) and to participate fully in classroom environments.

Although English learners are able to attain well-taught word-level skills such as decoding, word recognition, and spelling that are equal to their English-speaking peers, the same is not typically the case with text-level skills such as reading comprehension and writing (Goldenberg, 2008). One reason for the disparity between word-level and text-level skills among English learners is oral English proficiency. Well-developed oral proficiency in English, which includes English vocabulary and syntactic knowledge plus listening comprehension skills, is associated with English reading and writing proficiency. Therefore, it is insufficient to teach English learners the components of reading alone; teachers must also incorporate extensive oral language development opportunities into literacy instruction. Further, English learners benefit from more opportunities to practice reading, check comprehension, and consolidate text knowledge through summarization. They also need instruction on the features of different text genres, especially those found in subject area classes—such as textbook chapters, online articles, laboratory directions, diagrams and other graphics, and primary source materials. Since reading is the foundation for learning in school, it is critical that teachers use research-based practices to provide English learners with high-quality instruction that will lead to the development of strong reading skills.

Academic writing is an area that is affected significantly by limited English proficiency. While oral skills can be developed as students engage in meaningful activities, skills in writing must be explicitly taught. The writing process, which involves planning, drafting, editing, and revising written work, allows students to express their ideas at their level of proficiency with teacher (or peer) guidance and explicit corrective feedback. However, for English learners, it is critical that a lot of meaningful discussion take place prior to asking students to write because such dialogue helps connect ideas in support of writing and provides students with the English words they will use. Writing is also facilitated by such things as teacher modeling, posting of writing samples, providing sentence frames, and even having students copy words or text until they gain more independent proficiency (Graham & Perin, 2007). This kind of constant exposure to words and sentence patterning allows ELs to become familiar with the conventions of how words and sentences are put together in the language (Garcia & Beltran, 2003).

Systemic functional linguistics (SFL) is a research field that gives us some insights into the writing process. It looks at linguistic features of different genres (see, for example, Schleppegrell, 2004) and considers the writing purpose and role of the author in communicating with an audience. Cloud, Lakin, Leininger, and Maxwell (2010) have interpreted SFL information for teaching ELs. They point out that *factual writing* is the least language-demanding genre. These types would include lists, procedures, and reports.

They utilize simpler verb tenses (e.g., simple present and simple past) and simpler sentence structures that may follow patterns. Some use of transition words may occur, but they are more likely sequence terms. The next category would be *personal writing.* This is more creative writing, often relying on past and perfect tenses, longer, more complicated sentences, and less common transitions and connectives (e.g., terms to indicate comparisons, causation, exceptions). It is also more subjective. Cloud and colleagues argue that *analytical writing* is the most difficult for ELs. The writer is outside of the action, interpreting or evaluating it. Claims must be backed by evidence, arguments must be written persuasively. In history and social studies, biases must be analyzed and multiple perspectives considered. A wide range of verb tenses, transitions, and connectives are used and diverse agents may be discussed. The purpose may be to synthesize or analyze. All in all, this latter category requires the most proficiency with academic English.

English learners should be encouraged to write in English early, especially if they have skills in their native language, and should be provided frequent opportunities to express their ideas in writing. Errors in writing are to be expected and should be viewed as part of the natural process of language acquisition. Providing scaffolded writing tools, such as partially completed graphic organizers for pre-writing and sentence frames for organizing key points and supporting details will help ELs write in the content classroom and advance them toward success with the more difficult genres as well.

# What Is the Academic Language of Social Studies and History?

There are myriad terms that are used in academic settings. As mentioned previously, some of these are used commonly across the curricula and others are content specific. The metaphor of bricks and mortar may be useful here. Think of some words as representing bricks, such as content-specific words (e.g., *latitude, migration, communism*), and other words as mortar, such as general academic words (e.g., *discover, represent, factor*) (Dutro & Moran, 2003). Understanding both types of terms is often the key to accessing content for English learners. For example, while most students need to have terms related to economics explicitly taught, English learners also require that general academic words be included in vocabulary instruction. In addition, economics often utilizes words with multiple meanings for specific purposes and students may know one meaning but not another. Consider *cycle, depression,* and *market.* ELs are likely to know of bicycles, mental illness, and stores that sell goods, but may not know the economic usage of these terms. So those terms need specific attention as well.

In truth, the development of academic English is a complicated endeavor that involves more than just learning additional vocabulary and grammar. The writing of a scientific lab report is not the same as the writing of a persuasive speech or the writing of an essay comparing the Allied and Axis countries' goals and actions during World War II. Students need semantic and syntactic knowledge and facility with language functions. English learners must merge their growing knowledge of the English language with the content concepts they are studying in order to complete the academic tasks associated with the content area. They must also learn *how* to do these tasks, such as generate a timeline, negotiate cooperative group roles, and interpret maps and graphs. Figure 1.3 shows how the knowledge of

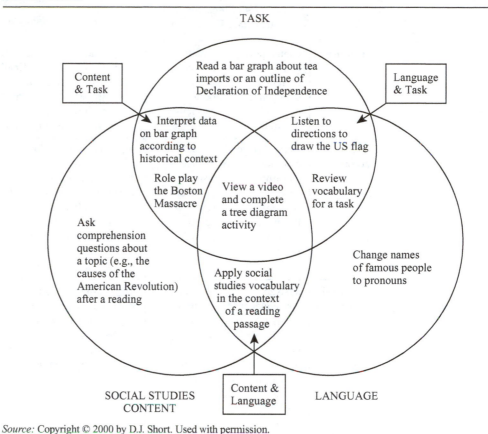

**FIGURE 1.3** *The Language–Content–Task Framework Applied to Middle School Social Studies Lessons*

TASK

Content & Task

Language & Task

Read a bar graph about tea imports or an outline of Declaration of Independence

Interpret data on bar graph according to historical context

Listen to directions to draw the US flag

Role play the Boston Massacre

View a video and complete a tree diagram activity

Review vocabulary for a task

Ask comprehension questions about a topic (e.g., the causes of the American Revolution) after a reading

Apply social studies vocabulary in the context of a reading passage

Change names of famous people to pronouns

SOCIAL STUDIES CONTENT

Content & Language

LANGUAGE

*Source:* Copyright © 2000 by D.J. Short. Used with permission.

language, content, and task intersects and identifies the type of academic language practice that can occur, using activities from a middle school social studies unit on the American Revolution as an example (Short, 2000).

As you plan for lessons that teach and provide practice in both social science-specific academic language and more general academic language, use your teacher's guides from the textbook to note the highlighted vocabulary, but consider other terms and phrases that may need to be taught. Also, you may use your state social studies/history standards and English language proficiency standards to assist you in selecting the general academic language to teach and reinforce. Using categories from Coffin (1997), contributor Seidlitz and colleague Perryman organized such terms and phrases in Figure 1.4. Other resources include the "1,000 Most Frequent Words in Middle-Grades and High School Texts" and "Word Zones™ for 5586 Most Frequent Words," which were collected by Hiebert (2005) and may be found online at www.textproject.org. For those of you who are high school teachers, you might also want to take a look at the Coxhead Academic Word List (Coxhead, 2000). [Available at http://simple.wiktionary .org/wiki/Wiktionary:Academic_word_list]

While studying history and social studies, therefore, students are exposed to new terms that they are unlikely to encounter in other subjects, general academic words that have use across the curriculum, and polysemous words for which they know a common meaning but

**FIGURE 1.4** *Seidlitz's Historical Language Terms and Sentence Stems*

| | High Frequency Academic Vocabulary | | Sentence Stems |
|---|---|---|---|
| Historical recount | contemporary<br>context<br>currently<br>emergence<br>event<br>external | initially<br>instance<br>internal<br>occur<br>previously<br>sequence | • ____ occurred while/after/before . . .<br>• First . . . second . . . finally . . .<br>• Initially . . . . but later . . . .<br>• In the past___ but currently . . .<br>• In this instance . . .<br>• Previously/initially/earlier . . . however now/later . . . |
| Historical account | circumstance<br>consist<br>constitute<br>define<br>economic<br>factors<br>framework<br>function | identify<br>involve<br>issues<br>political<br>religious<br>social<br>specific<br>tension | • ____ is/has/looks like . . .<br>• ____ consists of . . .<br>• Some important issues were . . . .<br>• Some of the factors that contributed to ____ were . . .<br>• Social/religious/political/economic factors were important because . . .<br>• This circumstance is an example of . . . . because . . .<br>• Sometimes/few/many . . .<br>• Occasionally/often/seldom/rarely . . . |
| Historical explanation | analyze<br>consequences<br>contrast<br>cycle<br>derived<br>distinctive<br>excluding<br>interact<br>link<br>major | maximum<br>minimum<br>minor<br>modify<br>reaction<br>response<br>shift<br>similar<br>vary | • ____ differs from/is similar to ____ in that . . .<br>• This event/response/action implies . . . .<br>• ____ was a response/reaction to . . . .<br>• The shift is the result of . . . .<br>• ____however/ whereas/ nevertheless . . .<br>• ____on the other hand/on the contrary . . . |
| Historical argument | alternative<br>approach<br>benefit<br>considerable<br>criteria<br>debate<br>evidence<br>implies<br>interpretation<br>journal<br>justification<br>negative | option<br>perception<br>perspective<br>positive<br>primary<br>source<br>redefining<br>relevant<br>secondary<br>source<br>validity | • ____ is important.<br>• ____ is significant due to . . .<br>• ____ should have . . . .<br>• ____ implies . . . .<br>• From my point of view . . . .<br>• The evidence points to . . .<br>• The debate is about . . .<br>• Another approach/option might be . . .<br>• ____ would have a negative/positive impact because . . .<br>• It's important to note . . . since . . .<br>• ____ is especially relevant due to . . .<br>• Above all/of course/remember ____ because . . .<br>• Finally/therefore . . .<br>• As a result___ should<br>• We must . . . because . . .<br>• ____ proves ____ because . . . |

*Source:* © 2008 by John Seidlitz and Bill Perryman. Used with permission.

not the particular meaning used in the social science context. Let's take a look at the various terms that are present in a few sample composite standards from different states. The words that are specific to one of the social science areas are **bolded**, general academic words are underlined, and the polysemous words are in *italics*. Some words, you will see, are specific to an area, such as geography and also polysemous, so students may think they know what the words mean, but do not know the definition for the purpose intended by these standards.

**In grade 2,**

- The student will compare the lives and contributions of **Native Americans,** such as the **Iroquois** in the Northeast, the **Blackfeet** of the **Plains,** and the **Pueblo** of the **Southwest.**
- The student will demonstrate skills related to reading and constructing **maps,** using titles, *legends,* **compass** *roses,* and symbols.
- The student will explain the *rights* and responsibilities of **citizenship.**

**In grade 4,**

- The student will demonstrate knowledge of the **colonization** of North America by **English** *settlers* in America and of the relationships between the **English settlers** and the **Native Americans** they encountered.
- The student will demonstrate knowledge of **economics** by explaining the importance of **barter, credit,** *trade,* **supply** and *demand.*
- The student will demonstrate knowledge of the issues that led to the **Civil War** by identifying the events and *differences* between **northern** and **southern states** and the effect of the war on **territories** in the **western** part of North America.

**In grades 6–8,**

- The student will apply analytical skills to **historical** events, including the ability to identify and interpret *primary* and *secondary* **source** documents.
- The student will demonstrate understanding of the rise and influence of two **political** *parties* in the 1800s.
- The student will use **maps, globes,** charts, *tables* and photographic *evidence* to locate and identify the **geographic** features important to the development of **urbanization.**

**In grades 9–12,**

- The student will distinguish characteristics and contributions of ancient **civilizations,** such as those of Mali, India, Peru, and China.
- The student will compare and contrast the goals and actions of the **Allied** and *Axis powers* during **World War II.**
- The student will demonstrate knowledge of the organization and *powers* of the **federal** and **state governments** described in the **U.S. Constitution** and as developed over time through *key* **Supreme Court** decisions.

As you can see, many of the underlined words may be used across the content curricula, but students need to be explicitly taught their specialized meaning in a particular history or social science course. For students who speak a Latin-based language such as Spanish, cognates will help in teaching a number of words. For example, *decision* in English is *decisión* in Spanish; *civilization* is *civilización; construct* is *construir;* and *identify* is *identificar*. Words specific to the history or social studies course should be explicitly taught as part of each lesson.

John Seidlitz analyzed the language of social studies found in Texas's state social studies standards and state tests. The sentence stems and related language functions are listed in Figure 1.5. In addition, in Appendix B you will find a listing of academic vocabulary words found in several national and state social studies/history/geography/civics/ economics standards. Your state's standards and domains may differ somewhat, but we hope these extensive but not exhaustive lists will assist you in your lesson and unit planning, and in the writing of your content and language objectives.

You should also be aware that the national standards for English language proficiency (TESOL, 2006) clearly state that students need to learn about social studies language. They are similar to the WIDA (World-class Instructional Design and Assessment) standards that have been adopted by 22 states and the District of Columbia. The social studies language standard is:

> English language learners communicate information, ideas, and concepts necessary for academic success in the content area of social studies.

Model performance indicators are provided at five proficiency levels across grade-level clusters (PreK–K, 1–2, 3–5, 6–8, and 9–12) for the four domains—speaking, reading, writing, and listening, and ways to integrate these standards into classroom instruction is found in a resource by Gottlieb, Katz, and Ernst-Slavit (2009). Seidlitz (2008) also prepared a resource to help content teachers incorporate the Texas English language proficiency standards (ELPS) in their lessons, offering academic language frames as scaffolds for student oral and written discourse.

# Why Do English Learners Have Difficulty with Academic Language?

Developing academic language has proven to be quite challenging for English learners. In fact, in a study that followed EL students' academic progress in U.S. schools, researchers found that the ELs actually regressed over time (Suarez-Orozco, Suarez-Orozco, & Todorova, 2008). There are a multitude of influences that affect overall student learning, and academic language learning in particular. Some factors, such as poverty and transiency, are outside of the school's sphere of influence, but some factors are in our control, namely what happens instructionally for these students that facilitates or impedes learning.

Many classrooms are devoid of the kinds of supports that assist students in their quest to learn new material in a new language. Since proficiency in English is the best predictor of academic success, it seems reasonable that teachers of English learners should spend a significant amount of time teaching the vocabulary required to understand the lesson's topic. However, in a study that observed 23 ethnically diverse classrooms, researchers found that in the core academic subject areas only 1.4% of instructional time was spent developing vocabulary knowledge (Scott, Jamison-Noel, & Asselin, 2003).

The lack of opportunity to develop oral language skills hinders students' progress in all subject areas. Passive learning—sitting quietly while listening to a teacher talk—does not encourage engagement. In order to acquire academic language, students need lessons that are meaningful and engaging and that provide ample opportunity to practice using

FIGURE 1.5  *Sentence Stems Found in Texas Standards for Social Studies and the Texas Social Studies Test*

## Social Studies Questioning Stem Guide
### Based on Texas Standards for Social Studies and the Released TAKS Test

| | |
|---|---|
| **Analyze** | • The significance of ____ is . . . <br> • ____ contributed to ____ because . . . <br> • _____ did _____ because . . . <br> • ____ opposed ____ because . . . <br> • ____ said ____. What was he referring to? <br> • The concerns of ____ were satisfied through . . . <br> • Which of the following choices would best complete the diagram? <br> • In the cartoon, what is ____ trying to tell ____? <br> • Which would be the best title for the cartoon? <br> • This excerpt reflects . . . |
| **Analyze how** | • Which of the following . . . <br> • ____ does ____ through . . . <br> • ____ is reflected in ____. <br> • Which ____ does the chart illustrate? |
| **Analyze information** | • Based on the chart/map/timeline, what conclusion can be drawn about ____. <br> • From the chart/map/timeline, one can conclude . . . <br> • Which of the following tables/graphs/charts might indicate a need for ____. <br> • The largest decline/increase was in . . . <br> • The graph indicates that . . . |
| **Analyze the effects or impact** | • ____ resulted from . . . <br> • One reason ____ happened was . . . <br> • ____ affected/aided ____ by . . . <br> • ____ resulted in ____ experiencing . . . <br> • _____ was designed to . . . <br> • One effect/result of ____ was . . . <br> • ____ was important because . . . <br> • Which of the following is the correct cause-and-effect pairing of events? <br> • Which event is an example of *geographic factors* having a significant effect on ____? |
| **Apply chronology** | • Which of these lists shows the correct order/sequence? <br> • Which event best completes the timeline? |
| **Compare** | • A key difference is . . . <br> • It can be inferred that ____ is an example of . . . <br> • In addition to ____, ____ also . . . <br> • ____ might change/have changed ____ because . . . |

| | |
|---|---|
| **Compare the effects** | • ____ did ____ because . . . <br> • ____ was the result of . . . |
| **Define** | • Which of the following is an example of ____? |
| **Give examples** | • ____ is an example of . . . |
| **Describe** | • Which of these is correctly matched to his/her/its description? <br> • Which of the following describes . . . |
| **Describe the effect/ changes/ impact** | • According to the diagram ____ changed because . . . <br> • ____ occurred as a result of . . . <br> • Based on the map, what conclusion can be drawn about ____? <br> • Based on the map, what was one outcome of ____? <br> • Which of the following is a result of ____ shown in the diagram? <br> • What effect did ____ have on ____? <br> • ____ contributed to ____ by . . . <br> • ____ affected ____ by . . . <br> • One reason ____ were considered milestones was . . . <br> • What pattern can be deduced from the information in the chart? <br> • This poster shows that . . . |
| **Describe the conflicts/ responses** | • ____ became increasingly important to the conflict over ____ because of . . . <br> • ____ would have agreed with which of the following statements? <br> • One reason for ____ was ____. <br> • One of the primary goals of ____ was . . . <br> • ____ responded to ____ by . . . |
| **Explain** | • ____ organized/formed/created/wrote ____ in order to . . . <br> • Based on the cartoon, which best explains ____? <br> • Which item would best complete the list? |
| **Explain the effects** | • ____ led directly to . . . |
| **Explain the geographic factors** | • Based on the information found on the map, what geographic advantage did ____ have? |
| **Explain how** | • ____ established ____ through <br> • ____ increased because . . . <br> • ____ were addressed through . . . |

*(continued)*

**FIGURE 1.5** *Continued*

| Explain the issues | • _____ were viewed as _____ because . . .<br>• Some _____ believed/opposed _____ because . . .<br>• Which item would best complete the list?<br>• _____ was a turning point because . . .<br>• _____ established _____ in order to . . .<br>• The information in the box represents . . . | Identify bias/points of view | • Which claim is best supported by the illustration/quote/cartoon?<br>• Based on this excerpt, a reader can conclude _____ believed . . .<br>• In this excerpt, _____ is arguing that . . .?<br>• These comments reflect the speaker's view that . . .<br>• What does the speaker/writer mean by the word "_____" in this excerpt? |
|---|---|---|---|
| Explain the reasons | • What factor was most important?<br>• _____ occurred because _____ wanted . . . | Identify influences | • _____ was relevant to _____ because. . . |
| Explain the roles | • The person who _____ was . . .<br>• The accomplishments shown are associated with . . .<br>• _____ played an important role by . . .<br>• _____ made an important contribution when . . .<br>• Which action/document is correctly paired with the right person/author? | Identify reasons | • _____ supported _____ because . . . |
| | | Interpret/Observe geographic, spatial, and other patterns | • The map suggests . . .<br>• According to the map . . .<br>• The feature shared by _____ on the map is . . .<br>• Which of the following conclusions does the map best support?<br>• Based on the information on the map, which _____ was _____? |
| Explain the significance | • _____ was significant because . . .<br>• _____ is important because . . . | | |
| Explain | • For what reason did _____ do _____? | Locate | • What geographic feature would . . .<br>• Which of the following on the map is ___? |
| Evaluate | • This cartoon represents which of the following views?<br>• _____ is significant because . . .<br>• The reason _____ did _____ was . . . ?<br>• What was established through _____?<br>• One result of _____ was . . .<br>• The efforts of _____ led to . . .<br>• What prompted _____? | Summarize | • _____ refers to . . .<br>• Which of the following is included in ___? |
| | | Use/Acquire Information/ | • Based on _____ what conclusion can be drawn about _____?<br>• Based on the quote, an important effect of _____ was . . . |
| Identify | • _____ addresses . . .<br>• _____ happened in which era?<br>• Which of the following best describes ___?<br>• _____ gained prominence when . . . | Apply methods (about social studies resources) | • In this excerpt _____ suggests/symbolizes . . .<br>• The quote illustrates that . . .<br>• In which situation would a historian need to ___?<br>• This photograph portrays an important historical event in the . . .<br>• What is described in this excerpt? |

*Source:* © 2004 by John Seidlitz. Used with permission.

language orally. Successful group work requires intentional planning and teaching students how to work with others effectively; expectations need to be made clear. Grouping students in teams for discussion, use of partners for specific tasks, and other planned configurations increase student engagement and oral language development.

Another related reason that ELs struggle is lack of access to the language and the subject matter. Think about a situation where you hear another language spoken. It could be the salon where you get a hair cut or your favorite ethnic restaurant. Just because you regularly hear another language, are you learning it? Typically not. Likewise, many English learners sit in class and hear what amounts to "English noise." It doesn't make sense to them and thus, they are not learning academic language or the content being taught. Without the kinds of practices that are promoted by the SIOP® Model, much of what happens during the school day is lost on English learners.

We must also consider the types of classroom cultures students have experienced in the past. As Lemke (1990) noted, competence in content classes requires more than mastery of the subject matter topics; it requires an understanding of and facility with the genres and conventions for spoken and written interaction and the skills to participate in class activities. Some ELs who are recent immigrants may never have experienced a lesson where students collaborate in order to create a project or reach a common understanding. They may have learned their subjects through rote memorization of teacher lectures. Therefore, teachers will need to introduce these ELs to a new classroom culture in which students are expected to participate orally, work in cooperative groups, solve problems, participate in debates, express opinions, and so forth. Because communication patterns in class may be very different from those in their native culture, teachers need to engage in culturally responsive teaching (Bartolomé, 1998), being sensitive to and building upon culturally different ways of learning, behaving, and using language. Working together, respectfully, the students and teacher can create a classroom culture in which they will all feel comfortable and learning can advance.

Finally, some teachers have low expectations for EL students (Lee, 2005). They are not motivated to get to know the students, their cultures, and families. Poor performance is not only accepted but expected. Rather than adjusting instruction so that it is meaningful to these students, teachers attribute lack of achievement to students' cultural background, limited English proficiency, and, sadly, ability. This attitude is unacceptable and staff who hold this view need to be re-educated in appropriate ways to teach these students and to learn that all students can reach high standards, although the pathways by which they attain them may vary.

# How Can We Effectively Teach Academic Language with the SIOP® Model?

In a recent synthesis of existing research on teaching English language and literacy to ELs in the elementary grades, the authors make five recommendations, one of which is to "Ensure that the development of formal or academic English is a key instructional goal for English learners, beginning in the primary grades" (Gersten, et al., 2007, pp. 26–27). Although few empirical studies have been conducted on the effects of academic language instruction, the panel of researchers conducting the synthesis made as a central theme of their work the importance of intensive, interactive language practice that focuses on developing academic language. This recommendation was made based upon considerable expert opinion with the caveat that additional research is still needed. Additional reports offer similar conclusions (Deussen, Autio, Miller, Lockwood, & Stewart, 2008; Goldenberg, 2008; Short & Fitzsimmons, 2007).

Because you are already familiar with the SIOP® Model, you know that effective instruction for English learners includes focused attention on and systematic implementation of the SIOP® Model's eight components and thirty features. The SIOP® Model has a dual purpose: to systematically and consistently teach both content and language in every lesson. Content and language objectives not only help focus the teacher throughout a lesson, these objectives also (perhaps even more importantly) focus students on what they are to know and be able to do during and after each lesson as related to *both* content knowledge and language development. Therefore, use the SIOP® protocol to guide lesson design when selecting activities and approaches for teaching academic language in your history, social studies, geography, economics, civics, and government courses.

## Academic Vocabulary

Within the SIOP® Model, we refer to academic vocabulary as having three elements (Echevarria, Vogt, & Short, 2008a, p. 59). These include:

1. *Content Words:* These are key vocabulary words, technical terms, and concepts associated with a particular topic. Key vocabulary, such as *continent, democracy, political, land bridge,* and *Mayan,* typically come from history and social studies texts as well as other components of the curriculum. Obviously, you will need to introduce and teach key content vocabulary when teaching about ancient civilizations, market economies, regions of the United States, the Monroe doctrine, and civic engagement.

2. *Process/Function Words:* These are the words and phrases that have to do with functional language use, such as how to *make an argument, compare historical events, state a conclusion, "state in your own words," summarize, ask a question, interpret bias*, and so forth. They are general academic terms. Tasks that students are to accomplish during a lesson also fit into this category, and for English learners, their meanings may need to be taught explicitly. Examples include *list, explain, paraphrase, identify, create, monitor progress, define, share with a partner,* and so forth.

3. *Words and Word Parts that Teach English Structure:* These are words and word parts that enable students to learn new vocabulary, primarily based on English morphology. While instruction is this category generally falls under the responsibility of English-language arts teachers, we also encourage teachers of other content areas to be aware of the academic language of their own disciplines. The English language arts (ELA) or English as a second language (ESL) teacher may teach the formation of the past tense (such as adding an *-ed* to regular verbs), yet you might reinforce past tense forms when discussing and reading about historical events. Primary source documents may be written in arcane language, but students may be able to use knowledge of word parts and cognates to determine meaning.

    ELA teachers will likely teach morphology (base words, roots, prefixes, suffixes), but you may teach many words with these word parts as key vocabulary (such as so- cial*ism* or *im*migra*tion*). History and social studies courses are well suited to activities with roots and affixes because so many terms utilize these word parts. Think about the root **geo**, for instance. If we teach students it means "earth," it might help them figure out *geography* and *geology*.

    For a usable and informative list of English word roots that provide the clue to more than 100,000 English words, refer to pages 60–61 of *Making Content Comprehensible for English Learners: The SIOP® Model* (Echevarria, Vogt, & Short, 2008). This is a must-have list for both elementary and secondary teachers in ALL curricular areas.

In sum, picture a stool with three legs. If one of the legs is broken, the stool will not function properly; it will not support a person who sits on it. From our experience, an English learner must have instruction in and practice with all three "legs" of academic vocabulary (content vocabulary, process/function words, and words/word parts that teach English structure) if they are going to develop the academic language they need to be successful students.

Zwiers (2008, p. 41) notes that "academic language doesn't grow on trees." Rather, explicit vocabulary instruction through a variety of approaches and activities provides English learners with multiple chances to learn, practice, and apply academic language (Stahl & Nagy, 2006). This requires teachers to provide comprehensible input (Krashen, 1985), as well as structured opportunities for students to produce academic language in their content classes. These enable English learners to negotiate meaning through confirming and disconfirming their understanding while they work and interact with others.

In addition to explicit vocabulary instruction, we need to provide a variety of scaffolds, including ones that provide context. Writing a list of social studies terms or pointing out terms that are in bold print in the textbook only helps if students know what they mean. Remember that research reveals that we can only read independently if we know 90–95% of the words in a text (Nagy & Scott, 2000). To create a context for learning new words, teachers preteach the terms, explain them in ways that students can understand and relate to, and then show how the terms are used in the textbook or classroom discourse. Scaffolding involves providing enough support to students so that the learners gradually are able to be successful independently.

Another way to scaffold academic English is to display word walls or posters of key terms with illustrations, definitions, and/or sentences that use the term in context. Posters of signal words such as lists of Comparison Words (e.g., *both, and, alike, similar, in contrast to, different from, unalike, neither*) are useful too. These terms are more difficult to capture through visuals, but are important for academic discourse. These aids reduce the cognitive load for English learners. Moreover, English learners can work in pairs or groups to create these posters. As students refer to and use these posted academic language words and phrases, the terms will become internalized and will later be used independently by students.

If English learners have opportunities to read, write, and orally produce words during history, math, science, and English classes, the words are reinforced. And, if this reinforcement occurs throughout each and every school day, one can assume that English learners' mastery of English will be accelerated, much like repeated practice with any new learning.

## Oral Discourse

Researchers who have investigated the relationship between language and learning suggest that there should be more balance in student talk and teacher talk to promote meaningful language learning opportunities for English learners (Cazden, 2001; Echevarria, 1995; Saunders & Goldenberg, 1992; Tharp & Gallimore, 1988; Walqui, 2006). In order to achieve a better balance, teachers need to carefully analyze their own classroom interaction patterns, the way they formulate questions, how they provide students with academic feedback, and the opportunities they provide for students to engage in meaningful talk.

Not surprisingly, teacher questioning usually drives the type and quality of classroom discussions. The IRE/F pattern discussed previously is characterized by questions to which the teacher already knows the answer and results in the teacher unintentionally expecting students to "guess what I'm thinking" (Echevarria & Silver, 1995). In fact, researchers have found explicit, "right there" questions are used about 50% of the time in classrooms (Zwiers, 2008) and that history and social studies "discussions" can devolve into a series of factual exchanges.

In contrast, open-ended questions that do not have quick "right" or "wrong" answers promote greater levels of thinking and expression. During social studies lessons there should be more of an emphasis on promoting classroom discourse by students questioning one another, separating fact from opinion, reasoning rather than memorizing positions and outcomes, making connections or generalizations, and drawing conclusions. For example, questions such as, "Which achievement or invention of the Incas is most significant to you and why?" and "Explain the importance of Marco Polo's travels along the Silk Road to civilizations in Europe and China" not only engender higher-level thinking about historical events but also provide an opportunity for students to grapple with ideas and express themselves using academic English.

The Interaction component in SIOP® Model promotes more student engagement in classroom discourse. The features of the Interaction component, which should be familiar to you, include:

- Frequent opportunities for interaction and discussion between teacher/student and among students, which encourage elaborated responses about lesson concepts;
- Grouping configurations support language and content objectives of the lesson;
- Sufficient wait time for student responses consistently provided;
- Ample opportunities for students to clarify key concepts in L1 as needed.

These features promote balanced turn-taking between teachers and students, and among students, providing multiple opportunities for students to use academic English. Notice how each feature of Interaction encourages student talk. This is in considerable contrast to the discourse patterns typically found in both elementary and secondary classrooms.

Something as simple as having students turn to a partner and discuss an answer to a question first, before reporting out to the whole class, is an effective conversational technique, especially when the teacher circulates to monitor student responses. Speaking to a peer may be less threatening and also gets every student actively involved. Also, rather than responding to student answers with "Very good!" teachers who value conversation and discussion encourage elaborated responses with prompts such as "Can you tell us more about that?" or "What made you think of that?" or "Did anyone else have that idea?" or "Please explain how you figured that out."

Zwiers (2008, pp. 62–63) has classified comments teachers can make to enrich classroom talk; by using comments like these, a greater balance between student talk and teacher talk is achieved. Further, classroom interactions are less likely to result in an IRE/F pattern. Try using some of the comments below and see what happens to the interaction pattern in your own classroom!

### To Prompt More Thinking

- You're on to something important. Keep going.
- You're on the right track. Tell us more.
- There is no right answer, so what would be your best answer?
- Can you connect that to something else you learned/saw/experienced?

### To Fortify or Justify a Response

- That's a probable answer . . . How did you come to that answer?
- What evidence do you have to support that claim?
- What is your opinion/impression of . . . Why?

### To Report On an Observation or Problem

- Tell us more about what you noticed.
- What do you think caused that to happen?
- How else might you study the problem?
- Can you generalize this to another situation? How?

### To See Other Points of View

- So you didn't get the result you expected. What do you think about that?
- If you were in that person's shoes, what would you have done?
- Would you have done it like that? Why or why not?

### To Consider Consequences

- Should she have . . .?
- What if he had not done that?
- Some people think that . . . is wrong/right. What do you think? Why?
- How can we apply this to real life?

A conversational approach is particularly well suited to English learners who, after only a few years in school, often find themselves significantly behind their peers in most academic areas, especially when instruction is in English, usually because of low reading levels in English, weaker vocabulary knowledge, and underdeveloped oral language skills. Students benefit from a conversational approach in many ways because conversation provides:

- A context for learning in which language is expressed naturally through meaningful discussion
- Practice using oral language, which is a foundation for literacy skill development
- A means for students to express their thinking, and to clarify and fine-tune their ideas
- Time to process information and hear what others are thinking about
- An opportunity for teachers to model academic language, use content vocabulary appropriately, and through think-alouds, model thinking processes and learning strategies

- Opportunities for students to participate as equal contributors to the discussion, and as such they are provided with repetition of both linguistic terms and thinking processes which result in eventual acquisition and internalization for future use

A rich discussion, or conversational approach, has advantages for teachers as well, including the following:

- Through discussion a teacher can more naturally activate students' background knowledge and assess prior learning.
- When students work in small groups and each participates in a discussion, teachers are better able to gauge student understanding of the lesson's concepts, tasks, and terminology, while areas of weakness are made transparent.
- When teachers and students interact together, a supportive environment is fostered which builds teacher-student rapport.

When contemplating the advantages of a more conversational approach to teaching, think about your own learning. In nearly all cases it takes multiple exposures to new terms, concepts, and information before you can use them independently. If you talk with others about the concepts and information you are learning, you're more likely to remember them. English learners require even more repetition and redundancy. When they have repeated opportunities to improve their oral language proficiency, ELs are more likely to use English and more frequent use results in increased proficiency (Saunders & Goldenberg, in press). With improved proficiency, ELs are more adept at participating in class discussions. Discussion and interaction push learners to think quickly, respond, construct sentences, put their thoughts into words, and ask for clarification through classroom dialogue. Discussion also allows students to see how other people think and use language to describe their thinking (Zwiers, 2008).

Productive discussion can take place in whole-class settings but it is more likely that small groups will facilitate the kind of high-quality interaction that benefits English learners. Working to express ideas and answers to questions in a new language can be intimidating for students of all ages. Small-group work allows them to try out their ideas in a low-stress setting and gauge how similar their ideas are to those of their peers. Working with partners, triads, or in a small group also provides a chance to process and articulate new information with less pressure than a whole-class setting may create.

Earlier in this chapter, you read an interaction between a teacher and her students in which the IRE/F pattern prevailed. In contrast, read the following interaction from a sixth grade newcomer history class that was part of a SIOP® Model professional development project[1], and reflect on the differences in the two classroom interaction patterns:

MR. GLENN:    Yesterday we saw a video clip about Native Americans. Turn to a partner and name the Native Americans and tell where they lived.

*Students pair up and talk.*

MR. GLENN (*one minute later*):  Okay, who can come to the map and show us where the tribe lived and tell us its name? Carmela? Yes, come on.

CARMELA (*pointing at Rhode Island on the map*):  The Narragansett lived here, along the water.

---

[1]All names are pseudonyms.

MR. GLENN:   Carmela, thanks. Who can tell us more about the Narragansett?

TOMMIE:   They fished and ate clams.

MR. GLENN:   Yes . . .

JOAO:   English people took their land.

MR. GLENN:   Good memory for both of you. Okay, everyone, let's do a Quickdraw. On a piece of paper, draw a picture of the Narragansett people's winter home. It was called a *longhouse*.

MR. GLENN (*one minute later*):   Show your picture to your partner. Do you have the same drawing? Now hold your picture up so I can see it. Look around. Many of you have similar drawings. Who can tell us about the drawing? (*He pulls a name stick from a jar and checks to see if that student's hand is raised.*) Josue?

JOSUE:   The house is long. Many families sleep inside. They make it from trees.

MR. GLENN:   Thank you, Josue. Now let's look at our objectives. For the language objective, you will watch another video and take notes. For content, you will compare the way three Native American tribes live. Who can predict what we will do today? (*He pulls another stick from a jar and checks to see if that student's hand is raised.*) Anna?

ANNA:   Watch a video.

MR. GLENN:   Yes, can you tell me more?

ANNA:   Write notes.

MR. GLENN:   Yes, take notes. That means I have to show you how to take notes too. Anything else? (*He pulls another name stick.*) Luciana?

LUCIANA:   Compare, but what compare?

MR. GLENN:   I like the way you look at the verbs in the objectives. Yes, we will compare three different Native American groups. You will learn about two new groups in the video. But first let's start by taking notes about the Narragansett. Here is a chart to use. Ricardo, please pass these out. (*He projects a version of the chart on the smart board.*) (See Figure 1.6.)

MR. GLENN:   We can use a chart like this to take notes and later to compare groups. (*Pointing to the columns*) These are the three tribes we are studying. Say them after me: Narragansett, Wampanoag, and Iroquois. (*Students echo repeat.*) Let's look at the categories in the first column. Tell a partner what these are (*He points to categories in first column*). Tell me what we write for the Narragansett. Where did they live?

**FIGURE 1.6** *Native American Tribes Chart*

|  | *Narragansett* | *Wampanoag* | *Iroquois* |
|---|---|---|---|
| Where the tribe lived | Rhode Island | | |
| What they ate | Fish, clams, corn, berries | | |
| What work they did | Fishermen, warriors | | |
| What the families lived in | Longhouse | | |

STUDENTS:   Rhode Island.

MR. GLENN:   So I write Rhode Island here (*He writes in first box under the tribe's name*). Now you copy on your chart. (*He continues to model how to complete the first column with student input.*) Next, try to fill in the boxes under Wampanoag (*pointing to the boxes*) and we'll discuss . . .

In this newcomer class, the students of Spanish and Portuguese backgrounds do not yet have strong oral English skills. As you read the transcript you saw that they spoke in short sentences. Mr. Glenn, however, resisted lecturing and answering questions fully for them. He has students recall information from the prior day, using a Turn and Talk technique, the U.S. map, and a Quickdraw and then connects the information to the current lesson. Because these are newcomer students, they need a good deal of support. Mr. Glenn scaffolds the question-and-answer discussion. He prompted for more ideas with queries such as "Who can tell us more?" He had the learners talk with a partner before sharing out with the class. So as not to call on the same students each time, he used a jar with name sticks. He would draw a student name stick and then call on that student, if that student were ready to respond. Further, he modeled with them an important academic skill, note-taking, that would be handy in the regular history classroom once they exited the newcomer program.

Teaching students to share conversational control and stepping back, trusting them to get the job done takes some risk-taking on the part of the teacher, and practice on the part of students who may be used to just answering questions with monosyllabic responses. Simply telling students to "have a discussion among yourselves" is rarely successful. We need to teach students how to engage in meaningful conversation and discussion and provide the support they need to do it well. Rather than sitting as "quiet cornstalks," students, including English learners, can learn to express themselves, support their viewpoints, advocate their positions, and defend their positions. When this occurs, we establish a classroom environment in which conversational control is shared among teachers and students alike.

# Concluding Thoughts

Proficiency in English is the best predictor of academic success, and understanding academic language is an important part of overall English proficiency. In this chapter we have discussed what academic language is, why it is important, and how it can be developed in social studies and history classes and across the curriculum. In all content areas, teachers need to plan to explicitly teach both content area terms and general academic terms so that English learners can fully participate in lessons and acquire knowledge about social studies, history, geography, government and civics concepts.

For our students to achieve academically and meet state standards, they need to have practice with all four language skills so they can read for a purpose, summarize information in writing, use persuasive language compellingly in arguments, and compare events or points of view. When you teach students how to participate in classroom conversations and structured discussions, and how to read and write and think like a historian, you not only improve their English skills but also prepare them for the academic language skills used in school and in professional settings. If students are to become adults capable of making informed choices and taking effective action in the twenty-first century, then they must possess a set of skills that merges the knowledge of social science concepts, facts, events, and perspectives with the ability to use language to articulate, converse about, and debate those ideas.

In the lesson plans and units that appear in Chapters 5–8, you will see a variety of instructional techniques and activities for teaching, practicing, and using academic language in social studies and history classrooms. As you read the lesson plans, reflect on why particular activities were selected for the respective content and language objectives. Additional resources for selecting effective activities that develop academic language and content knowledge include: Buehl's *Classroom Strategies for Interactive Learning* (2001); Vogt and Echevarria's *99 Ideas and Activities for Teaching English Learners with the SIOP® Model* (2008); Reiss's *102 Content Strategies for English Language Learners* (2008); and Marzano and Pickering's *Building Academic Vocabulary: Teacher's Manual* (2005). Secondary teachers will also find the following books, among many others, to be helpful: Zwiers's *Building Academic Language: Essential Practices for Content Classrooms (Grades 5–12)* (2008) and *Developing Academic Thinking Skills in Grades 6–12: A Handbook of Multiple Intelligence Activities* (2004); Fisher and Frey's *Word Wise and Content Rich: Five Essential Steps to Teaching Academic Vocabulary* (2008); and Cloud, Genesee, and Hamayan's *Literacy Instruction for English Language Learners* (2009).

# Activities and Techniques for SIOP® History-Social Studies Lessons: Lesson Preparation, Building Background, Comprehensible Input, & Strategies

By John Seidlitz, Robin Liten-Tejada, and Deborah Short

## Mr. Michaels's Vignette

John Michaels loves teaching history. Latin American studies is his passion and he enjoys sharing his knowledge with his middle school students. He has many artifacts to display from his trips to Mexico, Peru, Argentina, and Brazil, and he can tell the class many anecdotes

about the Inca and Maya and the Aztecs. He has collected video clips over the years—some even produced in Spanish—that he uses in his lessons to convey the beauty of South America's geography and the ancient civilizations of its peoples. He frequently finds himself veering off the day's lesson plan when students ask questions, but he knows so much that he can't resist telling the students. And they respond well. They like listening to his stories; some even imagined themselves as Amazonian natives or Mayan mathematicians. He loves that the state didn't test history or social studies the way it did math, reading, and science, so he doesn't feel the pressures of teaching to the test and the kids can have fun.

But this year has been a wake-up call. As a teacher with only three years of experience, John doesn't have a lot of seniority. Over the summer he was told that he'd be switched to the ESL team at the school. That meant he would work only with English learners in sheltered history classes. He would have two periods of seventh grade and two of eighth. Except for the recently arrived newcomer students, who had a self-contained classroom for their first year, his classes would have beginning, intermediate, and advanced level students. Sure, the class size would be a bit smaller; he would have 18–20 students, rather than the typical 25, but wow, what would he do about their language skills? He couldn't just tell his stories, could he? Would students understand him?

Near the end of summer break, the lead teacher for the ESL team, Ms. Feehan, had a cookout for fellow team members. John didn't know most of the teachers well except for her. She was the language arts teacher, and he co-sponsored the yearbook club with her. After an hour of relaxing and snacking, he confessed to her that he was apprehensive about working with the English learners. He explained that he hadn't had any methods courses in college or graduate school that addressed techniques for reaching these kids and he hadn't paid much attention to the occasional workshops they'd had at school.

Ms. Feehan explained that she had been in the same boat a few years ago: "I too was unsure whether I could reach these kids. I wondered how would they be able to read the novels we have in the curriculum, like *Monster* and *Night*. So I investigated strategies and approaches on my own and found one called the SIOP® Model. I've been using it for three years now and think I understand it pretty well. Last year our team read *Making Content Comprehensible for English Learners* as a book study project and we are all seeing positive effects in class. I want it to continue to be a focus of our PLC[1] this year. One new thing we agreed to do was observe a class of another teacher on our team once a month. We thought it would be good to see how the others use the SIOP® Model in their content areas and how the kids we share act and respond in these classes. I'll make sure you get a copy of the book. You should probably read it before school begins."

# Introduction

Mr. Michaels has some techniques already in his repertoire that are likely to help his English learners, but he didn't realize it yet. History and social studies can be motivating and engaging subjects for students of all ages and all language backgrounds when teachers personalize the historical narrative, explain how applications of historical events and results affect lives today, and tap into students' cultural backgrounds. Mr. Michaels has stories and artifacts to share with the students to bring history alive and he uses visual supports like video clips to develop background knowledge about places and events unfamiliar to many

---

[1]Professional learning community

of his learners. With the support of his ESL team members and the PLC meetings, he was trying to incorporate new techniques and activities into his lessons, focusing especially on vocabulary development and reading strategies. He highlighted words commonly used in history that were also beneficial across the curricular areas, such as *circumstances, conflict, effect, goal, maintain, position, result*, and *struggle*. He helped students read for the main idea and supporting details, ask questions about actions and decisions historical figures took, and compare and apply past events to current ones. He still had much to learn, but the support of his colleagues and the enthusiasm of his students made his task easier.

In this chapter and the following one, we present a variety of proven techniques and activities that teachers can use in their history and social studies lessons so students actively take part in the learning process, have access to the content, and develop proficiency in academic English. You will see that after the steps for each technique are explained, the technique is applied in a classroom scenario depicting a SIOP® history, geography, government, or social studies lesson. Note that the social studies and history curriculum topics vary by grade level across the states. Our scenarios reflect topics taught in some states at that grade level, although in some instances, the topic might match a different grade level in your state. In Appendix C you will find a list of these techniques along with the grade level and sub-subject of the classroom scenarios.

Given the realities and challenges of working with diverse groups of students, it was also important for us to consider not only that our students are second language learners but also that they have different language levels and academic needs. So, with the scenarios, we have also identified how the various techniques that are used to support the development of content and language can be modified for students at different proficiency or grade levels.

As you read and reflect on planning lessons yourselves, remember that the activities alone are not the lesson. The focus should always be on the content and language objectives that the activities are meant to support. Select appropriate activities and techniques that allow students to practice new learning or reinforce new concepts, language structures, and processes. Remember that in history the big picture can get lost in the facts, and so establishing a key concept for each unit of study is advisable.

# History and Social Studies Techniques and Activities

The activities and techniques in this chapter are organized around the first four SIOP® Model components: lesson preparation, building background, comprehensible input, and strategies. Chapter 3 presents techniques and activities for the final four components. We recognize that a number of the techniques are suitable for multiple components, and have indicated those alternatives. The techniques may be used across various recommended grade levels; they are not restricted to the grade level we discuss in the application scenarios or show in the sample lessons in the following chapters. Each technique's description identifies the optimal grades for use.

The following information is included for each technique in this chapter and Chapter 3.

**Name of Activity or Technique**—In cases where we have drawn from the techniques in the *99 Ideas* book, we indicate that here. In other cases, our contributors have included techniques and activities that they have named or ones that are familiar to many ESL educators.

**SIOP® Component**—Here we identify the SIOP® component that this technique or activity addresses in the application we present. We recognize that several of these techniques may be used with different components as well.

**Grade Level**—Often we provide a range of grade levels suitable for the technique or activity. While the classroom application is grade-specific, teachers will likely be able to modify the technique to a different grade within the range suggested.

**Grouping Configurations**—We explain what type of student configuration is most effective for this technique or activity. As you know, the way students are grouped is an important component of the SIOP® Model. We recommend deliberate, thoughtful groupings of students that match a lesson's objectives. Teachers may group students in pairs to promote more conversation and lower anxiety levels. They may create small groups of students with different abilities to give more advanced students a chance to teach and less proficient students an opportunity to have peer role models. Teachers may at times group students by first language so the ELs can process the new information through a language they are more comfortable with before completing a task using English. There will also be times when a teacher wants to present new information to the whole group, but wants to ensure it is comprehensible and the students stay focused.

**Approximate Time Involved**—This information gives the teacher a sense of how long the activity may take in a lesson. It is useful for considering the pacing while preparing a lesson plan. It does not include the time needed to prepare for the activity.

**Materials**—Materials needed for the activity are listed here.

**Description**—We describe the technique or activity here, including its general purpose and the steps of the procedure. Some suggestions for topics pertinent to specific subjects may be included, such as using gestures to represent key concepts of the French Revolution.

**Application**—In this section, we explain how the technique or activity might be used in one specific class (with the grade or subject identified). The lesson concept is listed and content and language objectives that this technique can help student meet are presented. As needed, key vocabulary terms are identified, particularly when the language objective is related to vocabulary learning. Then a classroom vignette illustrates how a teacher would use the technique or activity in the lesson.

**Differentiation**—Many of the techniques lend themselves to differentiation. As appropriate, we suggest some modifications. The adjustments might help apply the technique to students who are at different proficiency or grade levels or to students who are underschooled or who have wide gaps in their formal educational backgrounds. In some cases, the differentiation options extend the activity or provide challenges.

# Lesson Preparation

- Building Language Objectives from Content Objectives
- Differentiating Sentence Starters

The specific techniques described below offer targeted suggestions for preparing SIOP® History or Social Studies lessons and ensuring strong language objectives.

# Building Language Objectives from Content Objectives

**SIOP® COMPONENT:** Preparation

Grade Level: All
Grouping Configuration: None (teacher planning)
Approximate Time Involved: 30 minutes during unit preparation
Materials: Language Objectives graphic organizer (Figure 2.1)

## Description

Once unit content objectives have been determined, teachers need to design language objectives that flow naturally from the content, and that will reinforce content knowledge as well as all four language domains. This graphic organizer (Figure 2.1) helps teachers connect the content and language objectives. It can be used for individual lessons or as a unit planner. Teachers identify the focus topic, the academic vocabulary, the language function(s) to be taught and practiced, and the speaking, listening, reading, and writing objectives for each unit.

---

### Grade 6 Geography Application

**Unit Concept:** Migration

**Content Objective:** Students will be able to (SWBAT) determine the reasons for migration of peoples in the past.

At the start of each school year, the Grade 6 curriculum calls for a unit on migration. The overall goal of the unit is for students to determine reasons for the migration of large groups of people in the past. Typically, this unit takes about five days, and so the teacher considers what key concepts need to be shared and which language functions the students should learn and practice. The topics will be the migration of northern Asians into North and South America hundreds of years ago and the present-day migration of Eastern Europeans into Western Europe and North America.

For this unit, the teacher plans the following language functions: 1. Ask and answer questions, and 2. Make comparisons. Academic vocabulary includes *compare, migrate, resources, economy, cause, reason*. The speaking objective is SWBAT (students will be able to) compare reasons for migrating in the past to the present. The listening objective is SWBAT listen to an audio tape and mark the migration route on a map. The reading objective is SWBAT ask questions before reading a text about migration and find answers in the selection. The writing objective is SWBAT write diary entries for a child on a migration journey.

---

**FIGURE 2.1** *Integrate Content and Language Objectives for Effective Instruction!*

*1. Select a content topic. 2. Determine the applicable academic vocabulary and language functions. 3. Write a content objective. 4. Write a language objective for each of the four language domains of speaking, listening, reading, and writing that address the academic content.*

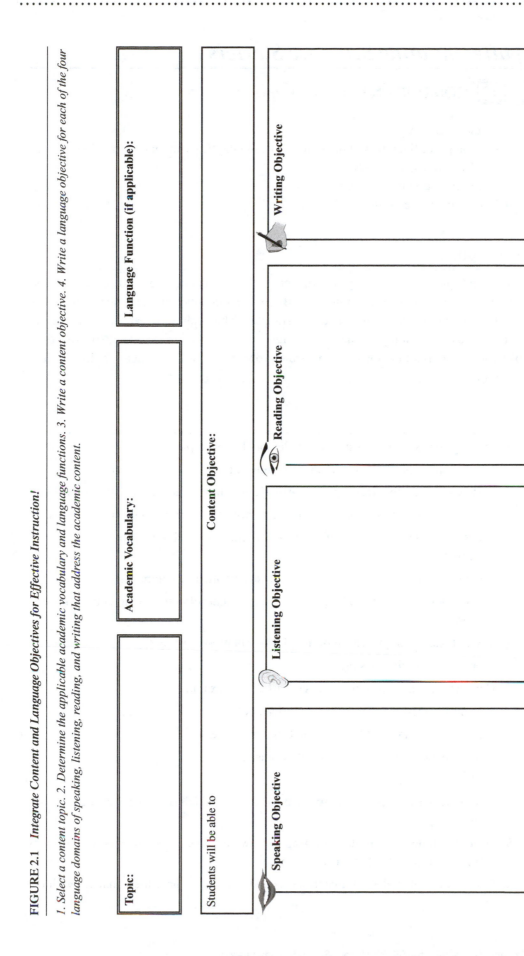

| Topic: | Academic Vocabulary: | Language Function (if applicable): |

**Content Objective:**

Students will be able to

**Speaking Objective**

**Listening Objective**

**Reading Objective**

**Writing Objective**

# Differentiating Sentence Starters

**SIOP** **COMPONENT:** Lesson Preparation

Grade Level: All
Grouping Configuration: Small groups: beginning ELs with intermediate, advanced
  ELs, or native speakers
Approximate Time Involved: 5 minutes
Materials: Posted sentence frames

## Description

This technique provides a way for students with various language proficiency levels
and background knowledge to interact. By giving students sentence starters to organize their thoughts, more students can participate. This technique can be used with a
wide range of lesson topics such as the significance of historical events, perspectives
of various historical persons, and possible problems for various social, political, and
economic issues.

## Procedure:

1. Identify the essential question of the lesson. For example:
   - What changes resulted from the development of Renaissance humanism?
   - How did Manifest Destiny affect American political and cultural development?
   - Describe the significance of push/pull factors on global immigration patterns.

2. Write questions at a variety of levels of difficulty for each question. For
   example:
   - How did Manifest Destiny affect American political development?
   - What actions did the U.S. government take that reflected the idea of Manifest
     Destiny?
   - What was the significance of the idea of Manifest Destiny?
   - What is Manifest Destiny?

3. Convert the questions into sentence starters. For example:
   - Manifest Destiny affected the American political system by/because. . .
   - Because of Manifest Destiny, the U.S. government . . .
   - Manifest Destiny was significant because . . .
   - Manifest Destiny is . . .

4. Post sentence starters and allow students to select which sentence starter they wish
   to use.

5. Have the students share their answers with two or three other students who may have
   selected a different starter or the same starter.

6. Choose several students for each starter and have them share their answers with the
   class.

**Grade 8 U.S. History Application**

**Lesson Concept:** Controversial Acts of Parliament before the American Revolution

**Content Objective:** SWBAT explain the significance of the French and Indian War.

**Language Objective:** SWBAT orally recall previously studied information using a variety of sentence structures.

**Key Vocabulary:** agree, disagree, position, debate, taxes, acts of Parliament, significance

In this middle school lesson, students are studying the aftermath of the French and Indian War. The essential question is: What was the significance of the French and Indian War? The students may use the following sentence starters:

- Yesterday we talked about . . .
- The French and Indian War was between . . .
- The colonists were angry with Parliament after the French and Indian War because . . .
- I agree/do not agree with position of the colonists because . . .

Students *choose* two of the sentence stems to discuss what they remember about the French and Indian War. This activity helps the students prepare for a debate later in this unit by accessing prior knowledge about key issues.

# Building Background

- Concrete Personal Experiences
- Post a Connection
- Oh Yesterday + Year!
- Predict Definitions
- Vocabulary Scan

The techniques described below help connect to students' personal lives and background knowledge, build additional knowledge they need for understanding the essential themes of history or social studies curricula, tie new learning to prior lessons, and develop the academic vocabulary they need to participate effectively in class.

## *Concrete Personal Experiences*

**SIOP®** COMPONENT: Building Background

Grade Level: All
Grouping Configuration: Varied, depending on activity
Approximate Time Involved: Varied, depending on the activity; from 10 minutes to a
class period
Materials: Varied, depending on the activity

## Description

Effective teaching starts with a concrete experience linked to the students' own lives that connects to the key concept of the unit. If students have no related background experience, it is essential to create an experience at the start of a new unit that will build hooks upon which the students can hang their new knowledge. Learning always moves from the concrete to the abstract. If teaching begins with the abstract, without any personal connections for students, the students have no mental hooks, and the learning slides right off.

## Procedure:

1. Create a concrete experience related to the students' own lives that connects to the key concept of the unit.

2. Have students reflect on the experience.

3. Connect the personal experience to the new learning; that is, make a bridge to the new learning by introducing the topic and moving to the abstract concepts.

   In planning the background or hook to a unit, three questions for teachers to consider are:

   a. What concrete experience will introduce the topic, activate background knowledge, and help make a meaningful connection to students' lives and prior learning?

   b. How will students analyze and reflect on this concrete experience?

   c. How will you make the connection between the concrete experience and the new concept, while previewing the topic and emphasizing the key vocabulary?

The choice of an opening background building experience depends on the nature of the key concepts and content objectives. Some options include:

- Participating in a simulation
- Viewing visuals
- Handling realia
- Writing or speaking about a personal experience related to the topic
- Taking a stand on a provocative opening question
- Listening to a story

### Grade 5 U.S. History Application

**Lesson Concept:** Transcontinental Railroad

**Content Objectives:**

- SWBAT identify the factors that contributed to the completion of the transcontinental railroad.
- SWBAT describe the impact of the transcontinental railroad on American life.

**Language Objective:**

- SWBAT write a reflection after participating in a simulation.

*(continued)*

**Key Vocabulary:** transcontinental, mountain range, competition

The race to complete the transcontinental railroad is an abstract concept for children. Introducing the unit with a simulation in which students race to build a popsicle stick "railroad" is an excellent strategy for building background.

**Procedure:**

1. Prior to class, place two strips of masking tape on the floor about 15 feet apart as starting points. Place another strip in the middle. Place pictures of Native Americans on the floor between each half. Also place chairs upside down between each half (representing the Rocky Mountains and Sierra Nevada Mountains). Place two bowls full of popsicle sticks near each starting point.

2. At the beginning of the lesson, ask students to think of a time they were in a race against someone else. How did they feel? Did they win? Did they try to win? What happened and why? Students can either draw a quick picture of their experience or write in their journals, then share with a partner. Tell students that today they will experience a race that will help them learn about their next topic of study. As they participate, they should make connections to their previous experiences in races.

3. Divide students into two groups. Have them line up at each starting point. Explain that each student will take three sticks. One at a time, they will place their sticks on the ground in the shape of an "H", beginning at each end tape. When one person finishes, s/he goes to the end of the line and the next person goes up and places his/her sticks on the floor, touching the "H" of the previous person (thus they are "building a railroad"). When they encounter a picture on the floor, they build right over it. When they encounter a chair, they have to figure out a way to get past it, but all the popsicle sticks must be touching (just like the railroad workers had to go around or through mountains). [Note: They can adjust sticks previously laid, but don't tell them this unless they ask specifically to do so.] The first group to reach the middle point wins. When they finish, you will have an excellent visual of the transcontinental railroad, with its various dilemmas.

4. Next is the most important step—the reflection. Students must understand why they did this activity and its connection to the content. Students will be excited, and the losers may be annoyed with each other. To diffuse the emotion and help students understand the purpose of the activity, have them complete a written reflection, answering questions such as:

   - What happened today?
   - Why do you think students tried hard to win?
   - What do you think the pictures on the floor represent? What about the chairs?
   - Why does competition motivate people?
   - Was this simulation a good way to learn? Why or why not?

5. If possible, leave the railroad in place throughout the unit as a visual representation. Otherwise take a photograph and post it on a bulletin board. Students will make the connections!

# *Post a Connection*

**SIOP** **COMPONENT:** Building Background

Grade Level: Grades 2–12
Grouping Configuration: Whole class
Approximate Time Involved: 10 minutes
Materials: Self-stick notes

## Description

As you start a new unit, ask students to "make a connection" by asking them what the new topic makes them think of or how it is similar to something else they learned. Before writing about these connections, have a few students share their ideas with a partner. Then ask a few volunteers to share with the class. To help students make explicit connections and to understand that making connections is an important learning strategy, have students write down their connection on self-stick notes and place them on a large chart paper posted in the room, titled "Connecting With [topic]." If desired, provide sentence starters for these connections. Repeat the process periodically throughout the unit, asking students to make personal connections, sharing, and then posting.

---

### Grade 2 Social Studies Application

**Lesson Topic:** Hispanic Civil Rights Leaders

**Content Objective:** SWBAT connect lessons on Cesar Chavez or Dolores Huerta to prior learning or life experiences.

**Language Objective:** SWBAT describe a personal connection orally and in writing.

**Key Vocabulary:** civil rights, discrimination, separate, connection, reminds me of

Many teachers begin a unit on Hispanic civil rights leaders by having students experience a simulated discrimination or by viewing photos (e.g., migrant workers' field and housing conditions, signs in storefronts "No Mexicans Allowed"). At the conclusion of this type of introduction, ask students to make a personal connection with the information, reminding them that effective learners look for connections between new information and prior learning or personal experiences, in order to have a hook on which to hang the new knowledge. Before asking the students to write, have a few students share their connections with a partner; then ask a few volunteers to share with the class.

With younger students, it is helpful to provide an academic sentence starter to jump-start the connection writing. Possible sentence starters that may be posted are:

- This information makes me think of . . .
- These pictures remind me of . . .
- One connection for me is . . .

*(continued)*

**Differentiation**

- Younger students can share their thoughts orally, or draw images on self-stick notes.

- An extension activity can take place after the notes are posted on the chart paper. The class can try to organize the ideas and personal connections into categories.

# *Oh Yesterday + Year!* (suggested by Lindsey Hillyard)

## SIOP COMPONENT: Building Background

Grade Level: K–12
Grouping Configuration: Individual
Approximate Time Involved: 5 minutes
Materials: None

## Description

Oh Yesterday + Year! is a fun method for students to recall and relate information they learned in the prior lesson about a historical event. The student selected to begin stands and states something he or she learned or remembered from the lesson the day before, in a theatrical manner, using the sentence starter, "Oh, Yesterday, I learned that . . . in [year]." The student may spread his/her arms wide or take a bow, for example, and speak loudly, or in a stage whisper, or in a funny voice. The year changes according to the time period being studied. For example, a student might say "Oh Yesterday I learned that Christopher Columbus made a second voyage to the Caribbean in 1493." Because this is an oral activity, students of all ages and language proficiencies can participate.

Sentence starters may vary:

- Oh Yesterday I learned that . . . in [year]!
- Oh Yesterday we studied about . . . in [year]!
- Oh Yesterday I discovered that . . . in [year]!
- Oh Yesterday our class found out that . . . in [year]!

Oh Yesterday + Year! should be done quickly, with students speaking one after the other. The teacher may select the speakers or the first student may choose the second, who chooses the third, and so on. Usually only four to six students do this any given day.

## Grade 7 U.S. History Application

**Lesson Concept:** Industrial Revolution

**Content Objective:** SWBAT review machines and other technologies developed during the Industrial Revolution.

*(continued)*

**Language Objective:** SWBAT use gestures, intonation, and word choice to convey an understanding of the role of inventions during the Industrial Revolution.

**Key Vocabulary:** telegraph, telephone, sewing machine, steamboat, phonograph, light bulb, electric motor, diesel engine

The class has been studying the Industrial Revolution for two days, with a focus on mechanical inventions that assisted the development of industry. At the beginning of class the third day, the teacher asks the students to make Oh Yesterday + Year! statements to review what they had been studying. She models one dramatically: "Oh Yesterday, we learned that Robert Fulton constructed the steam boat in 1807." She reminds the students to use gestures, such as bows or arm sweeps, and intonation to indicate their surprise, pleasure, fear, or confusion about the new inventions. She then calls on one student to begin and the process proceeds for about 4 minutes with several students taking turns.

**Differentiation**

The teacher might provide rehearsal time before having students perform. Newcomers and beginners might be paired up with other students to generate Oh Yesterday + Year! sentences and practice before being called on. More advanced students might be challenged to make an analytical statement or draw a conclusion about the prior lesson.

## *Predict Definitions*

**SIOP® COMPONENT: Building Background**

Grade Level: 3–12
Grouping Configuration: Individuals, partners, small groups
Approximate Time Involved: 20 minutes
Materials: Vocabulary flash cards (optional), student copy of word list and definitions

### Description

Teaching key vocabulary at the start of a unit (after the concrete personal experience) is an effective way to build background, but is often not engaging for the students. Rather than just having students copy words and definitions, Predict Definitions will engage students by creating excitement and giving them a personal stake in finding out the definitions.

### Procedure:

1. Post new vocabulary words for students using the flash cards or a list on the board. Have students look at the words and think of which ones they know. Have them pronounce each word after you.

2. Distribute a list of the new words. Have students put a check mark next to the words they think they know.

3. Distribute a list of the definitions. Instruct students to match the words with the definition they predict is correct. Stressing that these are just predictions eliminates student anxiety of trying to be correct.

4. As students finish, have them compare predictions in small groups or pairs to see if they agree or disagree. Those who disagree should be encouraged to explain their thinking to each other.

5. Review definitions. Students will be eager to know which ones they had predicted correctly. Have them make corrections to their definitions as necessary.

## Grade 4 Virginia State History Application

**Lesson Concept:** Settlements in Colonial Virginia

**Content Objective:** SWBAT explain hardships that settlers faced in establishing colonies in Virginia.

**Language Objective:** SWBAT define words related to the early settlements in colonial Virginia.

**Key Vocabulary:** colony, settlement, explore, resources, soil, treaty, compact, starvation

In a unit on colonial Virginia, the teacher presents the key words to students. After the students chorally pronounce each one in turn after the teacher's model, they consider their knowledge of the words. The teacher states each word and has the students raise one hand if they think they know it; two hands if they don't. The teacher then distributes a definition sheet (Figure 2.2), and students predict which words match which definitions. Newcomer and beginning students work with partners.

After the predictions, the teacher reviews the correct definitions and introduces the topic for the day. The class previews the section of the textbook they will read next and the teacher points out key words that occur in the headings, subheadings, and captions.

### Differentiation

This technique can be adapted for kinesthetic learners, or just for variety. The words and definitions can be written on individual index cards. In step 2, students can separate the words into two piles: one for words they think they know, one for words they don't. In step 3, the words and definition cards can be physically matched.

Beginning students can be paired with a more advanced classmate to make the predictions in step 3. Classmates may also translate the definitions on the handout into the native languages of newcomers. Advanced students and native English speakers can try to write predictions for the definitions as a self-assessment before receiving the handout.

FIGURE 2.2   *Predicting Definitions Handout*

**Predicting Definitions**

**Directions:** Draw a line to match each word on the left with its definition on the right.

| | |
|---|---|
| colony | dirt; land on Earth's surface used for farming |
| settlement | not having enough food to eat; feeling very, very hungry |
| explore | permanent village established in a new place |
| resources | formal agreement or contract between two countries or political groups |
| soil | go to new places to discover new things |
| treaty | region where people live and are ruled by a government in another country |
| compact | agreement between two or more groups to act in a certain way |
| starving | things we need in nature, such as water and clean air |

# Vocabulary Scan

**SIOP** **COMPONENT: Building Background**

Grade Level: 4–12

Grouping Configuration: Individual, then whole class

Approximate Time Involved: 5–10 minutes

Materials: Social studies text to scan

## Description

One of the challenges we face in teaching social studies to English learners is selecting the vocabulary words to teach. Scanning enables us to bring students in on the process by having them select key vocabulary found in content area texts for the class to preview before reading. We often underestimate the power of teaching the vocabulary students are about to encounter in a meaningful context. Marzano, Pickering, and Pollock (2001) discuss how prior instruction on words greatly enhances the probability that students will understand the new words from context when they encounter them later in reading. Scanning is a powerful tool for enabling teachers to provide vocabulary instruction in context on words that students will encounter in new content.

## Procedure:

1. Select a text (or set of texts) for students to read.

2. Have students begin scanning the text from the last page forward, page by page, for unfamiliar vocabulary. The purpose of starting from the end of the text is to dissuade students from reading the text and skipping unfamiliar words. By starting at the end, students develop the habit of scanning rather than reading a text.

3. Ask students to call out unfamiliar terms or write them on white boards. List the new terms on the board in front of the class.

4. Define the vocabulary briefly using student-friendly language, giving only the definition that fits the context of the text to be read. Have students copy unfamiliar terms and definitions into their notebooks.

5. Pronounce the unfamiliar terms and have the students repeat them.

6. Have students read the text.

7. Leave the list on the board for students to refer to when engaged in content area discussion and writing activities.

---

### Grade 10 World History Application

**Lesson Concept:** Ancient Japan

**Content Objective:** SWBAT compare the feudal system in Japan with the feudal system in Europe.

**Language Objective:** SWBAT define unfamiliar terms and be able to use the new words in context.

**Key Vocabulary:** shogun, samurai, daimyo, feudal, emperor, Imperial Court, artisan, ceremonial

Students backward scan the section of textbook discussing the time periods in Japan when the emperor and shogun ruled the country, looking for unfamiliar terms. They write the unfamiliar terms on their white boards or in their notebooks. In this lesson, possible terms are *shogun, samurai, daimyo, feudal, emperor, Imperial Court, artisan*, and *ceremonial*. The teacher then lists the terms on the board and provides a short, written definition. The teacher then pronounces the unfamiliar words for the students, which they repeat in turn. For example, the teacher writes the word *artisan* and says, "Repeat after me, artisan. This word means *someone who is skilled in a craft*." The teacher writes the definition and students copy it in

*(continued)*

their notebooks. Later, when the students are comparing feudal Japan to feudal Europe, the teacher encourages the students to use the words during the activity.

### Differentiation

**Beginner:**
Use native language when possible to provide definitions, making sure to limit the definition to words that fit the context of the passage. When scanning a textbook, newcomer and beginning students may scan captions, titles, and subtitles rather than the text. Be sure to point out cognates to students.

**Intermediate:**
Provide the students with adapted text to scan when possible or limit the scope of a scan to a portion of a text rather than a whole text. Encourage these students to consider prefixes, suffixes, and cognates when they try to figure out the words' meanings.

**Advanced:**
Point out characteristics of the words selected including roots, affixes, word origins, and features of English spelling and pronunciation when discussing the words with the class.

# Comprehensible Input

- Prop Box Improv
- Listen for Information
- Move It!

History or social studies lessons can be very dense, full of facts and unfamiliar events, places, and people. It is important for teachers to chunk the information to give students greater access to the concepts, patterns, and enduring understandings they need to learn. Familiar ESL techniques such as using visuals, demonstrations, gestures, movement, role plays, simulations, and the like are particularly well suited to the history or social studies classroom. The techniques and activities described below give teachers ideas for helping students access the necessary content.

### *Prop Box Improv* (developed by John Seidlitz and Bill Perryman)

**SIOP**
SHELTERED INSTRUCTION
OBSERVATION PROTOCOL

**COMPONENT:** Comprehensible Input

Grade Level: 6–12
Grouping Configuration: Small heterogeneous groups of 4–6 students
Approximate Time Involved: 50–75 minutes
Materials: Props for skits, chart paper, markers

## Description

This activity creates high levels of student engagement by having learners use props to create short skits that represent key content concepts. History and geography come alive as students use specific everyday items to demonstrate and communicate their understanding of ideas.

## Procedure:

1. Create a "prop box," which contains items that students can use to represent ideas relevant to a skit. Perryman and Seidlitz (2009) suggest including such items as feathers, rope, binoculars, sunglasses, canteen, cardboard, scarf, artificial flowers, crosses, colored cloth or fabric, markers, construction paper, chart paper, bandanas, cane, plastic crown, costume jewelry, and plastic toys.

2. Select a text and divide it into sections. Each section will be assigned to one group of students. Group size should range from four to six students.

3. Introduce the students to the text and then assign a section to each group. The group is to choose five key words and two or three big ideas contained in the section. They are to write their key words and big ideas on chart paper.

4. Give each group a set amount of time (15 to 20 minutes) to create a skit. The skits should represent as many details as possible from the passage. Skit guidelines include the following:

   - All students must speak at some point during the presentation.
   - All key words and big ideas must be represented using the props, movement, or dialog.
   - Students should use as many props and represent as many details as possible from the passage during the skit.

5. Have students present their skits in the order they appear in the text. Before each skit, students silently read the passage about to be represented. After the skit, students jot down the key words and big ideas in their notebooks with supplemental notes and clarifications added by the teacher as needed.

### Grade 7 Texas State History Application

**Lesson Concept:** The Texas Revolution

**Content Objective:** SWBAT describe the key events of the Texas Revolution.

**Language Objective:** SWBAT create and participate in a dramatization of key events of the Texas Revolution.

**Key Vocabulary:** revolution, tyranny, infamy, mission, repeal, outnumber, massacre

The teacher creates a prop box using the suggestions listed in the procedures. The teacher then divides up the textbook into four sections for her class size of 22: The Battle of Gonzales, The Goliad Massacre, The Battle of the Alamo, and The Battle of San Jacinto. Each group of students reads its section, chooses key vocabulary and ideas, and records them.

*(continued)*

For example, the group that selects the Battle of the Alamo may chose three key ideas and represent the ideas the following ways:

1. *The Alamo was a fort that used to be a mission.* Students create a mission using chairs and cut-out chart paper in the shape of a cross, placing the cross on the top of the fort. They take the cross down during the skit when the characters representing Texas soldiers enter the fort.

2. *The Texans were outnumbered.* If there are six people in the group, four play the parts of Mexican soldiers, and two play Texans. Students create small Texas and Mexican flags to represent both sides.

3. *The battle became a rallying cry for Texans in the revolt against Mexico.* Students use cloth fabric to represent a flag. At the end of the skit, one student waves the cloth saying, "Remember the Alamo, it will help you win the war."

The key words the students select could be represented the following ways:

- *Santa Anna* can be represented using a military hat.
- *Revolution, tyranny,* and *infamy* can be used during a dialog among the students.
- The repeal of the *Constitution of 1824* can be represented by having Santa Anna tear up a piece of paper at the beginning of the skit.

### Differentiation

**Beginner:**

Beginners may use native language resources to provide necessary background information. Resources could include a word bank or an article in the native language about the event. Beginners may need some practice with social and academic language terms necessary to understand the activity such as *prop, skit, role, part, represent,* and *demonstrate.* You may also grant beginners some flexibility about their speaking roles during the skit. They will need to practice pronouncing the words and phrases they have to say until they are comfortable.

**Intermediate and Advanced:**

Students at intermediate and advanced levels of proficiency can self-select their level of involvement in speaking and writing during the activity. This activity works best with heterogeneous grouping. Students who are more advanced tend to participate more in the speaking and writing portions.

An extension of this activity is to have two groups present skits that demonstrate different perspectives on the events.

## *Listen for Information*

**SIOP** **COMPONENT:** Comprehensible Input

Grade Level:  All
Grouping Configuration:  Whole class
Approximate Time Involved:  Varies
Materials:  Activity sheet with pictures or a list of questions to listen for

## Description

English learners at beginning and early intermediate levels of proficiency often need support to help focus their attention when viewing videos, listening to stories, and following a teacher's lecture because they struggle to comprehend rapid speech. They may get the main idea of the presentation but not important details. Helping students develop strategies that enable them to access more meaning from extended teacher talk or video clips is invaluable. This technique focuses on previewing information that will be shared orally. Younger students and beginning level students can be given various pictures related to the topic (clip art is a great source) to see if they appear in the video or are mentioned in the historical narrative. Older or more proficient students can be given a list of yes/no questions or true/false statements to respond to as they are listening.

## Procedure:

1. Design an activity sheet with pictures, yes/no questions, or true/false statements and give a copy to each student. This sheet can be laid out like an anticipation guide with one section or column to indicate a prediction and another to confirm or change after the presentation.

2. Review the pictures or statements beforehand, and have students predict which ones will be discussed in the video or talk. If some are associated with new vocabulary terms, briefly define the words. Then have the students listen to see if their predictions were correct. This form of an anticipation guide will provide even beginning students with a purpose for viewing a video or listening to a story or lecture. Also discuss with students the importance of listening for information as a key learning strategy.

---

### Grade 1 Social Studies Application

**Lesson Concept:** Neighborhood Resources

**Content Objective:** SWBAT identify community resources.

**Language Objective:** SWBAT listen and watch for specific information.

**Key Vocabulary:** elementary school, bank, police station, firehouse, supermarket, drug store, park, movie theater, library

The teacher distributes the handout with pictures of the key words and labels. The class reviews what each picture represents and discusses the function of each building and whether these buildings are near the school. The teacher explains they will be watching a video clip of a neighborhood in another state and asks them to predict which community resources will be present. The students take a few minutes to mark their papers.

The teacher reminds students to listen and watch carefully for the community resources. They can mark their sheets when they see a resource or hear it being discussed. The 4-minute clip includes narration and interviews with residents of a rural town in

*(continued)*

Appalachia. When it ends, the teacher encourages students to confirm their predictions and share their observations with a partner.

### Differentiation

For classes with mixed ability levels, several versions of the activity sheet can be prepared: one version with pictures for beginners; one with pictures and yes/no questions for intermediate students; one for true/false statements for advanced ELs and native English speakers.

# *Move It!*

**SIOP®** **COMPONENT:** Comprehensible Input

Grade Level:  All
Grouping Configuration:  Individuals, small group, partners, whole class
Approximate Time Involved:  8–10 minutes
Materials:  None

## Description

Teachers often struggle to find ways for students to understand the meaning of key concepts and remember the terms associated with those concepts. Move It! gives teachers a method for connecting key ideas and terms through the use of gestures and movement. The activity involves students moving their bodies to represent the key concepts. For example, in a lesson on the French Revolution, a teacher might share specific hand signs to represent key concepts such as

- holding up the index finger and smiling to represent the Enlightenment
- gripping hands in front of face while marching to represent the storming of the Bastille
- searching with one's eyes, cupping one's ears, and using a hand chop motion to represent the Reign of Terror

## Procedure:

1. Select key concepts from a lesson that could be represented using gestures and movement.

2. Introduce the key concepts to the students and either create or have students working in small heterogeneous groups create movements and gestures that represent those concepts.

3. Have students practice reviewing the gestures first as a whole class and then with a partner.

4. Review gestures during the lesson and at the end of the lesson.

## Grade 9 U.S. Government Application

**Lesson Concept:** Principles of American Government

**Content Objectives:** Students will be able to define significant political principles reflected in the U.S. system of government.

**Language Objectives:** Students will be able to create gestures that represent the terms: federalism, separation of powers, checks and balances, limited government, and popular sovereignty.

**Key Vocabulary:** gesture, represent, federalism, separation of powers, limited government, popular sovereignty, checks and balances

This lesson takes place after students have had a basic introduction to the American political system, including descriptions of the powers of the three branches of government and some of the distinctions between the powers of state and federal levels of government. The teacher provides students with the list of terms and practices pronouncing the terms with them. The teacher provides a brief explanation of the meaning of each term. The students are then divided into small groups; each has the task of creating a gesture that involves physical movement to represent one of the key concepts. For example, students might place one hand on top of the other to represent federalism—the top hand representing the national level of government and the lower hand representing the state level. Students might show separation of powers by using their hands to create an equal sign to show the equality between the three branches of government. Students might show popular sovereignty by raising their hand to represent voting for a particular choice.

### Differentiation

**Beginner:**
Beginners may be provided with a native language resource that would include definitions of the terms and important background information. Identifying cognates can be helpful when possible. Teachers may wish to practice pronunciation individually with students who are at the beginning level of language proficiency.

**Advanced:**
Students at this level of proficiency should be encouraged to justify the reasons particular gestures or movements were selected by linking the meaning of the term with the gesture or movement.

# Strategies

- Highlight Key Information in Text
- Cut and Match Answers
- Expert/Novice

The techniques described below offer teachers ideas to help students learn and practice metacognitive and cognitive strategies. They can be applied to tasks requiring listening and reading comprehension. The techniques also show how peers can scaffold information for their classmates.

# Highlight Key Information in Text

**SIOP® COMPONENT: Strategies**

Grade Level: 3–12
Grouping Configuration: Individual, partners
Approximate Time Involved: 15 minutes
Materials: Copy of selected text, highlighters

## Description

English learners often have trouble locating answers in text, as well as paraphrasing answers from text. To practice these skills, provide a copy of one to two pages of the text being studied and three to five questions for which answers can be found in the text. Review the questions with the class. First, have students read and highlight the text where they believe the answer is given, then compare their highlighted sections with a partner. Next, have partners work together to write their answers in their own words. After that, ask partners to exchange their answers with another pair to check for accuracy and paraphrasing versus copying straight from the text. This activity needs to be fully modeled by the teacher before the students try it independently.

### Grade 5 Social Studies Application

**Lesson Concept:** Ancient Greece

**Content Objective:** SWBAT determine important facts about Ancient Greece.

**Language Objective:** SWBAT read for specific information and paraphrase that information.

**Key Vocabulary:** religious beliefs, gods, goddesses, oracles, culture, trade, conquest, compare

The teacher prepares the list of questions below and selects the portion of the text where the answers may be found:

- Where was Ancient Greece located?
- What land features did Ancient Greece have?
- Tell about the religious beliefs of Ancient Greeks.
- Compare the Minoans and the Mycenaeans.

*(continued)*

Using a copy of the text on a transparency, the teacher models through a think-aloud how to look for the answer to the first question and how to highlight information that answers it. The teacher then orally paraphrases the answer and, when satisfied, writes it down. Students then use their own copies of the text to read and highlight sentences related to the remaining questions. In pairs they answer the questions and share responses with another pair.

The class reports out once all the groups have finished. The teacher records some of the answers to the third question and discusses how different groups phrased the response. This step reinforces the notion that answers can be written in different ways but still provide correct information.

### Differentiation

This activity is a follow-up to one where all students were taught the concept of paraphrasing and given some opportunities to practice paraphrasing sentences or paragraphs written for that purpose. If some students are still struggling with the concept or process, a review is merited before the work with the text begins.

As this classroom example indicates, it is useful to include a range of question types, including higher-order questions. In classes with mixed levels of proficiency, the teacher might want to assign different questions to different pairs, or identify some questions as "bonus queries" to challenge more advanced learners.

## *Cut and Match Answers*

**SIOP®** **COMPONENT:** Strategies (also suitable for Interaction and Practice & Application)

Grade Level: 1–12
Grouping Configuration: Individual, partners
Approximate Time Involved: 15 minutes
Materials: Answers to cut out, graphic organizer or questions, glue

## Description

Graphic organizers are common instructional scaffolds in many classes. However, to make graphic organizers more interactive, engaging, and hands-on, instead of having students write on an organizer, provide the answers for students to cut up (or precut them yourself and place them in individual envelopes) and have students arrange the cutouts on the organizer. Before students glue down their cutouts, have them compare their placements with a partner and discuss any differences of opinion. As students are working, circulate and assess what students know, so you will only need to discuss with the whole class the placements that many students missed. Students may glue their answers after determining that all are correct. This activity can be used with any other type of worksheet; instead of writing answers, students can arrange them, compare with partners, and then glue.

FIGURE 2.3 *Graphic Organizer on the Thirteen English Colonies*

**The Thirteen English Colonies**

|  | *New England Colonies* | *Mid-Atlantic Colonies* | *Southern Colonies* |
|---|---|---|---|
| Names of Colonies |  |  |  |
| Geography and Climate |  |  |  |
| Main Occupations |  |  |  |
| Settlers/Colonists |  |  |  |
| Reasons for Coming to America |  |  |  |

## Grade 3 Social Studies Application

**Lesson Concept:** The Thirteen Colonies

**Content Objective:** SWBAT describe and compare the characteristics of the New England, Mid-Atlantic, and Southern colonies.

**Language Objective:** SWBAT read a description and classify it on a graphic organizer.

**Key Vocabulary:** colony, geography, climate, occupation, New England, mid-Atlantic, southern

After reading a text or viewing a movie about the thirteen colonies, distribute a blank graphic organizer with the headings New England Colonies, Mid-Atlantic Colonies, and Southern Colonies (see Figure 2.3). The topics to address are Names of Colonies, Geography and Climate, Main Occupations, Settlers/Colonists, and Reasons for Coming to America. Give students the answers in random order on a sheet for them to cut up and place on the chart, or distribute envelopes with the answer pieces already cut up.

### Differentiation
This activity works well for all students, especially to introduce them to graphic organizers and to realize how much information should be included and how it may be worded. Teachers can continue this technique for the newcomers and beginners, but can slowly move more advanced students away from this, perhaps by giving them half the answers as the next phase and asking them to write in the rest.

*(continued)*

A variation, suggested by Jennifer Himmel and Emily Evans, is to treat the graphic organizers and pieces as a puzzle and have students work in rotating groups. They start at a table with the graphic organizers and cutouts. They have 2 minutes to start the task. When time is called, each group rotates to another table and works on that puzzle. After one minute, they move again, continuing the process until the graphic organizers are complete.

# *Expert/Novice*

**SIOP** **COMPONENT:** Strategies (also suitable for Interaction)

Grade Level: 6–12
Grouping Configuration: Heterogeneous groups of two or three
Approximate Time Involved: 15 minutes, after students have developed "expertise" on their topics
Materials: Primary and secondary sources for students to use to research topics

## Description

The Expert/Novice technique was created by Bill Perryman as a way to get his students to take on the roles of social studies professionals in the social studies classroom. Students develop expertise on a topic and then play the role of an expert in interactions with other students who have less understanding of the topic.

## Procedure:

1. Select two topics about which students will develop expertise.

2. Divide the class in two halves, A's and B's. The A's will research one topic; the B's will research another.

3. Ask the class as a whole to brainstorm research questions for the two topics. Evaluate the list as a class and select several for each topic.

4. Organize students so that A's partner with other A's and B's partner with other B's to research the topic and answer the questions. As they conduct the research, they also note other interesting and significant ideas they discover.

5. Pair up the A's with the B's. B's begin and ask A's about their topic. They may begin with the research questions identified, but should also ask extension questions using the following language stems:

   a. Why do you think . . . ?

   b. Is there another . . . ?

   c. Tell me more about . . . .

   The A's respond to the B's questions. If students are unable to answer the extension questions, they may respond, "That's an interesting question; let's write that down" and then record the question in their notebooks for later investigation.

6. Students switch roles and A's ask questions next.

7. The first set of pairs separate; the A's find a new B partner, the B's a new A partner. The A's begin by questioning their new partner. Then the B's ask the questions. This repetition of the process is done so that students have a chance to hear from more than one expert about the topic.

8. The teacher then conducts a whole-class discussion on the research questions. New questions the students wrote down can be raised with the whole group.

---

### Grade 10 World History Application

**Lesson Concept:** China: Past and Present

**Content Objective:** SWBAT identify characteristics of ancient and modern Chinese societies.

**Language Objective:** SWBAT research and compare significant features of ancient and modern Chinese societies.

**Key Vocabulary:** ancient, modern, dynasty, significant

This lesson takes place in a World Geography class during a unit on Asian societies. The teacher wants to use the activity to clear up misconceptions students may have about modern China. The teacher divides the class into two groups; one will research ancient Confucian Chinese society during the Ming dynasty (A's), the other will research contemporary Chinese society (B's). The teacher makes sure that both groups contain students of diverse levels of language proficiency.

The teacher then leads a discussion where the students brainstorm research questions. The final list of questions may include:

1. Who was/is in charge, and how did/do they decide who was in charge?

2. What was/is their religion?

3. How did/do they earn a living?

4. Who were/are their enemies? Why?

5. How were/are women treated? Why?

6. Who were/are the heroes? Why?

7. What did/do people do for fun?

The teacher then pairs A's with A's and B's with B's to research answers to the questions. Afterward, the teacher pairs A's with B's and encourages students to ask and answer the research questions and also extension questions using the stems: "Why do you think . . .", "Is there another . . .", and "Tell me more . . .". After the first round, A's and B's find new partners and repeat the process.

Once these partner discussions have been completed, the class has a discussion. Some new questions that might come up are "Why is Mao Zedong (Tse-tung) still considered a hero in modern China?"; "Why do women in China today have more rights than they did in the past?"; and "What other ways do modern Chinese people have fun besides sports and movies?"

*(continued)*

Differentiation

**Beginner:**

It is important to group beginners with more advanced classmates during the research phase of this activity. Beginners may need to practice responding to the research questions orally and to practice saying, "That's a good question; let's write that down." Beginners may be provided with a native language resource (written or audio-supported) that would include background information about the topic being studied. In addition, preteaching classroom and academic vocabulary for the activity is helpful for students at this level of proficiency.

**Intermediate:**

These students also need practice responding to the questions orally when working in their research group. They also may benefit from preteaching some academic vocabulary.

**Advanced:**

Students at this level of proficiency should be encouraged to elaborate responses to the extension questions. During the whole-class discussion the teacher might ask, "What was an interesting question you were asked about Chinese society? How did you respond?"

# Concluding Thoughts

This chapter is the first of two that offers a selection of activities and techniques that can help teachers meet the goals of SIOP® History or SIOP® Social Studies instruction. We encourage you to try these activities with your students. Although we have situated them in a particular grade with a particular lesson topic, you will find that these techniques can be applied in multiple contexts and differentiated for the range of learners in your classroom. The techniques should not, however, be treated as a grab bag of activities. Rather, select from them in service of your lesson goals, your language and content objectives, and the needs and interests of your students.

# chapter 3

# Activities and Techniques for SIOP® History-Social Studies Lessons: Interaction, Practice & Application, Lesson Delivery, Review & Assessment

By Robin Liten-Tejada, John Seidlitz, and Deborah Short

## Introduction

This chapter presents additional techniques and activities for history and social studies instruction, organized by the final four SIOP® components: Interaction, Practice & Application, Lesson Delivery, and Review & Assessment. As we did in Chapter 2, we describe the steps for each technique, contextualize it in a particular grade and lesson topic, and offer suggestions for differentiation. (If you haven't read Chapter 2 yet, look over the beginning of the section of History and Social Studies Techniques and Activities, page 26 to see the explanations and purposes of each section of a technique's description.) The techniques are generally useful across the range of K–12 grade levels, although some are more advantageous in a narrower range. You will notice again that some of the techniques are applicable to more than one SIOP® component. Remember, the activities alone do not constitute a lesson. Choose among these proven techniques so students will explore, practice, and meet your content and language objectives.

# Interaction

- Structured Conversations
- Learning Styles Debate
- You Are There

The techniques and activities described here offer multiple opportunities for students to interact with each other. By providing sentence starters and academic language frames, the teacher can scaffold the appropriate language for the students to use. Students may also select roles and tasks based on their interests and proficiencies.

## *Structured Conversations*

**COMPONENT:** Interaction (also suitable for Practice & Application)

Grade Level: All, depending on oral or written activity
Grouping Configuration: Partners
Approximate Time Involved: 15–20 minutes
Materials: Depends on activity

## Description

Teachers can turn many written activities into speaking and listening activities that reinforce the content and academic language by creating structured conversations. Any time students are practicing a skill, such as determining points on a map grid or identifying features on a map, teachers can provide them with sentence starters to enable them to discuss their work with a partner. Students then move to other partners to practice the conversation. Partners can also recite their conversation for the whole class; the class members listen to determine if the information is accurate. This is a powerful strategy to reinforce both language skills and content knowledge.

One suggestion is to consider a language function students should learn to express and then develop some sentence frames. For example, students need to be able to agree or disagree appropriately. While studying a map, the following frames for partners could be posted:

*Person A:* Point A is located at _____. It is in the _____ Hemisphere.

*Person B:* I agree [*or* I disagree] with you. It is located in the _____ Hemisphere.

After practicing several times, partners switch roles and practice the other language frame, using different content information each time. The teacher could wrap up the activity by having some partners demonstrate their conversations, with classmates listening for accuracy.

Partners or small groups can also write 5W questions and answers related to the topic being studied, practice saying the questions and answers, and then move to other partners to ask their questions. The final pairs can recite the questions and answers for the whole class, again with the class listening for accuracy.

## Grade 2 Social Studies Application

**Lesson Concept:** Map Reading Skills

**Content Objective:** SWBAT identify geographic features on a map.

**Language Objective:** SWBAT use comparative and superlative adjective forms.

**Key Vocabulary:** mountain, glacier, river, lake, park, farther, nearer, adjective + *-er*, adjective + *-est*

In this grade 2 classroom, students are learning to read maps. They have already learned about keys, legends, scales, and the compass rose, and today they are applying their knowledge to a map of Alaska. The teacher introduces sentence frames she would like the students to use and reviews how to form comparative and superlative adjectives. Some of the frames are:

- *Partner A:* The tallest mountain in Alaska is _____.
- *Partner B:* I agree [*or* I disagree] with you because _____.
- *Partner B:* The biggest glacier in Alaska is _____
- *Partner A:* I agree [*or* I disagree] with you because _____
- *Partner A:* The _____ river is longer than the _____ river.
- *Partner B:* Yes, but the _____ river is the longest.

### Differentiation

1. Simple frames can be prepared for beginners, with longer and more complex frames suggested for intermediate and advanced level students. Advanced students can also be encouraged to extend the conversation beyond two or three exchanges.

2. With younger students or beginning language proficiency students, or just to change the nature of the activity, each student can be given one teacher-written question that they practice saying to themselves. They then go around the room taking turns asking their question and answering their partners' questions. This can also be used as a vocabulary review. Each student has a vocabulary word, and is instructed to move around the room to different partners, asking and answering:

   - What is the definition of _____?
   - The definition of _____ is _____.

3. A follow-up activity can reinforce writing skills and academic vocabulary knowledge. Students should write their final question and answer in their journals, and then exchange journals with a partner so the partner can check for written accuracy.

# *Learning Styles Debate*

**SIOP®** **COMPONENT:** Interaction (also suitable for Practice & Application and Lesson Delivery)

Grade Level: 6–12

Grouping Configuration: Students self-select a task based on interest and ability, and then are grouped with other students who chose the same task.

Approximate Time Involved: 40 minutes

Materials: Chart paper and markers

## Description

Social studies teachers often use debate as a way to get students to reflect on a variety of points of view about issues. It is challenging, however, to get students to participate in a debate when they are at different language levels and have varying degrees of background knowledge. Often, students who are more extroverted and language proficient tend to dominate the debate, leaving English learners who are at lower levels of language proficiency as observers rather than as full participants in the conversation. The learning styles debate provides a way for teachers to have all students participate by asking them to self-select tasks that enable them to represent different viewpoints in assorted ways. As a result of the choice, students have more confidence and interest in the activity.

This technique may be used with numerous historical controversies, such as isolationism vs. imperialism, federalism vs. anti-federalism, divine right of kings vs. popular sovereignty, prohibition, immigration policy, and so forth.

## Procedures:

1. Prepare the following four labels for the classroom and display these labels in different corners of the room: **LETTER TO THE EDITOR, CARTOON, SPEECH,** and **CHANT.**

2. Set the debate topic and have the students list on the board reasons supporting both sides of the argument.

3. Ask students to choose an activity (letter to the editor, cartoon, speech, or chant) and stand by the sign representing it. If some stations are empty, ask students to consider moving so that you have at least two people at each station.

4. Have the students "letter" off as A's and B's at each station around the room. A's will represent one point of view, and B's will represent an opposing point of view. Make sure that each station has both A's and B's so that each point of view will have a letter to the editor, cartoon, speech, and chant.

5. Ask students to use the information on the board to prepare their respective letters, cartoons, speeches, or chants representing their points of view.

6. Debate presentation: All the A's and B's form separate teams facing each other. The debate occurs in this order: **Chants, Cartoon, Letter to the Editor,** and **Speech.** To add enthusiasm, two lines of the A chant can be repeated after each A team presents

and the same can be done with the B chant. Also, a cheer for each team can be created and taught to all members of the team.

7. After the debate, hold a secret ballot vote for all the students to determine whether the A or B point of view won the debate.

---

### Grade 8 U.S. History Application

**Lesson Concept:** Controversial Acts of Parliament before the American Revolution

**Content Objective:** SWBAT explain points of view regarding the various acts of the British Parliament that were protested by the American colonists.

**Language Objective:** SWBAT participate in a debate about the conflict between the British Parliament and the American colonists.

**Key Vocabulary:** debate, loyalty, revolt, freedom, rights, point of view

The class is divided into two teams: the Parliament and the Colonists. Parliament will argue that the colonists should be loyal and grateful to the British crown. The Colonists will argue that the British should respect their rights as Englishmen or expect a revolt. Each team will divide into four groups with different responsibilities.

- *Group One:* Write a chant supporting the view that the Colonists are spoiled and should remain loyal and stop complaining (A), or supporting the idea that the British have had no respect for the colonists and do not deserve respect and loyalty until they do (B).

- *Group Two:* Create a political cartoon either mocking the colonists' behavior (A), or mocking the British Parliament's behavior (B).

- *Group Three:* Write a brief letter to a local newspaper editor arguing that the colonists need to be loyal and grateful to the British Parliament and stop complaining and causing trouble (A), or that the colonists should think about revolting against England if the Parliament's behavior doesn't change (B).

- *Group Four:* Make a list of talking points and practice a short speech defending the idea that the colonists should submit loyally and be grateful to the British crown for the favors they have received (A), or that the British must respect the rights of the colonists or expect revolt (B).

Each group prepares its activity and then presents the debate to the class by alternating teams, with the chant group A beginning, the chant group B next, and so on.

---

## *You Are There* (Adapted from *99 Ideas*, p. 119)

**SIOP** **COMPONENT:** Interaction

Grade Level: 4–12
Grouping Configuration: Small groups, whole class
Approximate Time Involved: 30–45 minutes
Materials: Resources for research (e.g., books, articles, Web sites)

## Description

The teacher divides students into small groups of three or four. Each group is assigned a historical event to research. When the research has been completed, students use an interview format to present the information. They designate roles within their groups. One student plays the role of the interviewer and the others take on the roles of people who were present when the event took place. For example, one student may play Meriwether Lewis, another William Clark, and others members of different Native American tribes encountered during the expedition. The interviewer will prepare questions to ask the interviewees and the interviewees will prepare their responses. The teacher should remind students to use the key vocabulary and sentence structures when preparing their presentations.

Next, small groups will take turns acting out their interviews for the rest of the class. As the students watch the interviews, they can use prepared outlines to take notes on the information presented.

---

### Grade 12 Economics Application

**Lesson Concept:** Great Depression

**Content Objective:** SWBAT identify the effects of the financial collapse of 1929 on Americans' daily lives.

**Language Objective:** SWBAT ask and answer questions using cause-effect expressions, such as "As a result of ___," " Because of ___, we ___," "After the ___, I ___," and "If we had ___, then ___."

**Key Vocabulary:** cause, effect, impact, result, finance, collapse, stock market, crash, bread line, suicide, Depression, Wall Street, Dust Bowl, migration, stocks, bonds, shares

The class has been studying the stock market crash of 1929, including some of the financial decisions that led to Wall Street's demise. In this two-day lesson, the teacher asks students to consider the impact of the Depression on the lives of American families. The students form groups of four or five and select a card with a role designated on it: farming family in Oklahoma; family of a government worker in Washington, DC; family of a dockworker in New York City; wealthy family connected to the railroad trade in Chicago; a cattle ranch family in Texas. The teacher posts some causation sentence frames for students to use in their interviews, such as

- The impact of the stock market crash has been _____.
- We can no longer _____ because _____.
- If _____ had _____, then we _____.
- As a result of _____, I am now _____.
- After _____, we _____.

Each group conducts research on the effects of the stock market crash (and other catastrophes at the time, such as the Dust Bowl) and plans a You Are There interview.

*(continued)*

The teacher encourages multi-generational portrayals, such as assigning the roles of a grandparent, parent, and child in each family to be interviewed. The second day of the lesson is set aside for the interview presentations.

### Differentiation

- By working in mixed-proficiency level groups to develop the interviewer questions and interviewee answers, less proficient English learners have support as they develop their roles. Including time for rehearsal is beneficial for the lower level students as well.

- The interviews can be presented in a variety of ways, for example as a "reporter in the street" scenario, stopping people to ask questions; as a radio talk show; or as a panel interview.

# Practice & Application

- Reader's Theater
- Living Diorama
- Partner Listening Dictation
- Go Graphic – One Step Further

The SIOP® Model encourages teachers to include opportunities for students to practice and apply both their new content knowledge and the language skills and structures they are learning. Hands-on activities, projects, and other tasks that require critical thinking are valuable when they tap both oral and written modes. The following techniques engage students as they practice and apply historical or social studies content and language.

## *Reader's Theater*

**SIOP®** **COMPONENT:** Practice & Application

Grade Level:  All
Grouping Configuration:  Small group
Approximate Time Involved:  30 minutes
Materials:  Reader's Theater rubric (Figure 3.1)

### Description

Reader's Theater is a strategy that builds oral reading fluency for native speakers and English learners as they read and perform scripts. With strategically written scripts that incorporate academic vocabulary, Reader's Theater also reinforces content knowledge through oral practice. Reader's Theater is usually performed by small groups of four to six students to provide an interesting range of voices. Teachers can create their own scripts using key vocabulary in lines that will be read by the entire group, by pairs, and/or by individual students. Teachers may also find scripts from poems, chants, and other published dialogues.

In order to effectively introduce students to the scripts, teachers should model the script first, and then do a whole-class choral reading, followed by half-class alternating lines. This repetition will provide nonthreatening practice for beginning proficiency students to develop confidence to perform with their groups. The groups then practice their scripts separately and finally perform them for the class. During the performance, classmates in the audience can use a simple rubric to assess the speakers.

## Grade 6 Social Studies Application

**Lesson Concept:** Achievement of Black Americans

**Content Objective:**
- SWBAT connect achievements with famous Black Americans.

**Language Objectives:**
- SWBAT speak fluently while performing a Reader's Theater script.
- SWBAT listen to classmates' performances to assess the accuracy of content and pronunciation.

**Key Vocabulary:** dream, humanity, freedom, achievement, vision, goal

Before beginning the lesson, the teacher selects two children's poems about or by famous Black Americans, such as Martin Luther King Jr., Maya Angelou, Langston Hughes, and Nikki Giovanni. At the start of the lesson, the teacher preteaches key vocabulary terms and explains accomplishments of the Black Americans. The teacher then models both poems, one at a time, for students while they read along silently. This allows students to hear the correct pronunciation, fluent speech, and an energetic presentation. After each teacher model, the whole class does a choral reading, which provides less proficient students an opportunity to practice speaking in a nonthreatening situation. After that, the class reads, alternating lines between two groups, such as all boys and all girls, or one half of the room and the other half.

After the choral practice, the class is divided into groups of five or six; group members decide which poem they want to read and who will read which lines. They practice together for several minutes as the teacher encourages them to speak with expression, as fluently as they can.

To encourage active listening when students are not performing, the teacher introduces the class to a rubric (see Figure 3.1) and explains that they will use the rubric to assess some of their classmates who are performing. The teacher assigns classmates for each student to observe. Students are to listen for the correct pronunciation, fluent speaking, and an energetic presentation. They will also complete the sentence frame at the bottom of the rubric.

*(continued)*

---

**FIGURE 3.1** *Reader's Theater Rubric*

Write the name of the student you will observe in the Reader's Theater. Use the following point system to observe that person as you listen to the presentations:

> 3 = excellent
> 2 = good
> 1 = tried, but needs lots more practice
> 0 = not at all

| Group | Student name | Correct pronunciation | Fluent speaking | Energetic presentation | Total |
|---|---|---|---|---|---|
| 1 | | | | | |
| 2 | | | | | |
| 3 | | | | | |
| 4 | | | | | |

One achievement of _____ is

_____

_____.

*Source:* Adapted from Liten-Tejada, 2009.

---

Finally, groups perform the Reader's Theater by reciting the lines. After each performance, audience members use the rubric to score the assigned person who performed.

**Differentiation**

- The teacher may assign lines or roles to readers according to their English proficiency levels.
- Newcomers may read chorally with one partner.

## *Living Diorama*

**SIOP®** **COMPONENT:** Practice & Application (also suitable for Interaction, Lesson Delivery, and Review & Assessment)

Grade Level: K–12

Grouping Configuration: Small or large group, or whole class, depending on number of roles

Approximate Time Involved: 10 minutes

Materials: Index cards with a role written on each card, posted sentence frames if needed

## Description

Students create a living diorama by posing in a scene, such as representing well-known people at an historic event. They are given index cards with their assigned roles. As a group, they discuss their roles and create the scene. The scene should be frozen—once students are in place, they do not talk or move. However, one or two students should remain outside the scene and act as reporters to interview the characters. When they approach a character, that character unfreezes to respond to the question. Teachers may post sentence frames to scaffold the interview process.

The diorama scene can be enhanced through props that the teacher makes available to the students (e.g., scroll and quill pens to depict the signing of the Declaration of Independence, a U.S. flag and a headset to represent the Moon landing and mission control). Two related scenes could be set as well.

### Grade K U.S. History Application

**Lesson Concept:** Thanksgiving

**Content Objective:** SWBAT physically re-create an historic scene.

**Language Objectives:** SWBAT ask and answer questions about the role of their historical figure in an event.

**Key Vocabulary:** Pilgrim, Native American, harvest, corn, squash, turkey, fish, Plymouth

The kindergarteners have been studying the history associated with Thanksgiving. They have learned about Pilgrims and Native Americans in the Plymouth area. They know that the Thanksgiving dinner was in celebration of a successful harvest. The teacher shows the class the index cards, which assign roles such as Native American child, Native American man, Native American woman, Pilgrim man, Pilgrim woman, and Pilgrim child. Although she has written these words on the cards, she also has drawn pictures on each card to reinforce the character. She assigns the role of "reporter" to three of her most proficient students. She explains that the class will create a Thanksgiving scene and then some of them will be interviewed by a reporter. She also posts the following sentence frames and goes over them orally with the students, many of whom are not reading yet.

Q: Who are you?
A: I am _____.

Q: What do you do in _____?
A: I am a _____.

Q: Why are you _____?
A: I am _____ because _____.

*(continued)*

Students then create the scene in an open area of the classroom, and the reporters interview individuals.

### Differentiation

With older students, less support may be needed. Students who can read the role assignments will not need pictures. Students who are familiar with interview questions may not need the sentence frames.

## *Partner Listening Dictation*

**COMPONENT:** Practice & Application (also suitable for Interaction)

Grade Level: 2–12
Grouping Configuration: Partners
Approximate Time Involved: 15 minutes
Materials: Paper, pencil, class notes or text

### Description

Too often, listening dictation is a one-way street, with the teacher dictating and the students listening and writing. However, listening dictation is also a wonderful opportunity for students to practice listening, speaking, reading, and writing with a partner, while reinforcing content knowledge. Students can select a vocabulary word and write their own sentence using that word, or can write one fact they have learned about the lesson topic. They then dictate their sentence to a partner. After writing, partners compare sentences to see if they agree on the spelling and accuracy. If not, they decide who is right. They then switch roles. Students can also move around the room and dictate their sentences to new partners.

### Grade 11 Sheltered U.S. Government Application

**Lesson Concept:** Three branches of the U.S. government

**Content Objective:** SWBAT identify roles and responsibilities of the branches of the U.S. government.

**Language Objectives:**
- SWBAT write sentences using key vocabulary.
- SWBAT listen to a sentence and record what they hear.

**Key Vocabulary:** executive, legislative, judicial, laws, advise, vote, rule, power, veto, appoint

*(continued)*

This class of beginning- and intermediate-level ESL students has been studying the three branches of the U.S. government. After reading and discussing the roles and responsibilities of each branch, the teacher sets up this listening activity. She pairs the students and asks them to write a sentence stating one fact about one of the branches' roles or responsibilities. In pairs, students take turns reading and recording their sentences. They compare the written work and use their text or other sources to check for errors as necessary.

### Differentiation

- For newcomers, the teacher might provide the sentences to be read to partners. Then the pairs can check the words and spelling against the original.

- More advanced students might also check the accuracy of the facts.

# *Go Graphic – One Step Further* (modified from *99 Ideas*, p. 135)

**SIOP®** **COMPONENT:** Practice & Application

Grade Level: 3–12
Grouping Configuration: Individual, then pairs
Approximate Time Involved: 20–30 minutes
Materials: Depends on activity

## Description

Go Graphic involves using graphic organizers that conform to the text structure of a passage students have read and taking notes within the organizer. Teachers can take Go Graphic one step further and add a speaking component. First, introduce students to the different structures of expository text, such as description, explanation, comparison-contrast, cause-effect, sequence, and problem-solution. Show them different graphic organizers associated with these text structures and help them use the organizers to record key information while reading. Then point out that graphic organizers have specific signal words associated with them, such as compare-and-contrast words with Venn diagrams, cause-and-effect words with flow charts, sequence words with flow charts and timelines, and descriptive words with webs. After students complete the appropriate graphic organizer for the task, have partners work together to form oral sentences about their ideas using the appropriate signal words. They practice their sentences, and then state them to the class. The class listens for accuracy. As a follow-up, students write their sentences either as a list or as a paragraph with an introduction and conclusion.

## Grade 9 Geography Application

**Lesson Concept:** The influence of human actions on the environment

**Content Objective:** SWBAT analyze causes and consequences of human actions on the environment.

*(continued)*

**Language Objective:** SWBAT use comparative, persuasive, and cause-effect language to discuss information presented in reading passages on the environment.

**Key Vocabulary:** impact, unintended consequences, urbanization, environment, deforestation, pollution, desertification, limitation

The teacher selects three different texts that examine the impact of human actions on the environment. Each text represents a different text structure. One has a problem-solution format and discusses what needs to be done now to save the environment in the future. Another compares the impact of urbanization and population growth on the United States in the 1800s to the impact of urbanization and population growth in western Africa today. The third uses a cause-effect structure to discuss agricultural technologies and their effects on ecosystems.

The teacher divides the class into three groups, assigns a text, and distributes the appropriate graphic organizer (i.e., flow chart, Venn diagram, sequence chain). As a class, students review signal words to show comparisons, causation, possibility, and certainty. Each student then reads and records information on the organizer and then pairs up with another classmate who read the same passage. They use the signal words to discuss their texts. If time is available, the teacher regroups the students so at least one reader of each passage is in the group. Students summarize the different readings to one another using the signal words. To wrap up the activity, the teacher has several students report out to the whole class.

### Differentiation

The teacher might want to display Signal Words Posters that show key words associated with different text structures and language functions, such as *because, as a result, is caused by, so,* and *therefore* to reflect cause and effect. (More information on Signal Words can be found in *99 Ideas*, p. 36.)

# Lesson Delivery

- Group Response with a White Board
- Chunk and Chew Review
- Stand Up/Sit Down

The techniques and activities for this component should be closely aligned to a lesson's content and language objectives. When teachers incorporate these ideas into their lessons, they help the students master the content concepts and academic language goals.

# *Group Response with a White Board*

SIOP® **COMPONENT:** Lesson Delivery

Grade Level: 1–12

Grouping Configuration: Students should be grouped heterogeneously based on writing level, preferably with a high, middle, and a low writer in each group

Approximate Time Involved: 5–10 minutes

Materials: White boards, markers

## Description

White boards have often been used by teachers as a way to check for understanding at any point in a lesson. This technique provides an easy way for social studies and history teachers to assess their students' level of knowledge. It offers a means for student–student interaction as well.

## Procedure:

1. Prepare questions for the students. The teacher may either ask the questions in the standard question form or develop sentence stems that students must complete. The questions should relate to information that students have studied or have some background knowledge of, such as a topic previously discussed in class or a topic taught already in the current lesson.

2. Organize the students into heterogeneous groups of two or three, making sure students of high levels of proficiency in writing are grouped with students at lower levels of proficiency. Each group should have one marker and a white board.

3. Have each group select a writer.

4. Ask students one question. Give students a predetermined amount of time (30 seconds or more) to discuss the answer. After the time has passed, the designated writer writes their responses on the white board.

5. When all groups have finished recording their answers, a student other than the writer should hold up the board for the teacher to see.

6. Call on a group member to read the response to the question. All students with the same or nearly the same answer should put down their boards.

7. Call on one of the remaining groups to read its response. All students with the same or nearly the same answer should put down their boards.

8. Repeat the procedure until all answers are shared. As answers are shared, the teacher should confirm, correct, or clarify the information, or call on other students to do so.

9. Have each group select a new writer.

10. Ask a new question and repeat the procedure.

## Grade 11 World History Application

**Lesson Concept:** The Reformation

**Content Objective:** SWBAT explain the significance of the Reformation.

**Language Objective:** SWBAT describe causes and effects of the Reformation using a variety of sentence stems.

**Key Vocabulary:** Reformation, theses, indulgences, Lutheran, Catholic, Protestant, printing press, protest, doctrine, nationalism

This activity takes place after students have studied about Martin Luther's protests, his 95 theses, and the beginning of the reform movement. The teacher asks students to scan their notes about the Reformation silently. Then the students form pairs or triads, with each group sharing one white board. The teacher provides a sentence stem (see below) and has the students discuss the prompt. The writers complete the sentence on their group's board. When all groups have a response, the teacher has the students hold up their boards so all can see. The teacher then has the students share, making sure all the various responses are read aloud.

**Sentence stems:**

- The Reformation started as a reaction to . . .
- Martin Luther's 95 theses were significant because . . .
- The Catholic Church tried to stop Martin Luther because . . .
- The impact of the printing press on the movement was . . .

### Differentiation

**Beginner:**
Beginning English learners should not be forced to be writers during this activity. They may write with the help of other students or practice reading the response written by the writer and then share the response with the whole group if they are comfortable.

**Intermediate:**
Providing sentence frames for intermediate English learners may help them to have more confidence to share and practice correct English syntax in an academic context.

**Advanced:**
After students share, ask the groups extension questions to give more advanced students an opportunity to provide elaborated responses about lesson concepts.

# *Chunk and Chew Review*

**SIOP®** **COMPONENT:** Lesson Delivery (also suitable for Strategies)

Grade Level: 3–12

Grouping Configuration: Heterogeneous groups based on reading level, preferably including a high, middle, and low proficiency reader

Approximate Time Involved: 10 minutes or more, depending on the length of the passage

Materials: Textbook, posted sentence starters

## Description

One challenge facing social studies teachers of English learners is finding ways to enable students at different levels of proficiency to gain experience reading content area texts. Chunk and Chew Review, which is an adaptation of Chunk and Chew, provides a way for students to feel comfortable reading content area texts in small groups while developing reading proficiency and fluency. This technique is also helpful when students are reading primary source material, which often is at a high reading level and/or is written with archaic language.

## Procedure:

1. Post the following stems in a location visible to students:

   - You read about _____
   - _____ reminds me of _____
   - _____ happened because _____
   - _____ is significant because _____

2. Select a passage for students to read.

3. Organize students into groups of three or four, making sure that each group has students at a variety of language proficiency levels.

4. Have students select a reader to begin reading. The reader will read one to three paragraphs.

5. Ask every other student in the group to respond to the section read using one of the posted stems.

6. When the reader finishes, the student to the reader's right becomes the new reader. If a student does not wish to read, he or she can say "Pass" and the next student will become the reader.

---

### Grade 7 Ancient Civilizations Application

**Lesson Concept:**  Trade routes in Africa in the Middle Ages

**Content Objectives:**

- SWBAT analyze the political, economic, and social significance of African trade routes in the Middle Ages.
- SWBAT identify contributions Africans made to European civilization in the areas of science, mathematics, medicine, and art.

**Language Objectives:**

- SWBAT summarize text about African–European trade in the Middle Ages.
- SWBAT discuss the influence of African knowledge on European culture.

**Key Vocabulary:**  salt, books, trade, exchange, influence

Students take turns reading one to three paragraphs from the textbook section discussing the interaction between North Africans and Europeans in the Middle Ages, including the

*(continued)*

exchanges of ideas, commodities, art, technologies, and religious beliefs. One student reads first and the other students summarize the section orally using the stems listed below. Students may "pass" if they do not wish to read, but must respond to what is read using the stems.

- You read about . . .
- _____ exchanged _____ because . . .
- _____ is significant because . . .
- _____ benefited from . . .
- I wonder why . . .

### Differentiation

If a text includes archaic language, it can help to preview the text and practice pronouncing difficult words before beginning the activity.

**Beginner:**

Beginners should understand that "passing" is an option if they are not comfortable reading aloud. Providing a native language text, adapted text, or a native language summary by another student during the activity can be helpful. Also, it is important to explain the meaning of the stems to beginners. Some beginners may be able to use the stems to share what a passage is about, particularly if the passage has a high number of cognates or visuals that make the content comprehensible.

**Intermediate:**

Intermediate students may read one paragraph or stop and say "pass" during the reading if the text becomes difficult to decode. They may also ask for help from other students when pronouncing individual English words.

**Advanced:**

Advanced students should be encouraged to use the more advanced stems that require elaboration such as "____ happened because..." and "____ is significant because. . . ." If the text includes primary source documents, advanced students might read and interpret those.

## *Stand Up/Sit Down*

**SIOP®**

**COMPONENT:** Lesson Delivery (also suitable for Review & Assessment)

Grade Level: 6–12
Grouping Configuration: Whole class
Approximate Time Involved: 3–5 minutes
Materials: None

## Description

Stand Up/Sit Down uses a basic physical response signal to instantly check for students' understanding or point of view on a topic. Teachers may use it at various points during a lesson to check on how students are processing the information they are studying.

## Procedure:

1. The teacher prepares a series of questions or statements with only two possible responses: *yes/no, agree/disagree, fact/opinion, Asia/Africa, liberal/conservative,* and so forth.

2. The teacher reads the questions or statements and assigns a position (standing or sitting) to each response. For example, "Stand if you agree; sit if you disagree" or "Stand if the statement characterizes a liberal point of view; sit if you think it characterizes a conservative point of view."

3. After reading each question or statement, the teacher has the students describe to a partner why they chose to stand or sit.

---

### Grade 12 U.S. Government Application

**Lesson Concept:** Federal vs. state power

**Content Objective:** SWBAT distinguish between liberal and conservative viewpoints in current American political debate.

**Language Objective:** SWBAT orally justify their reasons for believing a certain viewpoint is liberal or conservative.

**Key Vocabulary:** liberal, conservative, viewpoint, belief, position

This lesson takes place after a discussion on the history and roles of political parties in the United States. Students must have sufficient background knowledge about liberal and conservative viewpoints to participate in this activity.

The teacher creates a list of statements representing conservative, liberal, and neither liberal nor conservative viewpoints such as:

1. We need to have a social safety net to protect the weaker members of our society, even if it involves increasing taxes. (liberal)

2. Participating in elections is important. (both)

3. Lower taxes are a fiscal priority. (conservative)

4. California should keep medical use of marijuana legal. (liberal)

5. We should interpret the Constitution strictly, as written by the founding fathers. (conservative)

6. Moral values are important to society. (both)

After the class has read a section on contemporary liberalism and conservatism in the textbook, the teacher explains that she is going to read a series of statements. The students are to stand if a statement's viewpoint is liberal and sit if it is conservative. Students must then justify their response using the following stems:

*(continued)*

- _____ is a liberal view because . . .
- _____ is a conservative view because . . .

The students should use information from the textbook and their own background knowledge to justify their opinions. Viewpoints that can be considered both liberal and conservative can provoke interesting discussions among the students and help elaborate key ideas underlying liberalism, conservatism, and democratic ideals common to both.

### Differentiation

**Beginner:**
It can be helpful to provide beginners with a translation of the statements before and during the task. Beginners may also benefit from a small group discussion or interaction with the teacher that clarifies key ideas about liberalism and conservatism prior to the discussion. Having students practice pronouncing the terms and stems is also helpful.

**Intermediate:**
Preteaching academic vocabulary found in the passage on liberalism and conservatism helps students at this level of language proficiency. Students also benefit from being given added wait time when asked to justify their selection. If students have trouble articulating their response, they can be provided with an opportunity to confer with a neighbor who chose the same point of view.

**Advanced:**
Advanced students have an easier time articulating their point of view because of their familiarity with English vocabulary and syntax. These students still may be unfamiliar with the content-specific vocabulary involved in a discussion of American government that native speakers might already know. For this reason, it is wise to consider pre-teaching of key content area vocabulary for these students as well.

# Review & Assessment

- Oral Number 1–3 for Self-Assessment
- Writing Self-Assessment Rubrics
- Number Wheels
- Whip Around, Pass Option
- Numbered Heads Together with Movement
- Differentiated Tickets Out

Activities and techniques for this final component of the SIOP® Model serve several purposes. They review the content concepts and vocabulary goals of the lesson. They also help the teacher assess student comprehension of the material presented, and they allow the teacher to give feedback to students on both their production of the language and the tasks they perform.

## *Oral Number 1–3 for Self-Assessment* (from *99 Ideas*, p. 179)

**SIOP® COMPONENT:** Review & Assessment

Grade Level: All
Grouping Configuration: Whole class
Approximate Time Involved: 3–5 minutes
Materials: None

### Description

Self-assessment is an effective informal strategy for determining one's progress toward meeting objectives. This technique offers a quick and easy way for students to self-assess how well they think they have met a lesson's content and language objectives. At the end of the lesson, the teacher should review the objectives with the students and ask them to indicate with one, two, or three fingers the degree to which they think they met them:

1 = I didn't (or can't) meet the objective.
2 = I didn't meet the objective, but I made progress.
3 = I met (or can do) the objective.

Depending on how students indicate their understanding of a lesson's key concepts and objectives, the teacher can reteach, provide additional scaffolding, work with a small group of students for further instruction and practice, or move forward.

### Grade 1 Social Studies Application

**Lesson Concept:** Past and Present

**Content Objectives:**
- SWBAT sequence personal photographs chronologically on a timeline.
- SWBAT identify personal changes between past and present.

**Language Objective:**
- SWBAT describe photographs of the teacher using two sentence structures:
  - In the past, Ms. X _____.
  - In the present, Ms. X _____.

**Key Vocabulary:** past, in the past, present, in the present, before, after, 10 years later, the year before, now

During this lesson, the class learns how to organize information chronologically by placing pictures in order along a timeline. To teach this skill, the teacher uses photos from her life as a child, teenager, and adult. The students also practice making sentences describing the teacher in the past and present-day photos. At the end of the lesson, the teacher reviews the content and language objectives with the students. She asks the following questions, and after each one, students should hold up one, two, or three fingers to self-assess their mastery for the day.

*(continued)*

- How well did you place the photographs in order on the timeline?
- How well did you describe how I changed between the past and present?
- How well did you make sentences about the past?
- How well did you make sentences about the present?

## Self-Assessment Rubrics (from *99 Ideas*, p. 180)

**SIOP®** **COMPONENT:** Review & Assessment

Grade Level:  All
Grouping Configuration:  Individual
Approximate Time Involved:  5–10 minutes
Materials:  A copy of the rubric for each student (Figure 3.2)

### Description

Another technique for student self-assessment is the use of self-assessment rubrics. The teacher reads aloud several statements about what the students should have learned or been able to do as a result of the lesson and the students indicate on a self-assessment rubric the degree to which they know the information or can do something related to the lesson. In grades K–2, students may mark rubrics that display smiley faces, question marks, and sad faces to describe their knowledge. Older students can circle or mark the number on the rubric that best matches how they interpret their knowledge. Sample rubrics are shown in Figure 3.2.

**FIGURE 3.2**  *Self-Assessment Rubrics*

| Kindergarten Self-Assessment Rubric | | | |
|---|---|---|---|
| 1 | ☺ | ? | ☺ |
| 2 | ☺ | ? | ☺ |
| 3 | ☺ | ? | ☺ |

| Grades 3–5 Self-Assessment Rubric | | | | |
|---|---|---|---|---|
| A | 0 | 1 | 2 | 3 |
| B | 0 | 1 | 2 | 3 |
| C | 0 | 1 | 2 | 3 |
| D | 0 | 1 | 2 | 3 |

0 = I don't understand
1 = I understand a little but have questions
2 = I understand but can't explain it
3 = I understand and can explain it well

**Grade 3 Social Studies Application**

**Lesson Concept:** Famous Americans in History

**Content Objective:** SWBAT identify Ben Franklin's inventions.

**Language Objective:** SWBAT explain what one particular invention does.

**Key Vocabulary:** invent, create, invention, inventor, post office, bifocals, printing press, newspaper

During a lesson on Benjamin Franklin's inventions, students look at illustrations of his devices. They describe several of the items and compare them with how the items look today. At the end of the lesson, the teacher reviews the content and language objectives with the students. She distributes a self-assessment rubric that students have used before. She reminds them how to mark the form and then reads each statement. Students self-assess by putting an X on the number that describes their knowledge level. The statements are

- Ben Franklin wrote a book to help farmers predict the weather.
- Ben Franklin made eyeglasses to help people see better.
- Ben Franklin's printing press made pamphlets and newspapers.
- Ben Franklin discovered facts about lightning.

**Differentiation**

For older students and more advanced English learners, the statements may be written in the first column of the rubric and the students may mark their knowledge level in the second column. Also, more detailed statements may be provided for them. In classes with younger and/or less proficient students, the teacher will still want to read the statements aloud.

## *Number Wheels*

**SIOP** **COMPONENT:** Review & Assessment

Grade Level: 6–12
Grouping Configuration: Whole class, small group
Approximate Time Involved: 3–5 minutes
Materials: None

## Description

Number wheels provide an opportunity for teachers to assess students' knowledge and opinions about a topic in a fun and easy manner.

## Procedure:

1. The teacher prepares one number wheel for each student. Number wheels consist of a binder clip or key ring with five index cards (or pieces of card stock) attached. Each card has a number on it: 1, 2, 3, 4, and 5.

2. The teacher distributes one number wheel to each student.

3. The teacher prepares questions or statements that have one of five responses. For example: 1 = Africa, 2 = Asia, 3 = Europe, 4 = North America, and 5 = South America; or 1 = strongly disagree, 2 = disagree, 3 = not sure, 4 = agree, and 5 = strongly agree.

4. The teacher then reads questions or statements and each student holds up his or her number wheel responses. Afterward, students may turn to a neighbor to justify their answers or participate in a class discussion justifying their points of view.

Note: If clips for number wheels are not readily available, each student could have a number card. Use an index card in the portrait position and write the five numbers down the middle, leaving space between the numbers. Students must point to or touch the number of their selection to indicate their responses. Tell students not to point *between* two numbers.

---

### Grade 12 U.S. Government Application

**Lesson Concept:** Behaviorism vs. Humanism

**Content Objective:** SWBAT distinguish between behaviorist and humanist explanations for human behavior.

**Language Objective:** SWBAT orally justify their reasons for describing a point of view as behaviorist or humanist.

**Key Vocabulary:** behaviorist, humanist, mildly, environment, individual responsibility

This lesson takes place after a discussion on two different explanations for human behavior: behaviorist and humanist. Behaviorists favor an environmental explanation of human behavior and humanists favor explanations that focus on individual choice. The teacher creates a list of statements representing behaviorist and humanistic explanations for an individual's behavior. Students rate each statement as one of the following:

1. Strongly behaviorist
2. Mildly behaviorist
3. Neither behaviorist nor humanist
4. Mildly humanist
5. Strongly humanist

*(continued)*

The statements include:

a. Alcoholism contains a genetic component.

b. Intergenerational poverty is the result of poor parenting.

c. It's up to the individual whether he or she becomes poor or rich.

d. If we provide higher quality education, we can reduce the number of people in prisons.

e. He's not guilty because he's insane.

f. People who are violent should have to take anger management classes.

g. Above all, people should treat one another with dignity and respect.

h. Children are born as blank slates; input by their parents and peers makes them who they are.

i. We all decide who we are going to be based on our moral choices.

j. We need to have a society where everyone is provided their basic needs, and then people will treat one another better.

Students justify their answers during the discussion, using sentence frames such as "I believe this statement is _____ (behaviorist/humanist) because. . . ."

## Differentiation

**Beginner:**

It can be helpful to provide a translation of the statements for the beginners to view before and during the task. Beginners may also benefit from a small group discussion or interaction with the teacher to clarify key ideas about humanism and behaviorism prior to the discussion. Practice pronouncing the terms and stems is also helpful.

**Intermediate and Advanced:**

These students may be able to access prior knowledge and experiences when justifying their ideas. Providing sufficient wait time and having students clarify their ideas with partners before discussing the idea with the whole class can help students at more advanced levels provide more elaborated responses about lesson concepts.

Younger students might use number wheels (or number cards) with only three numbers. These would represent three options, such as 1 = disagree, 2 = not sure, 3 = agree; or 1 = Past, 2 = Present, 3 = Future; or 1 = Continent, 2 = Country, 3 = State.

## *Whip Around, Pass Option* (adapted from Harmin, 1994)

**SIOP®**

**COMPONENT:** Review & Assessment (also suitable for
Building Background)

Grade Level: All
Grouping Configuration: Whole class
Approximate Time Involved: 5–10 minutes, depending on class size
Materials: None

### Description

At the conclusion of a lesson, teacher posts Outcome Sentences for students to consider, such as

- Today I found out that _____.
- The most interesting thing I learned today is _____.
- I'm surprised about _____.
- I wonder _____.
- I would like to know more about _____.
- I'm still not sure about _____.

The teacher quickly "whips around" the room, giving each student a chance to answer, or providing the option for a student to say "Pass." This option allows students to take responsibility for the decision to speak, and most usually choose to do so, especially when provided with the sentence starters. The interest level of the students rises as they listen to their peers, since they are curious to know who will pass or who will have a similar idea or opinion to their own.

The Whip Around, Pass Option can also be used at other points in a lesson that call for students to share ideas, such as after completing a Venn diagram comparing and contrasting two topics, or during Building Background to share what they know or want to know about a topic. It offers teachers an opportunity to quickly assess learning.

### Kindergarten Social Studies Application

**Lesson Topic:** State Geography
**Content Objective:** SWBAT draw landforms on a state map.
**Language Objective:** SWBAT watch a video and discuss key information.
**Key Vocabulary:** river, lake, mountain, capital city

A kindergarten class is working on basic map skills. The teacher shows a video about some geographic features in their state. The students watch brief clips of the video and then draw the feature on their own copy of an outline of the state map. For example, the video shows scenes from one of the state's big lakes. Students watch for two minutes, and

*(continued)*

then the teacher models how to draw and position the lake on the map. The students copy this on their own maps.

At the end of the lesson, the teacher reviews two outcome sentence starters with the class: "Today I learned _____" and "I want to know more about _____." Students choose one outcome sentence to share with the class through a Whip Around, Pass Option.

## Numbered Heads Together with Movement

(modified from *99 Ideas*, p. 183)

**SIOP®** **COMPONENT:** Review & Assessment

Grade Level: 3–12
Grouping Configuration: Small groups
Approximate Time Involved: 15 minutes
Materials: Blank paper for each student, prepared questions

## Description

In Numbered Heads Together, students work cooperatively to review and respond to questions about the lesson. After the teacher poses a question, peers support each other as they decide on an answer and practice responding using academic language. In this variation on the technique, students move from their seats and write answers on the board.

## Procedure:

1. Prior to class, develop a list of review questions, ranging from easy to hard. The questions can cover facts, vocabulary, historical people, analyses, and so on.

2. Divide students into groups of four. Assign each student a different number between 1 and 4. Each student should have a piece of paper on which he or she will write the answers.

3. Divide the classroom board into the number of groups present, or place sheets of chart paper around the room, if board space is not available.

4. Pose a review question to the class. Review questions should require short answers, or students will get bogged down writing lengthy responses. Have the students confer quietly with their group to decide on their answer. When they have decided on an answer, everyone writes it down. One person per group can be designated the "checker" and can review the written responses.

5. Choose a number 1, 2, 3, or 4, and call it aloud. (It is best if you have the numbers written on cards or sticks that you can pull at random.) When you say "Go," all the students who have that number will walk to the board or poster paper, carrying their

answer with them. When everyone is in place, say, "Write," and those at the board should write the answer. Note: This is not a race! Students do not need to run, and they should not start writing until you have directed them to do so.

6. Give a point to each team that has the correct answer, but keep the competition friendly. Remind students that the objective is to review and to help everyone learn. There need not be a prize for winning.

7. After the game, have students reflect on which questions they knew and which they discovered that they need to review further.

## Grade 4 Social Studies Application

**Lesson Concept:** Native American ways of living
**Content Objective:**
- SWBAT relate environment and climate to Native American lifestyles.

**Language Objectives:**
- SWBAT listen to, discuss, and respond to questions in writing.
- SWBAT collaborate politely with classmates.

**Key Vocabulary:** plains, woodlands, longhouse, tepee, wigwam, totem pole, salmon, buffalo, kiva

At the end of a several lessons on different Native American groups that lived in the United States prior to 1820, the teacher sets up student groups for this Numbered Heads Together technique. Some of the questions the teacher poses include

1. What is the name of the fish that was significant to the food supply and beliefs of the Tlingit tribe?
2. List two ways that the Plains Indians used bison.
3. Draw a picture of a longhouse.
4. What are two things that the Northwest and Northeast Native American groups had in common?
5. Why did Pueblo Indians build kivas?
6. How did the climate influence the Plains Indians' way of living?

Afterward, students should note which information they didn't know and spend extra time studying those particular topics.

### Differentiation

During Numbered Heads Together, the vocabulary words, concepts, and pictures can be posted in the room, particularly for beginning language learners. If the class consists of native speakers and highly proficient students, or to provide an extra challenge, the review game can be played without the words in sight. This option should only be used if the teacher is certain that students will be able to recognize the answers.

# *Differentiated Tickets Out*

 **COMPONENT:** Review & Assessment

Grade Level: 6–12
Grouping Configuration: Individual
Approximate Time Involved: 5 minutes
Materials: Posted list of ticket out choices, half sheets of paper

## Description

Tickets Out is an easy way for teachers to bring closure to a lesson and check student understanding of key lesson concepts. This variation of the Tickets Out activity enables teachers to assess the individual understanding of students who have various levels of background knowledge and language proficiency. The differentiated tasks may be selected by students according to their interests and abilities.

## Procedure:

1. Create a poster or overhead transparency, or write on the board a list labeled "Possible Tickets Out" such as the following:
   - Create a stick figure drawing representing what we discussed today and label it.
   - Write a short rhyme/rap describing what we discussed today.
   - Finish the sentence "What we learned about today reminds me of_____ because. . . ."
   - Draw a graphic organizer—Venn diagram, timeline, T chart, or flow chart representing what we discussed today.

2. At the end of a lesson, pass out half sheets of $8^1/_2$" by 11" paper.

3. Give the students five minutes to choose and complete one activity from the list to summarize their understanding of the lesson concepts on the paper.

4. Collect the students' Tickets Out as they exit the room.

---

### Grade 11 U.S. History Application

**Lesson Concept:** Communism in the United States before World War II

**Content Objective:** SWBAT describe American fears of communism in the era before World War II.

**Language Objective:** SWBAT summarize information in a variety of visual and textual formats.

**Key Vocabulary:** communism, socialism, leftist, immigrant, sentiment, conservative, anti-

During a lesson on anti-immigrant and anti-communist feelings in the United States in the 1920s and 1930s, students analyzed political cartoons reflecting various points of view from the era. They discussed the sentiments among different groups of Americans

*(continued)*

---

regarding communism and socialism. Near the end of the lesson, the teacher posted the following list of activities on the board and gave the students a choice to complete one of them on a half sheet of $8^1/_2$" by 11" paper:

- Draw a picture that represents one sentiment among Americans about communism.
- Write a short rhyme, chant, or rap describing what we discussed today.
- Finish the sentence: "What we learned about today reminds me of ___ because...."
- Draw a T chart representing the pros and cons of communism in the 1920s and 1930s.

## Differentiation

**Beginner:**
Beginning English learners may be more comfortable drawing and labeling a picture than writing. Allow students to use their primary language as well as English when labeling their pictures. Newcomer and beginning students may be grouped with more advanced peers who speak the same native language to clarify directions before starting the assignment.

**Intermediate:**
Avoid assessing students' English language usage during this activity. The goal is to assess content understanding.

**Advanced:**
Encourage more advanced students to be playful with language usage in rhymes, raps, and drawing labels. Direct advanced students to the word wall and encourage them to use the words in their Tickets Out.

# Concluding Thoughts

In this chapter, we have presented a variety of techniques and activities for the final four components of the SIOP® Model and applied them to history and social studies classroom scenarios. It is important to keep in mind that although we described these techniques by SIOP® component for organizational purposes, the techniques are intended to support each lesson's language and content objectives; they should not be presented as isolated activities. Our research has shown that lessons are most effective for English learners when all of the components of the SIOP® Model are incorporated. Lessons are ineffective when teachers pick and choose only their favored SIOP® features or use only preferred techniques. Go ahead and try out these techniques in your lessons. We hope your students will find them as meaningful and engaging as ours have!

# Revisiting Mr. Michaels

Halfway through the school year, John Michaels (who was introduced in Chapter 2) is more comfortable as a sheltered history teacher of English learners. He has participated actively in the PLC and has sought advice from other teachers on his team. He rereads sections of the book Ms. Feehan gave him from time to time; and when he tries a new technique, he shares the results with his team. If it doesn't work out well, he explains what he tried and what the result was to his fellow teachers. Sometimes they advise him how to adjust the activity, or more frequently, how to explain the task more clearly to the students. Yet at other times, he realizes that not all techniques appeal to his classes. One important advance he and the team have made this semester has been to jointly choose six techniques they all will use in their classes. Now, for example, when he tells the class they will review the prior lesson through the Oh Yesterday + Year! technique or end the class with Number Wheels, no time is wasted setting up the procedure. Having six techniques as regular routines has really helped his classroom management. His colleagues confirmed they are experiencing similar results in their classes.

# chapter 4

# SIOP® History and Social Studies Unit Design and Lesson Planning

## Ms. Parry's Vignette

Marge Parry had taught third grade for two years in her midwestern city. She enjoyed working with the young learners and felt she had good routines set up for them to participate in math and reading learning centers. Her school requires one hour of math each day and two and a half hours of reading/language arts. With specials like gym, library, and music, that didn't leave a lot of time for science or social studies. Recently the state decided that fourth-grade students would take the state science test, so she couldn't neglect that subject with her third graders now—but how was she going to cover all the social studies material?

Third grade is the year to cover basic geography like landforms and regions of the United States. Not too many of her students have personal experience outside of the plains region. Their ancestors were farmers, and although some families have different professions now, there are plenty of megafarms dotting the landscape just outside the city. Two refugee resettlement agencies in the city recently announced the pending arrival of families from Somalia and Burma. She would have refugee children in her class this year, arriving early in September. From what she had been told, it was unlikely that they would speak English. That could be problematic because she wasn't a trained ESL teacher. Yet as Ms. Parry thought about it, having students from countries with different geographic features and cultural backgrounds could really spice up her social studies lessons.

Ms. Parry began to think about a landforms unit she would prepare for the second month of school. She wanted to take advantage of the students' backgrounds and planned to incorporate visuals from Google Maps and other Web sites that showed areas of Africa and Asia, as well as the United States because she knew her incoming students would need to learn about the United States, too. She jotted down some questions she would consider at she prepared the lessons.

1. What must students learn in this unit? How will I organize objectives across the lessons themselves?

2. How will I assess students' learning of the unit's content concepts? What kind of ongoing project could wrap up this unit?

3. How much do my students already know about the topic? Will my newcomers have background knowledge that can enhance the lesson?

4. How many lessons will it take to teach the concepts and lead students to mastery?

5. What materials will I use to supplement the textbook? Are they already available or do I need to search on the Internet or in the school library?

6. What vocabulary do students already know, and what additional vocabulary must be taught?

7. How will I make the lessons meaningful so students are engaged and motivated to learn?

As Ms. Parry looked over these questions, she realized that with the non-English speaking newcomers expected in her classroom, she needed some help. She called the district offices and asked to speak with Dr. Levine, an ESL specialist. They set up a meeting and Dr. Levine looked over the plans Ms. Parry had for the unit. She explained that adding some activities to support language development would help both the newcomers and her regular English-speaking students. Further, because many of these students may have lived in refugee camps for several months to several years, Ms. Parry will need to work on building their background knowledge. Dr. Levine added some additional questions to Ms. Parry's list:

8. What language objective can be added to each lesson to complement the content objectives and address student learning needs?

9. What activities could be included that give students a chance to practice listening and speaking, reading, and/or writing skills?

10. What background knowledge or additional content concepts might students with limited formal schooling need to learn to participate in this unit and how can it be shared with them?

Dr. Levine worked with Ms. Parry on outlining her unit and identifying objectives and language activities. She offered to meet again closer to October when the unit was more fleshed out to review and generate additional activities if needed so Ms. Parry could successfully integrate language learning with her social studies content.

# Introduction

This chapter focuses on unit design and lesson planning processes that social studies, history, government, geography, and civics teachers undertake as they implement the SIOP® Model. Its aim is to demonstrate how meaningful, engaging activities with academic language practice, such as those described in Chapters 2 and 3, can be incorporated into appropriate lessons and units. Effective SIOP® teaching includes explicit instruction of the content material and associated academic language, plus teacher modeling, guided practice, and independent practice.

As educators we seek the gradual release of responsibility, so our students can engage with social studies and history tasks independently. (See Figure 4.1.) As teachers, we present information and model through focused mini-lessons "the type of thinking required to solve problems, understand directions, comprehend a text, or the like" (Fisher & Frey, 2008, p. 5). We then plan guided instruction activities so we can monitor student practice and application of the information from the mini-lesson. We give students an opportunity to collaborate so they discuss ideas and information they learned during the focus lessons and guided instruction—not new information. As we plan lessons within units, we incorporate techniques and activities for students to apply learning strategies, answer higher order questions, and use hands-on materials and manipulatives. When students have acquired background knowledge from the first three phases and are ready to

**FIGURE 4.1** *Gradual Release of Responsibility*

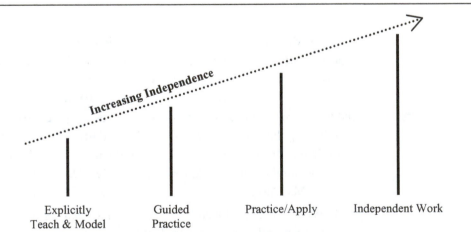

Explicitly Teach & Model     Guided Practice     Practice/Apply     Independent Work

*Source:* From Echevarria, J., Vogt, M.E., & Short, D. (2004). *Making Content Comprehensible for English Learners: The SIOP Model*, Second Edition. Boston: Allyn & Bacon.

apply the information, we offer them independent tasks. For English learners, this process may take some time, depending on their academic English proficiency and educational backgrounds.

In our own practice of planning and delivering effective SIOP® instruction, we also consider the process the teacher will take to guide students in mastering the concepts and language and what the final product, outcome, or academic expectation is for all students based on their literacy and language abilities. You'll see that the lessons in the units in Chapters 5–8 demonstrate how the objectives drive the selection of meaningful activities and the vocabulary that must be developed and how the students will demonstrate their understanding and progress in meeting the learning goals. The units wrap up with a variety of assessments so the teachers can be sure the students have mastered the content and language objectives.

# SIOP® Unit Design

We know from our interactions with teachers, schools, and districts implementing the SIOP® Model that there are multiple ways to design SIOP® lessons and units. Some are prescribed by the school or district; some are individual department or teacher preferences. All models are feasible if the lessons incorporate all the SIOP® features. In some districts such as the Clifton (NJ) Public Schools and Charlotte-Mecklenburg (NC) Schools, teachers have been paid for summer curriculum work to design new SIOP® units or siopize existing units. In other sites, such as Lela Alston Elementary School (Phoenix, AZ), grade-level teams have worked together to write language and content objectives to be used in units throughout the school year. Some districts have begun posting units and lessons on the district website.

For those of you who do not yet have an established process for developing your history and social studies units, we would like to share two SIOP® unit planners that we have used with several districts during our SIOP® research projects. You might select the one that best suits your approach. The first option, SIOP® Unit Planner 1, may be used as a brainstorming tool at the start of the process. The second option, SIOP® Unit Planner 2, may be used for existing units that need to be siopized.

## SIOP® Unit Planner 1

Figure 4.2 lists the steps we have undertaken with teachers to design units using the first planner. In the first step, we identify the critical topics to cover in a given unit. This is usually done by reviewing the state standards (for social studies, U.S. history, geography, or another similar subject), the local curriculum, and the textbook. In some cases, experienced teachers with knowledge of the state history test may also suggest critical topics to include. During this step, a large list of topics may be created, but it may be winnowed down as essential topics are highlighted.

The second step is derived from the first. Looking at the content topics and the likely materials to be used (chapters, primary source documents, video clips, etc.), teachers begin listing historical terms, general academic words, and language functions that may be taught in conjunction with the topics. Teachers may consult the state English language

**FIGURE 4.2** *SIOP® Unit Planning Steps*

**Step 1: Identify the Content Topics**

- Review the state content standards, grade-level curriculum, textbook, tests
- Examine graphs, charts, tables, diagrams
- Decide what's essential

**Step 2: Identify Language and Literacy Skills**

- Review the state ESL and ELA standards
- Review the grade-level curriculum and textbook to
  - Identify key scientific terms and academic words
  - Determine text structure and language functions
- Consider the reading and writing skills needed for the unit
- Consider tasks students will be assigned and the embedded language of the language tasks

**Step 3: Begin the Unit Planner**

- List the key concepts
- Draft the content objectives
- Draft the language objectives
- If useful, reference related state content and language standards

**Step 4: Generate Language Activities**

- Brainstorm activities for vocabulary, reading, writing, grammar, and listening/speaking while keeping the content topics in mind
- Identify possible learning strategies students might practice

**Step 5: Gather Supplementary Materials**

- Secure materials and multimedia that build background
- Look for related fiction or expository readers that have instructional scaffolds in the text, or offer on-level options
- Collect and organize hands-on materials such as manipulatives and realia

**Step 6: Plan Lessons**

- Organize content into lessons
- Use SIOP® lesson plan template
- Incorporate "interactivities" for language practice, and supplementary materials
- Establish a unit project or other unit assessment

*Source:* Adapted from Short, D. (2009, June). *Sheltered instruction: Curriculum and lesson design.* Paper presented at the 31st Sanibel Leadership Conference, Sanibel, FL. Used with permission.

proficiency standards and the English language arts standards. They consider listening, speaking, reading, and writing skills needed to complete tasks in the unit as well as their students' proficiency levels.

The first two steps may be done on scratch paper. It is in step three where teachers start completing the SIOP® Unit Planner 1 (in Figure 4.3). They list the key concepts they have decided on and then draft the content and language objectives. As they work through the rest of the planner, teachers may return to these sections to adjust the objectives. Usually the objectives are further refined during the actual writing of the lesson plans. Because some schools and districts require teachers to indicate what particular standards are being met in the units or lessons, teachers may want to reference the particular state history/social studies and language standards on the planner as well. Finally, teachers might record related topics that have been studied and might be useful for helping students make connections.

Step four is very important for the unit and is the crux of what will make the lessons appropriate for English learners. Here, teachers generate a list of activities they might include in the unit that will advance their students' academic language skills yet be applicable to the social science concepts being taught. These activities will be developed to promote historical and other academic vocabulary knowledge, reading skills, writing assignments (e.g., comparative essays), listening and speaking tasks, and, if feasible, related grammar points (e.g., comparative forms of adjectives, use of adverbs of time and place). In addition, learning strategies that might be useful (e.g., how to use Internet resources, how to take notes on a T-chart, how to memorize key facts) can be planned. As noted, this is a brainstorm list. Not all the activities may end up being used in the lessons; some may be better suited for later units in the course.

For the fifth step, teachers begin gathering the supplementary materials they will need for the unit. For social studies and history teachers, this may mean materials that can build background or make the content more comprehensible for English learners (e.g., video clips, audio files, visuals, Internet sites, computer programs, books on specific topics written at lower reading levels). Scaffolds such as graphic organizers, study guides, glossaries, and the like can also be collected.

The final step of the unit design process is writing the SIOP® lessons. This step will involve some back and forth with the unit planner as the content topics are organized into individual lessons and the objectives and tasks are allocated. As the writing takes place, the content and language objectives will be sharpened. Some new tasks may come to mind and replace ones in the planner. Those changes are to be expected. This is also the step where teachers can create a unit assessment, perhaps a project students will do, a performance they might present, a writing piece for their portfolio, or another significant wrap-up activity to measure the knowledge they have gained during the course of the unit.

## SIOP® Unit Planner 2

SIOP® Unit Planner 2 (see Figure 4.4) provides another option. You might use this template if you are siopizing a unit that you have used in the past or one that has been provided in your district curriculum guide. You already know the topics and order of the lessons, but you are adding language development and reconsidering some of the activities and grouping configurations to promote more interaction or building background, for example.

# SIOP® Lesson Planning

When planning effective SIOP® lessons, we always begin with explicit content and language objectives that are derived from content-specific standards and the academic language needs of our English learners. We know from our own experience as SIOP® teachers and SIOP® professional developers that language objectives are critically important to the development of academic language. As you noticed in our application sections of the techniques in Chapters 2 and 3 and as you will see in the lesson plans, social studies and history topics lend themselves to a rich variety of language objectives. This is a good thing! We want students to learn vocabulary, language structures and functions, reading and writing, and listening and speaking skills.

FIGURE 4.3  *SIOP® Unit Planner 1*

Subject: _____

Unit Focus: _____

Topic: _____

Related Topics:

| Key Concepts | Content Objectives | Language Objectives |
|---|---|---|
| | | |

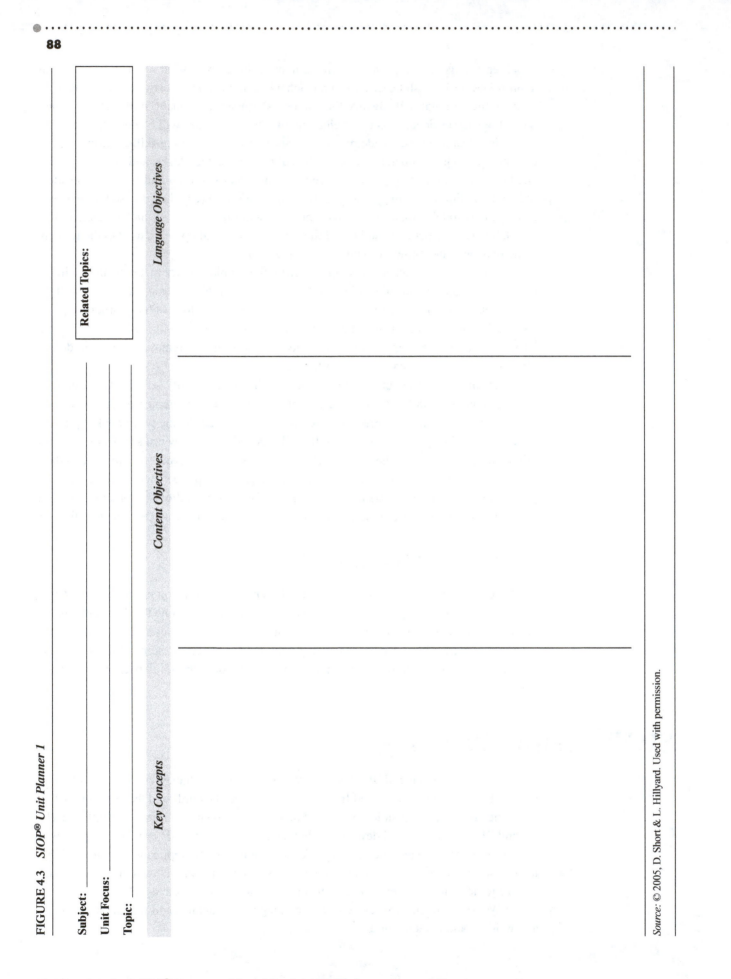

*Source:* © 2005, D. Short & L. Hillyard. Used with permission.

**Unit Project:**

| Vocabulary Tasks | Reading Tasks | Writing Tasks | Speaking/Listening Tasks | Grammar Focus | Student Learning Strategies |
|---|---|---|---|---|---|
| | | | | | |

*Source:* © 2005, D. Short & L. Hillyard. Used with permission.

FIGURE 4.4  *SIOP® Unit Planner 2*

| | |
|---|---|
| Grade Level: _____ | Subject: _____ |
| Unit: _____ | Approx. Time Involved: _____ |

| | |
|---|---|
| **Lesson Focus:** <br><br> **Content Objectives:** <br><br> **Language Objectives:** <br><br> **Reading/Writing/Discussion Activities:** <br><br> **Grouping Configuration:** | **Lesson Focus:** <br><br> **Content Objectives:** <br><br> **Language Objectives:** <br><br> **Reading/Writing/Discussion Activities:** <br><br> **Grouping Configuration:** |
| **Lesson Focus:** <br><br> **Content Objectives:** <br><br> **Language Objectives:** <br><br> **Reading/Writing/Discussion Activities:** <br><br> **Grouping Configuration:** | **Lesson Focus:** <br><br> **Content Objectives:** <br><br> **Language Objectives:** <br><br> **Reading/Writing/Discussion Activities:** <br><br> **Grouping Configuration:** |
| **Lesson Focus:** <br><br> **Content Objectives:** <br><br> **Language Objectives:** <br><br> **Reading/Writing/Discussion Activities:** <br><br> **Grouping Configuration:** | **Lesson Focus:** <br><br> **Content Objectives:** <br><br> **Language Objectives:** <br><br> **Reading/Writing/Discussion Activities:** <br><br> **Grouping Configuration:** |

If you use one of our SIOP® unit planners or a similar tool, you will already have a list of potential content and language objectives to draw from. In addition, you can review the six types of language objectives in the core SIOP® texts (Echevarria, Vogt, & Short, 2008, pp. 29–30; 2010a, pp. 32–33; 2010b, pp. 32–33). It is important to vary the types of objectives our students experience and the tasks they practice them with in every unit. A singular focus on only vocabulary or only reading comprehension strategies will not serve English learners as well as attention to the range of language uses will.

Besides writing the objectives in the lesson plan, we need to present them to the students and review them each day. In Figure 4.5, Melissa Castillo, a SIOP® National Faculty member, suggests a number of activities for making content and language objectives a relevant part of daily lessons (Castillo, 2008). We hope you find them useful in your own practice.

You have probably discovered that writing SIOP® lessons that incorporate the components and features of the model requires careful, detailed planning. If you use one of the lesson plan formats in the other SIOP® books, you know that it includes reminders of SIOP® features that should be present in the lessons. Incorporating all thirty features is a challenge, but well worth it for your students' academic progress. We encourage you to keep the SIOP® Protocol handy as a lesson plan checklist. The more you reflect on how

**FIGURE 4.5** *Ways to Present Objectives to the Class*

---

Read the objective as a shared reading piece with your entire class. Then ask students to **paraphrase the objective with a partner,** each taking a turn, using the frame: We are going to learn _____ .

---

Ask students to read the objectives on the board and add them to their Learning Notebooks in a paraphrased form. Then have them **read their paraphrased objectives to each other.** This could be done as a sponge activity during the first part of the class while you are taking roll!

---

Present the objective and then do a **Timed Pair-Share** asking students to predict some of the things they think they will be doing for the lesson that day.

---

Ask students to do a **Rally Robin** (taking turns) naming things they will be asked to do that day in that particular lesson.

---

Ask students to **identify important words from the objective** and highlight them, such as the action words and nouns.

---

Give students **important words to "watch" and "listen" for during the lesson** and call attention to that part of the objective when you mention the academic vocabulary in the lesson.

---

Reread the objectives using shared reading **during the lesson to refocus** your students.

---

Ask students to **rate themselves on how well they are understanding and meeting the objective,** using finger symbols that can be shown in class or hidden under the desk. For example: Thumbs up~ I got it! Thumbs down~I am completely lost! Flat hand tilting back and forth horizontally~I understand some of it, but I'm a bit fuzzy!

---

**Rate yourself 1–3,** how well did you meet the objective today?

  1. I can teach the concept to someone else because . . .

  2. I can demonstrate my learning and want to know more . . .

  3. I'm not sure, I need more . . .

---

Ask students to **write one or two sentences explaining what they learned in class and give an example.** This can be done on an index card, in a learning log, or on a sticky note left on the desk.

---

Have students do a **Round Robin** (taking turns talking for a specified time with a partner) about how they can prove they met their learning objective for the day.

---

Use **Tickets-Out**. Students write a note to the teacher (or a letter to a parent) at the end of the lesson telling what they learned and asking any clarifying questions they need answered.

---

*Source:* Castillo, 2008.

---

the features can be manifested in your lessons, the more comfortable you will become with the writing process. With regular practice, you will internalize the model and including the features in lessons will become second nature to you. As shown in Figure 4.6, less detailed lesson plans are needed over time.

**FIGURE 4.6** *SIOP® Lesson Planning over Time*

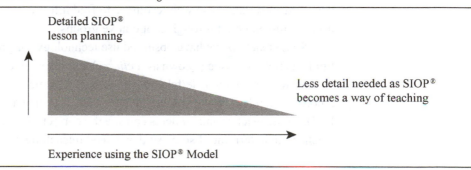

Detailed SIOP® lesson planning

Less detail needed as SIOP® becomes a way of teaching

Experience using the SIOP® Model

# Technology in SIOP® Lessons

The increasing use of technology in the classroom is an exciting trend, filled with many possibilities. Ten years ago, using PowerPoint slides in a lesson was innovative, but now it seems to be a standard and the students themselves are adept in designing animated slides and embedding video clips. More and more teachers use interactive white boards (e.g., smart boards, Promethean boards) as replacements for traditional white boards or overhead transparencies. Information can be projected, color-coded, merged, and edited. Some interactive white boards allow teachers to capture their instruction and post the material for review by students at a later time, providing much-needed opportunities for repetition for English learners.

Multimedia tools now not only allow teachers and students to access information but also to record and present information. Many districts have online video subscriptions (e.g., discoveryeducation.com or linked to their textbooks) and teachers no longer have to manage TV/video players or (to really date us) filmstrip projectors. With these video subscriptions and access to digital libraries, teachers regularly identify video clips that build background for students, on everything from castles and medieval life to Lewis and Clark's travels to Chinese dynasties to the Kennedy-Nixon television debate. Digital video and audio recording instruments are available with editing capabilities so teachers and students can fine tune a performance or project. Students not only listen to podcasts now, they can create their own. Think about an online Model United Nations event where—through video and audio recordings and live web feeds—students around a district or state can debate a global problem and negotiate possible solutions in real time.

Technology tools for students to use independently abound and have moved beyond a computer "spell-check" function. Some interactive software programs such as *Inspiration, Kidspiration,* and *Language Learner* are available on websites. Computerized reading programs have online coaches that monitor student comprehension of online text and adjust the readings offered as well as the questions posed based on their scores. With these programs, students can also record their own speech and check their pronunciation and fluency. Many of these programs print reports for teachers that show how well students are progressing.

Computer simulations allow students to adopt the role of a historical character and experience his or her daily life—as a Pilgrim, a pioneer in a wagon train, an explorer in the Amazon rain forest, or an anthropologist in New Guinea. In these roles, students face challenges and make decisions based on their knowledge of the time period and the resources available to the characters. Students may take on roles of historical figures or researchers in WebQuests, which are inquiry-based, online learning scenarios that are designed so students use web resources to find information and complete tasks. They are usually implemented through cooperative groups.

Some teachers we have observed use technology for group-administered reviews. Students hold a device (known as a *clicker*) and respond anonymously to a prompt from a teacher with a yes/no, true/false, agree/disagree, or multi-choice options. The computer records all student responses, collates the data, and displays the results quickly via an LCD, so the teacher and students can see the correct responses. Almost immediately, the teacher can determine if some students need reteaching of particular concepts.

In districts and schools that require graduation portfolios, technology is playing an increasing role as well. Students may video record simulations and debates, scan projects, show the evolution of a paper from first draft to final submission, and more. These electronic portfolios can be reviewed by staff on site or by invited reviewers who may live out of town.

Technology can be utilized in all the components of the SIOP® Model, as the following examples reveal:

**Preparation:** multimedia, WebQuests, computer simulations, and other technological tools to incorporate in lessons, online lesson planners

**Building Background:** digital libraries and video clips to build background on historical topics, online visuals for vocabulary development, digital photographs of historical people, events, and geographic features to recap activities from prior lessons

**Comprehensible Input:** software for semantic webs, concept maps, and graphic organizers, audio recordings of textbooks, embedded glossary links for words in online text

**Strategies:** audio recordings of think-alouds and other problem-solving processes, online note-taking charts and outlines

**Interaction:** student-developed and edited podcasts and video stories using digital media, WebQuests

**Practice & Application:** online historical simulations, computerized reading and writing programs, audio files of famous speeches and debates

**Lesson Delivery:** web timers to keep teachers and students on pace, multimedia to heighten student interest and engagement

**Review & Assessment:** hand-held clickers for quick informal assessment of the student learning in class, data management tools, computer adaptive tests and quizzes

By no means is this list exhaustive. Its aim is to show that it is not difficult to embed technology in SIOP® lessons if you have access to high-tech and low-tech tools.

However, we recognize that not all schools have these resources available due to lack of funds or a low commitment to technology use. Often, it is the schools with high numbers of English learners that are the most disadvantaged. In order to be sensitive to teachers of ELs who do not have access to state-of-the-art technologies, the lesson plans presented throughout this book are fairly "low tech." If you are one of the fortunate teachers who have these resources at your disposal, when the lesson plan calls for use of an overhead transparency or worksheet, you might use an interactive white board; when the lesson plan suggests showing a picture, you might project a website. We encourage the SIOP® teachers to integrate technology in their lessons to the extent feasible and appropriate.

# SIOP® History-Social Studies Lesson Formats

At present, there are a number of SIOP® lesson plan formats that teachers are using in schools and districts throughout the country. Some have been created by teachers, others have been adapted for the SIOP® Model from district lesson plans, and others have been created by SIOP® National Faculty and the SIOP® authors. You may remember that four lesson plan formats are included in the core text, *Making Content Comprehensible for English Learners: The SIOP® Model* (Echevarria, Vogt, & Short, 2008), and additional sample lesson plans and formats are included in *Implementing the SIOP® Model through Effective Coaching and Professional Development* (Echevarria, Short, & Vogt, 2008) and *99 Ideas and Activities for Teaching with the SIOP® Model* (Vogt & Echevarria, 2008). The lessons in this book use two different formats, which we present below. Although we, the SIOP® authors, do not endorse any particular lesson plan format, we advocate that you select one that works well for you. You may adjust any SIOP® lesson format to your preferences and district guidelines, and that is fine for SIOP® lessons, as long as all of the components and features are included.

The first lesson plan format developed by Robin Liten-Tejada, one of the contributors to this book, is a straightforward treatment of the lesson cycle. It is explained in Figure 4.7 and it is used for the lessons in the K–2 and 3–5 units. It follows a typical sequence for a lesson plan.

**FIGURE 4.7**  *History–Social Studies SIOP® Lesson Plan Template 1*

*Lesson Title:* _____

**Content Objective(s):**

*(List content objective(s).)*

**Language Objective(s):**

*(List language objective(s).)*

**Materials:**

*(List supplementary materials, visuals, realia, texts, handouts.)*

**Key Vocabulary:**

*(List key social studies and academic vocabulary.)*

**Introduce the Lesson:**

*(Begin with the objectives and explain the purpose of the lesson.)*

**Develop Understandings:**

*(Incorporate building background and comprehensible input activities and instruction in learning strategies.)*

**Practice:**

*(Promote student–student interaction; provide activities to practice the concepts and language.)*

**Apply:**

*(Promote student–student interaction; provide activities to apply the concepts and language.)*

**Wrap-Up:**

*(Review objectives, check comprehension, and offer self assessments.)*

Lesson plan format created by Robin Liten-Tejada.

The second format was developed by John Seidlitz, the other contributor to this book, and is described in Figure 4.8. In this plan, John records the comprehension checks, assessment tasks, and review activities in a separate column to remind teachers to monitor student learning throughout the lesson, not only at the end.

**FIGURE 4.8**  *History–Social Studies SIOP® Lesson Plan Template 2*

**Unit or Lesson Title:** _____

**Grade:** _____          **Topic:** _____
**Subject:** _____          **Date:** _____

| **Content Objective**: *List content objective(s).* | **Language Objective:** *List language objective(s).* |
|---|---|
| **Vocabulary:** *List key content and academic vocabulary.* | **Visuals, Materials, & Texts:** *List supplementary materials.* |
| *Activities* | *Review & Check for Understanding* |
| **Activating Prior Knowledge** *(Processes, Stems, and Strategies):* *List instructional techniques and activities, language stems or frames for speaking or writing, and learning strategies to help activate prior knowledge.* | *(Response Signals, Writing, Self Assessment, Student Products)* *List instructional techniques and activities to help students review, to provide feedback, and to assess student comprehension. This may include student work products, self assessment activities, and group response signals.* |
| **Building Vocabulary and Concept Knowledge** *(Processes, Stems, and Strategies):* *List instructional techniques and activities, language stems or frames for speaking or writing, and learning strategies to build vocabulary and content knowledge.* | |
| **Structured Conversation and Writing** *(Processes, Stems, and Strategies):* *List instructional techniques and activities, language stems or frames for speaking or writing, and learning strategies that will promote student interaction.* | |

Lesson plan format created by John Seidlitz.

# Concluding Thoughts

This chapter explores lesson and unit planning for SIOP® social studies and history classes and offers insights into the preparation processes involved. We have outlined how to effectively incorporate techniques and activities into thoughtful, standards-based

SIOP® lessons that give attention to language development every day. For English learners to make adequate progress in social studies, history, geography, civics, and economics—and all subjects—they must be given opportunities to use English for academic purposes. It is impossible to separate out the process of understanding and learning concepts, theories, points of view, events, and applications from their language requirements. Further, the cultural aspects of this subject area may give students a chance to share their background knowledge and become resources to other students in the classroom—a role reversal not common with many ELs. But in order for them to be able to act as cultural informants, they need to be capable of articulating their ideas and experiences.

To conclude our chapter opening scenario, you may be interested in knowing that Ms. Parry and Dr. Levine did meet before the landforms unit was taught, as well as several other times during the fall. As a result of her interaction with Dr. Levine when planning several units, Ms. Parry agreed to enroll in a course that Dr. Levine taught after school in the second semester, which was sponsored by the local university specifically for teachers in the district. Ms. Parry found this "Introduction to the SIOP® Model" course extremely helpful, specifically in learning how to write objectives that reflect what students should learn and in following through with appropriate activities that support the objectives in the lessons.

In the following chapters, you will hear from SIOP® social studies and history educators as they describe more details about the specific planning processes they undertook while developing and implementing the units. We hope that those units and lessons will illustrate clearly to you how to implement the features of the SIOP® Model in daily lessons, consistently and cohesively throughout a unit of study.

# chapter 5

# SIOP® Social Studies Unit, Grades K–2

### By Robin Liten-Tejada and Deborah Short

## Introduction

This chapter and the three that follow present complete units with lesson plans and student handouts for a variety of social studies and history topics. In this chapter, SIOP® social studies educator Robin Liten-Tejada (who was also one of the original SIOP® research teachers for the CREDE study) describes her planning process for this social studies unit for students in the primary grades. As you read this unit, look at how several of the techniques and activities from Chapters 2 and 3 are incorporated into the lessons. See how the activities in the detailed lesson plans map onto the components of the SIOP® Model (found in Appendix A). If you have not read Chapter 4 about SIOP® unit and lesson design for English learners, please read it now for an overview of the planning process and a discussion of the lesson plan format used in this and other chapters.

You will notice that there are some teacher Think-Alouds and Planning Points in these lessons. The teacher Think-Alouds, identified with thought bubble icons, reflect decisions Robin made as she wrote each lesson. The purpose of the Planning Points, identified with a flash drive icon, is to highlight or identify resources that support the implementation of the lesson.

The following section shows how Robin Liten-Tejada planned her social studies unit, *Past and Present.* You'll see that she identifies the main topic and the appropriate social studies and English language proficiency standards for her state, Virginia. She establishes enduring understandings students should develop as a result of the lessons, and she poses essential questions to guide her planning. She creates a list of potential language objectives organized by language skill, and records key vocabulary for the unit. Learning strategies that students can practice are noted and supplementary materials are identified.

This chapter then continues with the detailed lesson plans for the units. The student handouts are included as blackline masters (BLMs) in Appendix D.

# Past and Present

## Unit Overview, Grades K–2

Distinguishing between past and present is a key social studies concept for primary students. It is a fairly abstract concept, however, and requires the teacher to incorporate concrete experiences throughout the unit. As you see below, I always start planning by determining the big ideas of the unit, or the Enduring Understandings, to be sure that my lessons are focused around a central theme. Next I determine the Essential Questions that guide my instruction (Wiggins & McTighe, 2005). To plan the entire unit, I know that I need to start with concrete background building experiences, connecting the concepts to be taught to the students' own lives, then move to the abstract academic concepts, and finally return to the students' own experiences to apply their new knowledge. This unit follows that cycle through six lessons, each one incorporating specific content and language objectives. Throughout the lessons, there are frequent opportunities that are appropriate for young English learners to practice and reinforce reading, writing, listening, and speaking skills. At the start of each lesson, I include a Think-Aloud that explains why I chose those particular objectives and activities, and how they relate to the learning cycle.

### Topic

Past and Present

### Standards

- *Virginia Social Studies Standard of Learning (SOL) 1.1* about interpreting timelines
  *WIDA[1] English Standard 5* – English language learners will communicate information, ideas and concepts necessary for academic success in the content area of social studies.

---

[1]WIDA stands for World-Class Instructional Design and Assessment. It has a set of English language proficiency standards that have been adopted by 22 states and the District of Columbia, including Virginia, as of the time of this writing. These standards reflect the academic language of social studies, science, mathematics, language arts and the social/instructional use of English.

## Enduring Understandings

- Past and present times are different.
- Everyday life changes in different places and times.

## Essential Questions

- How have we changed over time?
- How has life changed over time?

## Content Objectives

Students will be able to (SWBAT):

- Sequence personal photographs chronologically on a timeline.
- Identify personal changes between past and present.
- Compare and contrast their lives between past and present.
- Identify changes between past and present in daily life.
- Classify activities as occurring in daily life of the past or present.

## Language Objectives

**Speaking**

Students will be able to (SWBAT):

- Describe photographs of the teacher using the sentence structure:
  - In the past, Ms. X _____.
  - In the present, Ms. X _____.
- Describe what they were like or did at the different times of their lives shown in their photographs using the sentence frames:
  - When I was a baby (or ___years old), I _____.
  - Now I am ___ years old and I _____.
- Justify their favorite picture using the sentence frame:
  - My favorite picture is _____ because _____.
- Orally compare and contrast personal abilities in the past and present, following a sentence frame:
  - In the past I _____ but now I _____.
  - In the past I _____ and I still _____.
- Work with a partner to classify activities and justify decisions using a sentence frame:
  - I think this picture is from the past (or present) because _____.
- Express an opinion about material they have read using a sentence frame:
  - In your flipbook, I like _____ or In your flipbook, I like how you _____.

**Listening**

SWBAT:

- Listen to a partner's descriptions of personal photographs and select a favorite.

- Listen to a story for details about life in the past.
- Listen to a description and identify the matching picture on a game card.

**Reading**

SWBAT:

- Read two poems aloud and relate them to their own lives.
- Read verbs and classify activities as occurring in the past or present.
- Classify details under appropriate topic headings.
- Read classmates' flipbooks.

**Writing**

SWBAT:

- Write descriptive sentences following a model.
- Create a flipbook comparing past and present characteristics of daily life.

## Key Vocabulary

- Past
- Present
- Timeline
- Change
- Variety of verbs describing everyday actions, such as *crawl, drink from a bottle, drink from a glass, listen to stories, play, sleep, use the toilet, walk, wear diapers*
- Communities
- Transportation

## Learning Strategies

- Classification
- Comparison and contrast
- Interpretation of concepts expressed by pictures
- Organization of information with timelines
- Sequencing of events in chronological order

## Materials

- Blackline masters 1, 2, 3, 4, 5, 6, 7, 8, 9, 10 (found in Appendix D)
- Poems: "The End," by A.A. Milne, and "When I Was Born," by Jill Eggleton
- Four photographs brought from home showing different ages of the teacher and students
- Antique or unusual household gadgets or pictures of items
- A book to read aloud that describes life in the past, such as *The Ox-Cart Man*
- Two sheets of 8-1/2" x 11" paper or 9" x 12" construction paper per student

# SIOP® LESSON PLAN 1: *My Personal Timeline*

**Developed by Robin Liten-Tejada**

## THINK-ALOUD, LESSON 1

- I know that an effective unit starts with a concrete experience that introduces the topic, activates background knowledge, and makes a meaningful connection to students' lives and prior learning. For my first lesson, I want to create a concrete experience that will capture the students' interest by making a personal connection to the concept of past and present and how we change over time. I know they will be interested in seeing pictures of the teacher at different stages of life, and this will entice them to bring in various pictures of themselves at different stages. In this way, we'll introduce the concept of past and present by starting with the students' own lives. Throughout the unit, I provide sentence frames to guide the discussion and to provide support for English learners so they can fully participate.

### Content Objectives

**SWBAT**
- Sequence personal photographs chronologically on a timeline.
- Identify personal changes between past and present.

### Language Objectives

**SWBAT**
- Describe photographs of the teacher using the sentence structure:
  - In the past, Ms. X _____.
  - In the present, Ms. X _____.

### Materials

Four photographs of teacher from different times in life, My Personal Timeline poster (BLM 1), self-assessment rubric (Figure 5.1)

### Key Vocabulary

past, present, timeline, change

### Introduce the Lesson

Start the lesson by reading today's objectives with the students. The wording should be simplified to meet the students' level of understanding. One possibility is
- "Today we will put my photographs in order on a timeline. Today we will tell how I have changed between the past and present. We will tell our ideas using these sentences:
  - In the past, Ms. X _____.
  - In the present, Ms. X _____."

### Develop Understandings

To introduce the concepts of past and present changes and a timeline, students view and analyze the teacher's personal timeline. The teacher should arrange four pictures of herself, beginning with childhood through the present, in a timeline with a line separating past and present (see BLM 1). Have students view the photographs, asking them what they notice. Discuss ways that you have **changed** (emphasizing key vocabulary *change*). Ask them why you have arranged the pictures in this way. Explain that

*(continued)*

Past and Present

## SIOP® LESSON PLAN 1: *My Personal Timeline* *(continued)*

your pictures are arranged on a **timeline**, from **past** to **present.** (With your arm, gesture a straight line from the students' left to right, saying, "This timeline shows pictures from **past** to **present**" while making the motion. Have students repeat this sentence after you while also making the motion.)

### *Practice*

Have students say a few sentences about your pictures following this example:

- In the past, Ms. X _____.
- In the present, Ms. X _____.

Give students a few seconds to think of one of each of the above sentences; then have them share their ideas with a partner. Conduct a Whip Around, Pass Option (described in Chapter 3) for students to share with the whole group their favorite ideas about one of your pictures.

### *Apply*

Have everyone answer and repeat the key vocabulary:

- How are my pictures arranged? (The pictures are arranged on a **timeline**.)
- What is a timeline? (The **timeline** shows my pictures from **past** to **present.**)
- Am I the same from past to present? (No, I have **changed** from **past** to **present.**)

### *Wrap Up*

At the end of the class, review the objectives with students and have them self-assess their own understanding using a Self-Assessment Rubric such as the one in Figure 5.1 (described in Chapter 3). Read each statement below, and have students put an X on the face (a smiley face ☺, question mark ?, or sad face ☹) that describes their feelings.

1. I could put my teacher's pictures in order on the timeline.
2. I could tell how my teacher has changed between the past and present.

**FIGURE 5.1**  *Self-Assessment Rubric*

| | | | |
|---|:---:|:---:|:---:|
| Statement 1 | ☹ | ? | ☺ |
| Statement 2 | ☹ | ? | ☺ |

### *Homework*

1. Have students bring in four photographs of themselves at different ages, starting with a baby picture and including a current one, which they will arrange on a timeline like yours. If necessary, send a letter home to parents ahead of time requesting the photographs.

2. To foster a home–school connection, students can ask their parents how their parents changed between the past and present, and what they were like as children.

## SIOP® LESSON PLAN 2: *My Life in Past and Present*

**Developed by Robin Liten-Tejada**

### THINK-ALOUD, LESSON 2

- To continue building background, I need to help the students make the connections to their own lives. We'll start off with a fun poem that the children can relate to. They'll arrange their own photographs in a timeline similar to mine, and then will talk and write about their own lives. I expect this to be an enjoyable activity for them since children like to talk about themselves. And starting with "the self" is the most effective way to teach abstract concepts like past versus present.

### Content Objectives

**SWBAT**
- Sequence personal photographs chronologically on a timeline.
- Identify personal changes between past and present.

### Language Objectives

**SWBAT**
- Describe what they were like or did at the different times of their lives shown in their photographs, using the sentence frames:
  - When I was a baby (or _____ years old), I _____ .
  - Now I am _____ years old, and I _____ .
- Listen to a partner's descriptions of personal photographs and select a favorite.
- Justify their favorite picture, using the sentence frame:
  - My favorite picture is _____ because _____ .
- Write descriptive sentences about their photographs.

### Materials

My Personal Timeline Sentences (BLM 2), photographs students bring from home

### Key Vocabulary

past, present, timeline, change

### Introduce the Lesson

Start the lesson by reading today's objectives with the students. The wording should be simplified to meet the students' level of understanding.

### Develop Understandings

To set the stage for creating personal timelines and thinking about personal change, open by reading aloud a poem about growing up, such as "The End" by A.A. Milne (first line: "When I was One, I had just begun."). Tell students that they will be thinking about their own lives as well in the **past** and **present.**

Review the teacher timeline, emphasizing that the pictures are arranged in order from past to present. Tell students that now they will be arranging their own pictures in order on a timeline. Distribute the timeline modeled from BLM 1, and help students arrange and stick their pictures on the timeline, dividing them between past and present.

### Practice

Think-Pair-Share Activity: Have students think of a sentence to describe each picture or what they were like at that age, which they will share with a partner. Partners will be instructed to listen and decide which of their partner's pictures is their favorite. The students should have Structured Conversations (see Chapter 3) following this model:

**Person A**
- When I was a baby, I _____ .
*or*
- When I was [age], I _____ .
*and*
- Now I am [age] and I _____ .

*(continued)*

## SIOP® LESSON PLAN 2: *My Life in Past and Present* (continued)

**Person B**

● My favorite picture is _____ because _____ .

The teacher should model a few sentences from her or his own pictures with a partner. Have students practice their own sentences to themselves, and then pair up for sharing.

### Apply

After sharing, students will write one sentence for each picture, completing the My Personal Timeline Sentences (BLM 2). These sentence strips should be cut up and affixed to their timelines under the correct photograph or picture.

### Wrap Up

At the end of the class, review the objectives with students and have them self-assess their own understanding using Oral Number 1–3 for Self-Assessment of Objectives (procedures in Chapter 3). Students can hold up fingers to indicate their response:

   1 = I didn't meet the objective.
   2 = I didn't meet the objective, but I made progress.
   3 = I met the objective.

---

## SIOP® LESSON PLAN 3: *Comparing the Past to the Present*

**Developed by Robin Liten-Tejada**

## THINK-ALOUD, LESSON 3

● Now that students have participated in the concrete background-building experience of thinking about their own lives in the past and present, we're ready to introduce the abstract concepts of comparison and contrast, and to organize ideas on a Venn diagram. But we don't just stop with the Venn diagram. I also provide the language for students to talk about comparisons and contrasts, which not only builds their language skills, but further reinforces the academic concepts through practice.

### Content Objectives

**SWBAT**

● Identify personal changes between past and present.
● Compare and contrast their lives between past and present.
● Classify activities as occurring in the past or present.

### Language Objectives

**SWBAT**

● Read a poem and compare its ideas to their own lives.
● Read verbs and classify activities on a Venn diagram as occurring in the past or present.
● Orally compare and contrast their personal abilities in the past and present, following a sentence frame:
     ● In the past I _____, but now I _____ .
     ● In the past I _____, and I still _____ .

*(continued)*

*Materials*

Poem or story about babies and children, My Life in the Past and Present Venn Diagram (BLM 3; Figure 5.2), vocabulary cards (BLM 4), comparison/contrast chart (Figure 5.3)

*Key Vocabulary*

change, could/couldn't, can/can't, and still, but now

*Action verbs:* crawl, drink from a bottle, drink from a glass, listen to stories, play, sleep, use the toilet, walk, wear diapers

*Introduce the Lesson*

Start the lesson by reading today's objectives with the students. The wording should be simplified to meet the students' level of understanding. Briefly explain the terms *classify*, *compare*, and *contrast*.

*Develop Understandings*

Bridge to a new concept by having students reflect on how they have changed. Tell students that people **change** from past to present. Ask students to think of things they **can** do now that they **couldn't** do in the past when they were younger—things that babies **can't** do. Ask a few volunteers to act out something they couldn't do in the past, and have the class guess the action. List the actions suggested by students on the board to provide support for the following oral activity. Some actions might be *walk, run, eat from a plate, drink from a glass, read, write,* and *talk.*

Read a story or poem about differences between babies and children, such as "When I Was Born" by Jill Eggleton (first line, "When I was born, I couldn't walk."). As you are reading, have students think about ways that they are the same as the person in the poem or story. Afterward, ask students to share one sentence about themselves, such as:

- In the past I couldn't _____, but now I can.

To help students understand that some things change for us from past to present, while other things stay the same, form small groups of students and have each group complete a Venn diagram using the Go Graphic—One Step Further technique to promote oral language practice too (see Chapter 3).

**Procedures:**

1. Create a large Venn diagram for each group of students, with labels similar to those in the example shown in Figure 5.2 and found on BLM 3.

FIGURE 5.2 *My Life in the Past and Present Venn Diagram*

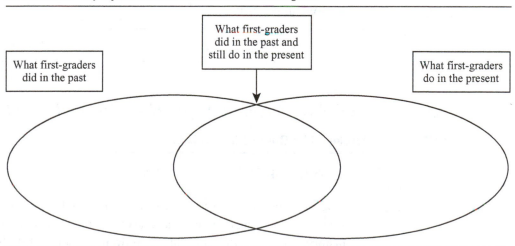

*(continued)*

## SIOP® LESSON PLAN 3: *Comparing the Past to the Present* (continued)

2. Cut out the vocabulary squares (see BLM 4), and give a set to each group of students. Have students categorize the pictures in the Venn diagram according to what students did in the past versus the present and what actions are the same in both time periods. There are three pictures for each category.

3. As students finish, review the Venn diagram on the board together. Have students suggest other activities to place on the graphic organizer, referring to the earlier action verb list for ideas if necessary. Keep the diagram in place for the following language activity.

### *Practice*

Teach students the comparison/contrast phrases by putting a chart like Figure 5.3 on the board. Point to the picture cards on the Venn diagram, and teach students how to form sentences from the graphic organizer. Point to the "same" section, and have them repeat after you:

- In the past I slept, and I still sleep now.
- In the past I played, and I still play now.
- In the past I listened to stories, and I still listen to stories now.

Next, point to the "contrasting pictures," and have students repeat after you:

- In the past I crawled, but now I can walk.
- In the past I drank from a bottle, but now I can drink from a glass.
- In the past I used diapers, but now I can use the toilet.

### *Apply*

Student partners should practice saying the sentences to each other while looking at their Venn diagram. After practicing the models, students should think of other sentences that are true for themselves, either from the other examples on the board or from new ideas.

### *Wrap Up*

Do a Whip Around, Pass Option (see Chapter 3) in which students share their favorite sentences describing how they have changed from the past, or what they can still do in the present. Beginning proficiency students who are not yet able to generate sentences can repeat one of the models. Then review the day's objectives with students and have them self-assess their own understanding.

**FIGURE 5.3** *Comparison/Contrast Word Chart*

| Comparison/Contrast Words | |
|---|---|
| **Words that indicate "same"** | **Words that indicate "different"** |
| • and I still _____ now | • but now I _____ |

## SIOP® LESSON PLAN 4: *How Do You Know It's from the Past?*

**Developed by Robin Liten-Tejada**

### THINK-ALOUD, LESSON 4

- After thoroughly exploring the concept of past and present in the students' own lives, we're ready to transition to the abstract topic of the changes in daily life throughout history. I'll start with a colorful visual from the Colonial Williamsburg website,

*(continued)*

which will allow students to brainstorm what changes they notice between the picture and today. To make the concept even more concrete, I'll bring in my collection of old and unusual household gadgets for students to handle and guess what they were used for. Then we'll read a picture book that will allow students to think of a variety of ways that daily life has changed between the past and the present.

### Content Objective

**SWBAT**

- Identify changes between past and present in daily life.

### Language Objectives

**SWBAT**

- Listen to a story for details about life in the past.
- Classify details under appropriate topic headings.

### Materials

Colonial Williamsburg picture (BLM 5), collection of outdated household objects, a picture book about life in the past (to be read aloud), blank sentence strips, tree map organizer (Figure 5.4)

### Key Vocabulary

communities, transportation (other words depending on story read)

### Introduce the Lesson

Start the lesson by reading today's objectives with the students. The wording should be simplified to meet the students' level of understanding.

### Develop Understandings

Explain that people's lives have all changed in many ways between the past and present and make the connection to the study of history. Display a picture from Colonial Williamsburg (see BLM 5) or another similar visual, and ask students how we can tell that this is a picture from the past. Draw a web on the board with "Life in the Past" in the center circle. Ask students what they already know about how life was different in the past, and record their ideas on the web. Tell them they are going to learn about how life has changed in important ways.

Use the Concrete Personal Experiences technique (see Chapter 2). If you have access to antique, outdated, or unusual household gadgets, bring them in to class, or obtain illustrations of such items from clip art (e.g., typewriter, record player, telegraph, washboard, transistor radio, eggbeater). Pass the items around and let students guess what they were used for. Afterward, name the object that we use in the present for a similar purpose, and discuss which is better.

### Practice and Apply

Select a picture book to read aloud that illustrates what life was like in the past. One possibility is *The Ox-Cart Man* (Hall, 1979). Instruct students to listen for ways that life was different in the past from today, and be prepared to make a list afterward. Depending on the story you are going to read, post key questions such as:

- How have communities changed from past to present?
- How has transportation changed from past to present?
- How has family life changed from past to present?

After reading, solicit ideas from the class on all the ways life was different in the past as seen in the book, writing each idea on a sentence strip. Draw a tree map organizer on the board with the title "Life in the Past" and with headings that are appropriate to the information in the book, such as in Figure 5.4. As a class, classify each idea by placing the sentence strips under the appropriate columns.

*(continued)*

## SIOP® LESSON PLAN 4: *How Do You Know It's from the Past?* *(continued)*

### *Wrap Up*

To wrap up, conduct a quick version of Stand Up/Sit Down (see Chapter 3). Elicit from students three interesting aspects of life in the past that they read today and write them on the board. Review the list orally. Then tell students to stand up when you read the one that is the most interesting to them. Read the items on the list one at a time and let students vote with their feet.

Review the day's objectives with students.

**FIGURE 5.4** *Life in the Past Tree Map*

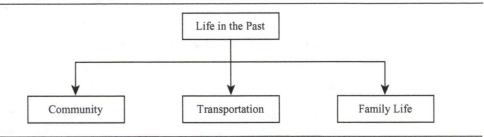

## SIOP® LESSON PLAN 5: *Living in the Past and Present*

**Developed by Robin Liten-Tejada**

 ### THINK-ALOUD, LESSON 5

- It's time to provide students with an opportunity to reinforce their new academic knowledge and language skills while interacting with their peers. Playing a game is a fun way to reinforce content and knowledge. I often use clip art to create pictures that the students will classify as occurring in the past or present, and then we will use the pictures to play Bingo.

### *Content Objective*

**SWBAT**
- Classify activities as occurring in daily life of the past or present.

### *Language Objectives*

**SWBAT**
- Work with a partner to classify activities and justify decisions, using the sentence frame: I think this picture is from the past (or present) because _____.
- Listen to a description and identify the matching picture on a game card.

### *Materials*

picture cards of aspects of daily life in the past and present (BLM 6) (see Planning Point), T-chart (BLM 7), Bingo game board (BLM 8)

### *Key Vocabulary*

communities, cooking food, getting clothes, getting food, homes, light, transportation, writing a letter

*(continued)*

*Introduce the Lesson*

Start the lesson by reading today's objectives with the students. The wording should be simplified to meet the students' level of understanding. Ask them to guess what they will do today.

*Develop Understandings*

Use the Cut and Match Answers technique (see Chapter 2) for students to learn more about classification. Distribute picture cards and the T-chart (BLM 7), and have students work in pairs to classify the pictures of daily life as either Past or Present, placing them in the T-chart in the appropriate category—for example "Transportation" or "Cooking food." Partners should tell each other why they made their choices. They can follow the model sentence:

- I think this picture is from the past (or present), because _____.

*Practice*

Play Bingo as a class. Tell student pairs to select nine pictures from the above activity and place each one in a different square on the Bingo game board (BLM 8). Randomly dictate one of the descriptions from the Teacher Script below and tell students if they have that picture on their board, they should place a marker on top of it. The first pair to get three in a row should call out "Bingo." The students must also read back their winning squares both to confirm their answers and to practice the language. Play several rounds, and after each round, students can choose to change their pictures or continue with the same ones. Explain that there is no prize and this is not a competition, but rather a fun way to practice what they have been learning.

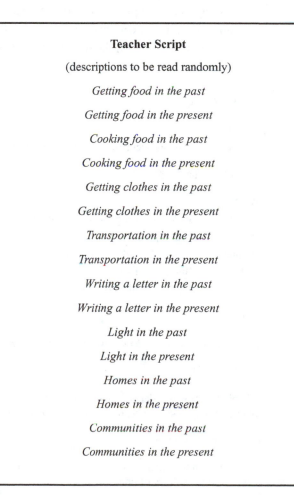

**Teacher Script**

(descriptions to be read randomly)

*Getting food in the past*

*Getting food in the present*

*Cooking food in the past*

*Cooking food in the present*

*Getting clothes in the past*

*Getting clothes in the present*

*Transportation in the past*

*Transportation in the present*

*Writing a letter in the past*

*Writing a letter in the present*

*Light in the past*

*Light in the present*

*Homes in the past*

*Homes in the present*

*Communities in the past*

*Communities in the present*

*(continued)*

## SIOP® LESSON PLAN 5: *Living in the Past and Present* (continued)

### Wrap Up

To wrap up, review the day's objectives with students and have them use Outcome Sentences such as
- Today I discovered . . .
- I want to know more about . . .

## PLANNING POINT

- The pictures on BLM 6 should be cut up into individual cards for the students to manipulate.

## SIOP® LESSON PLAN 6: *Flipping from the Past to Present*

### Developed by Robin Liten-Tejada

## THINK-ALOUD, LESSON 6

- To cement the new knowledge, it's important to provide students with an opportunity to apply the concepts in a personally meaningful way. Creating a flipbook is a good option for this concept because it entails different aspects that can be written on the tabs and illustrated on the pages. Students will enjoy reading each other's books and stating their opinions.

### Content Objective

**SWBAT**
- Classify activities as occurring in daily life of the past or present.

### Language Objectives

**SWBAT**
- Create a flipbook comparing aspects of daily life in the past and present.
- Read classmates' flipbooks.
- Express an opinion about the material read, using one of the sentence frames:
  - In your flipbook, I like _____.
  - In your flipbook, I like how you _____.

### Materials

Flipbook instructions (BLM 9), two sheets of paper per flipbook (see Planning Point)

### Key Vocabulary

flipbook, (other words depending on student choices, such as communities, cooking food, getting clothes, getting food, homes, light, transportation, writing a letter)

### Introduce the Lesson

Start the lesson by reading today's objectives with the students. The wording should be simplified to meet the students' level of understanding.

*(continued)*

### Develop Understandings

Explain to students that they will do a project to pull together what they have learned in this unit. The students will select the three aspects of daily life most interesting to them (e.g., transportation, homes) and compare life in the past and present by creating a flipbook. Model how to make a flipbook and have students generate some ideas orally as to what they might include. (See BLM 9 for instructions.)

### Practice

Have students make individual flipbooks. Newcomers and beginning students might be paired with more proficient students for assistance.

To assess the flipbooks, evaluate students' work for the following skills:

- Student was able to select three aspects of daily life.
- Student was able to compare life in the past and present for those aspects.

### Apply

Have students sit on the rug, and ask them to exchange their books with different partners and read their partner's books. After finishing each book, they will tell their partner one thing they liked, using the sentence:

- In your flipbook, I like _____.

*or*

- In your flipbook, I like how you _____.

### Wrap Up

To wrap up, review the day's objectives with students and have them self-assess their own understanding using Oral Number 1–3 or a Self-Assessment Rubric (procedures in Chapter 3).

## PLANNING POINT

- This lesson works best if the teacher constructs the flipbooks out of paper ahead of time for the students. They will add the drawings and text.

# Concluding Thoughts

Many elementary teachers enjoy teaching thematic lessons and look for cross-curricular opportunities. The unit could be linked to Reading or English language arts classes quite easily. For example, there are many literature books, both fiction and nonfiction, that describe daily life in the past. Science concepts, such as elapsed time during an experiment or inventions over time, can reinforce the past and present as well.

We hope this unit gave you new ideas for incorporating meaningful activities and attention to language development in your social studies lessons. Young ELs are emergent readers and writers, so the lessons rely on visuals, discussion, and kinesthetic activities more than reading and writing texts. Helping students articulate their social studies knowledge using oral sentence frames was one goal of the unit, as was developing their vocabulary base. Notice, too, we did not avoid higher-order tasks—the students were asked to compare and classify during the lessons and then synthesize information in their flipbook project.

We encourage you to read Chapters 6–8 for additional social studies and history units. Even if you currently teach grades K–2, you will find interesting SIOP® lessons and effective integration of the new techniques in these other sample units.

# SIOP® Social Studies Unit, Grades 3–5

### By Robin Liten-Tejada and Deborah Short

## Introduction

Like Chapters 5, 7, and 8, this chapter offers a complete social studies unit with lesson plans and student handouts. It has been designed for students in grades 3–5, although an extra lesson is included for students in grades 4 and 5. As you read the unit here, you will see how several of the techniques and activities from Chapters 2 and 3 are incorporated into the lessons, as well as how the activities in the unit lesson plans map onto the components and features of the SIOP® Model (found in Appendix A). If you have not read Chapter 4 about SIOP® unit and lesson design for English learners, please read it for an overview of the planning process and a discussion of the lesson plan format used in this and other chapters.

You will notice that there are teacher Think-Alouds and Planning Points in these lessons. The teacher Think-Alouds, identified with thought bubble icons, reflect decisions Robin made as she was writing the lessons and building the concepts over time. The purpose of the Planning Points, identified with a flash drive icon, is to highlight or identify resources that support the implementation of the lesson.

The following section shows how Robin Liten-Tejada planned her geography unit, *Where in the World Are You?* You'll see that she identifies the main topic and the appropriate social studies and English language proficiency standards for her state, Virginia. She establishes enduring understandings students should develop as a result of the lessons, and she poses essential questions to guide her planning. She creates a list of potential language objectives organized by language skill, and records key vocabulary for the unit. Learning strategies that students can practice are noted and supplementary materials are identified.

The chapter then continues with the detailed lesson plans for the units. The student handouts are included as blackline masters (BLMs) in Appendix D.

# *Where in the World Are You?*

## Unit Overview, Grades 3–5

This unit follows and builds upon prior lessons on identifying the continents and oceans and understanding cardinal directions. In this unit, students will discover that the Equator and Prime Meridian are used to demarcate the four hemispheres, and that lines of latitude and longitude describe exact locations on Earth. Students will learn the related academic vocabulary and reinforce the content knowledge through a variety of activities that develop language skills.

### Topic

Geography: Understanding Maps and Globes

### Standards

- *Virginia Social Studies Standard of Learning (SOL) 3.5* about labeling the continents and oceans and using the Equator and Prime Meridian to locate the hemispheres; and *USII.1* about doing historical and geographical analysis
- *WIDA[1] English Standard 5*—English language learners will communicate information, ideas and concepts necessary for academic success in the content area of social studies.

### Enduring Understandings

- There are seven continents and five oceans on the Earth.
- The Equator and Prime Meridian divide the globe into four hemispheres.
- Latitude and longitude are imaginary lines that help find locations on the Earth.

---

[1]WIDA stands for World-Class Instructional Design and Assessment. It has a set of English language proficiency standards that have been adopted by 22 states and the District of Columbia at the time of this writing. These standards reflect the academic language of social studies, science, mathematics, language arts and the social/instructional use of English.

## Essential Questions

- Where are the continents and oceans located on a world map?
- What imaginary lines are used to create hemispheres?
- How do latitude and longitude help us find locations?

## Content Objectives

Students will be able to (SWBAT):

- Identify the continents and oceans on a world map (prior knowledge that is reinforced).
- Identify the need for precise methods to identify locations on the Earth.
- Identify the Equator and Prime Meridian.
- Use the Equator and Prime Meridian to identify the four hemispheres.
- Identify the hemispheres in which their native countries and specific continents are located.
- Locate specific places using lines of latitude and longitude.
- Identify key terms related to locations on a map.

## Language Objectives

### Speaking

Students will be able to (SWBAT):

- Dictate directions, sentences, and locations to a partner.
- Describe a location to a partner using variations of:

  The (object) is in the _____ hemisphere because it is located _____ of the _____ .

- Speak fluently while performing a Reader's Theater script.

  Correctly pronounce a location's latitude and longitude following this structure: The _____ is located at _____° _____ latitude, _____° _____ longitude. [*For example,* Washington, DC is located at 39° north latitude and 77° west longitude.]

- Collaborate politely with classmates.

### Listening

SWBAT:

- Listen to directions and mark an X on a map to indicate a location.
- Listen to a description and identify the imaginary line or hemisphere being described.
- Listen to classmates' performances to assess accuracy of content and pronunciation.
- Listen to sentences identifying the hemisphere in which a continent is located and determine whether the sentence is true or false.
- Listen to a location described by its latitude and longitude and identify the location on a map.
- Listen to definitions and determine the correct vocabulary words.

**Reading**

SWBAT:

- Label key vocabulary terms on the world map after reading their definitions.
- Read a description of a location and converse with partners to identify the correct quadrant.
- Proofread a partner's paragraph.
- Read a location described by latitude and longitude and identify the location on a map.
- Read definitions and determine the correct vocabulary words.

**Writing**

SWBAT:

- Following a model, write two sentences about their native countries, identifying the two hemispheres in which the countries are located.
- Write two true sentences and one false sentence identifying the hemisphere in which a continent is located.
- Write a paragraph with a topic sentence, concluding sentence, and details that incorporate key vocabulary.
- Write a location's latitude and longitude following this structure:

  The _____ is located at _____° _____ latitude, _____° _____ longitude.

## Key Vocabulary

**Learned previously:**

- The 5 oceans
- The 7 continents
- compass rose
- cardinal directions (north, south, east, west)

**New:**

- location
- Equator
- Prime Meridian
- hemisphere (Northern, Southern, Eastern, Western)
- imaginary lines
- parallel
- lines of latitude
- lines of longitude
- degrees

## Learning Strategies

- Interpretation of maps
- Self-assessment
- Collaboration with partners

### Materials

- blank world maps for students to write on
- maps and globes for reference
- masking tape
- two colors of electrical tape
- sentence strips
- index cards for flash cards and tickets out

World maps can be downloaded from:

http://www.lib.berkeley.edu/EART/images/world-lg.gif

http://www.eduplace.com/ss/maps/pdf/world_phys.pdf

Interactive geography games can be found at:

http://kids.nationalgeographic.com/Games/GeographyGames/Geospy

http://www.kidsgeo.com/geography-games/latitude-longitude-map-game.php

Discovery Education video clips: "Using Maps and Globes" and "Understanding and Using Maps and Globes" are at http://streaming.discoveryeducation.com/

## SIOP® LESSON PLAN 1: *What's the Location?*

**Developed by Robin Liten-Tejada**

## THINK-ALOUD, LESSON 1

- To begin the new unit and get students thinking about the big ideas, I need to start with an engaging activity that will introduce students to the concept that imaginary lines help us locate places on the map. I decided to start with an interactive listening activity in which students will try to pinpoint a location in the middle of an ocean. I believe this will help them realize that precise ways to describe locations are needed and will pave the way to their understanding the functions of the Equator, Prime Meridian, and later lines of latitude and longitude.

*Content Objective*

**SWBAT:**
- Identify the need for precise methods to identify locations on Earth.

*Language Objectives*

**SWBAT:**
- Listen to directions and mark an X on a map to indicate a location.
- Dictate directions to a partner.
- Label key vocabulary terms on the world map after reading their definitions.

*Materials*

blank world maps, vocabulary definitions (BLM 10), index cards (optional), flash cards (one per vocabulary term: hemisphere, imaginary lines, Equator, Prime Meridian, Northern hemisphere, Southern hemisphere, Eastern hemisphere, Western hemisphere, parallel, lines of latitude, lines of longitude)

*(continued)*

### Key Vocabulary

location, Equator, Prime Meridian, hemisphere (Northern, Southern, Eastern, Western), imaginary lines, parallel, lines of latitude, lines of longitude

### Prior to Class

Prepare an overhead or a projection of a blank world map, with a small X marked somewhere in the ocean to represent the location where a ship is in trouble.

### Introduce the Lesson

Start the lesson by reading today's objectives with the students and explaining them.

### Develop Understandings

Create the experience to introduce the concept of finding locations on maps to the students. Distribute a blank world map to each student (a good one can be downloaded from http://www.lib.berkeley.edu/ EART/images/world-lg.gif). Create a scenario and tell students a ship traveling in the ocean has lost power and has radioed for help. Their job is to locate the ship and send help. Use the map you prepared prior to the lesson and tell them to listen to your directions and mark a small X where they think the ship is located. However, they will only hear a one-sentence direction.

Dictate your location. You might say something like, "The ship is located west of South America," or "The ship is located in the middle of the Pacific Ocean." After everyone has marked his or her map, have students compare maps to see how many marked the same spot. Then show students your map, and see if anyone came close to your location.

### Practice

Distribute another blank world map, and have students form pairs. Give each pair a file folder to set up between them to block the view of each other's map. Tell students to imagine that an earthquake has occurred, or a plane has gone down, or any other situation in which someone needs help somewhere on Earth. Have them mark a small X on their map, and then take turns dictating their location to their partner using one sentence ("The _____ is located _____"). Partners should then compare their marks to see if they agree.

Afterward, debrief with students as to why it was so difficult to pinpoint exact locations. Elicit suggestions for information that would have made it easier to find the same location on the map as their partner indicated.

### Develop Vocabulary and Apply

Introduce key vocabulary for the new concept. Explain that because the world is a big place, geographers have created a system to find locations on the map. Display key vocabulary on flash cards and ask students how many of these words indicate world map locations that they already know. Read each word and have students repeat them after you.

- hemisphere
- imaginary lines
- Equator
- Prime Meridian
- Northern hemisphere
- Southern hemisphere
- Eastern hemisphere
- Western hemisphere
- parallel
- lines of latitude
- lines of longitude

Distribute the vocabulary definitions (see BLM 10), and have partners work together to label the world map with the terms after reading the definitions. After a few minutes, label a large world map together. Have students correctly label their own maps, and then glue their maps and definitions into their social studies notebooks.

*(continued)*

## SIOP® LESSON PLAN 1: *What's the Location?* (continued)

### Wrap Up

Review the content and language objectives. Have students complete a Differentiated Tickets Out (see Chapter 3) on an index card or in their notebooks. They might draw a map and label what they learned today or complete the following sentence starter:

• Today I learned that _____.

## SIOP® LESSON PLAN 2: *What's My Hemisphere?*

**Developed by Robin Liten-Tejada**

## THINK-ALOUD, LESSON 2

• Now that we have completed a background-building activity that got students thinking about the key concept and have introduced the key vocabulary, I'm ready to actually teach the new information and have students read the text. Because reading a map can be confusing for students, I'm going to start with a concrete activity that will allow students to physically experience a representative map on the floor.

### Content Objectives

**SWBAT:**
• Identify the Equator and Prime Meridian.
• Use the Equator and Prime Meridian to identify the four hemispheres.
• Identify the hemispheres in which their native countries are located.

### Language Objectives

**SWBAT:**
• Listen to a description and identify the imaginary line or hemisphere being described.
• Describe a location to a partner using variations of "The _____ is in the _____ hemisphere because it is located _____ of the _____."
• Read a description of a location and converse with partners to identify the correct quadrant.
• Following a model, write two sentences about their native countries identifying the two hemispheres in which the countries are located.

### Materials

masking tape, electrical tape in two colors, sentence strips, paper to draw a compass rose, flash cards from Lesson 1, reference world maps or globes, 4 index cards labeled A, B, C, D

### Key Vocabulary

Same as in Lesson 1

### Prior to Class

Use masking tape to create a large rectangle on the classroom floor, large enough for the students to stand in. Use two different colored tapes, such as electrical tape, to represent the Equator and Prime Meridian and divide the rectangle into four equal quadrants. Create a large compass rose that can

*(continued)*

also be placed on the floor. (See Planning Point 1.) You will also need the vocabulary flash cards from the previous lesson to label the map on the floor.

Make the following four sentence strips for use in the Practice activity:

1. South of the Equator, east of the Prime Meridian
2. North of the Equator, west of the Prime Meridian
3. North of the Equator, east of the Prime Meridian
4. South of the Equator, west of the Prime Meridian

### Introduce the Lesson

Start the lesson with students by reading today's content and language objectives. Lead a brief discussion to review the previous lesson and to identify the need for more precise ways to identify locations on Earth. Quickly review the key vocabulary. Tell students that today they will have more practice in identifying hemispheres.

### Develop Understandings

Have the students gather around the rectangle. Explain that the floor represents the world map. Together, place the flash cards for the Equator and Prime Meridian on the appropriate colored tape. Hold up the cards for the Equator and the Prime Meridian. Have students refer to the compass rose and think to themselves which line they believe represents the Equator and which represents the Prime Meridian. After a few seconds of think time, have them turn to a partner to share their choices, explaining their decisions. Review together. Show students that the line running east to west represents the Equator and divides the Earth into the Northern and Southern hemispheres. Place the Equator flash card on the line, and place the flash cards for the Northern and Southern hemispheres in the appropriate halves. Show students that the line running north to south represents the Prime Meridian, and divides the Earth into the Eastern and Western hemispheres. Place the Prime Meridian flash card on the line, and place the flash cards for the Eastern and Western hemispheres in the appropriate halves.

Conduct a quick whole group listening response. Instruct students to raise one hand for Equator and two hands for Prime Meridian in response to the following phrases:

- This divides the Earth into the Eastern and Western hemispheres.
- This line runs from east to west.
- This line divides the Earth into the Northern and Southern hemispheres.
- This runs from north to south.

Have all the students standing on the side of the Northern hemisphere raise their hands. Refer to their location relative to the Equator and make sure everyone understands how that indicates the hemisphere. Repeat the same process with the Southern hemisphere, and with the Eastern and Western hemispheres relative to the Prime Meridian.

### Practice

Remove the hemisphere flash cards. Place a book in one of the quadrants and have students think to themselves if the book is located in the Northern or Southern hemispheres. Have them tell their partner where the book is located and how they know. You can provide the following language frames for students to use (see Planning Point 2):

- I think the book is in the (Northern/Southern) hemisphere because it is located (north/south) of the Equator.

Then have students decide if the book is located in the Eastern or Western hemispheres, and how they know. They can say:

- I think the book is in the (Eastern/Western) hemisphere because it is located (east/west) of the Prime Meridian.

Repeat the process a few more times.

Divide the class into groups of four, and have group members number themselves 1–4. Label four index cards with the letter A, B, C, or D. Place one card in each quadrant. Tell students you will hold up a sentence strip with a location and they will have to decide with their group which quadrant the strip describes, either A, B, C, or D. When you say "Number ___, go," the member of each group with that number will stand in the quadrant that the group decided was correct.

*(continued)*

## SIOP® LESSON PLAN 2: *What's My Hemisphere?* *(continued)*

Hold up one of the sentence strips made prior to the lesson and have students with the called number move to the location. After each group member stands in the chosen quadrant and errors are resolved, have each student name the two hemispheres in which he or she is standing.

### *Apply*

Have students find their native countries on a map or globe and complete the following sentences in writing:
- My country is in the (Northern/Southern) hemisphere because it is located (north/south) of the Equator.
- My country is in the (Eastern/Western) hemisphere because it is located (east/west) of the Prime Meridian.

### *Wrap Up*

Review the content and language objectives, and have students self-assess the degree to which they met the objectives for today using the Oral Number 1–3 for Self-Assessment technique (see Chapter 3).

### *Homework*

Students can complete a skill-builder from a social studies text or a map skills workbook, or students can use a world map to complete a review of the continents and oceans. (See BLM 11 for students with higher proficiency and BLM 12 for students with lower proficiency as worksheets that model the technique Questioning Prompts for Different Levels of Language Acquisition, described in Chapter 2.)

## PLANNING POINT 1

- You may want to leave this map on the floor for the unit. It will be used again in Lesson 5.

## PLANNING POINT 2

- You may want to post these language frames on sentence strips in the classroom.

## SIOP® LESSON PLAN 3: *Maps and Globes Reader's Theater*

**Developed by Robin Liten-Tejada**

## THINK-ALOUD, LESSON 3

- I've taught the concepts, but I know that students need more practice using the vocabulary before they really own the content and academic language. This point in the unit will be a good time to do a Reader's Theater. Reader's Theater is an effective technique for providing students with an opportunity to build oral fluency while reinforcing both the content and language. I write my own scripts, which allows me to select the vocabulary to practice and essentially the content to reteach at the same time. Having students listen to their classmates' performances also reinforces the content and academic language.

### *Content Objectives*

**SWBAT:**
- Identify the Equator and Prime Meridian.
- Use the Equator and Prime Meridian to identify the four hemispheres.

*(continued)*

*Language Objectives*

**SWBAT:**
- Speak fluently while performing a Reader's Theater script.
- Listen to classmates' performances to assess accuracy of content and pronunciation.

*Materials*

Reader's Theater Script (BLM 13), Reader's Theater Rubric (BLM 14)

*Key Vocabulary*

Same as in Lesson 1

*Introduce the Lesson*

Start the class by reviewing the day's objectives. Distribute a copy of the script to each student.

*Develop Understandings*

Begin the Reader's Theater (see Chapter 3) by modeling the entire script for students (see BLM 13) while they read along silently. This allows them to hear correct pronunciation, fluent speaking, and an energetic presentation. Be sure students understand these elements. Next, do a whole class choral reading, which provides less proficient students an opportunity to practice speaking in a nonthreatening situation. After that, alternate lines between two groups, such as all boys and all girls, or divide the classroom in half.

*Practice*

After the choral practices, divide the class into groups of six. Have the group members decide who will read which lines of the Reader's Theater script. Give them several minutes to practice together, encouraging students to speak with expression, as fluently as they can.

*Apply*

Tell groups they will now perform their scripts. To encourage active listening when students are not performing, tell them they will use a rubric to assess their classmates who are performing the same roles as they are. They will be listening for the correct pronunciation, fluent speaking, and an energetic presentation. Before the performances start, have each student list the names of performers under the proper role on the rubric (see BLM 14).

Groups should perform the script by reciting the lines. There is very little physical movement with Reader's Theater, as the point is to practice oral fluency. After each performance, the students will use the rubric to score the classmates who performed their same role.

*Wrap Up*

After all groups have performed, review the day's content and language objectives. Have each group complete a self-assessment using the rubric. Collect the rubrics and compile the responses to share with each student.

# SIOP® LESSON PLAN 4: *Maps and Globes: Student-Generated Writing*

**Developed by Robin Liten-Tejada**

## THINK-ALOUD, LESSON 4

- By now, students have had lots of teacher-led practice with the content and vocabulary. In order for students to truly own the new knowledge, I have to create an opportunity for them to process the content and generate language on their own. Since

*(continued)*

we've had so much practice, I think they are ready for this next step. We're going to start off with a quick interactive writing and partner listening dictation, and then we'll connect the content to writing by having the students write an expository paragraph, using the key vocabulary to explain their new knowledge about maps and globes. This will also give me an opportunity to assess their knowledge.

### Content Objectives

**SWBAT:**
- Identify the Equator and Prime Meridian.
- Use the Equator and Prime Meridian to identify the four hemispheres.
- Identify the hemispheres in which specific continents are located.

### Language Objectives

**SWBAT:**
- Write two true sentences and one false sentence identifying the hemisphere in which a continent is located.
- Dictate sentences to a partner.
- Listen to sentences identifying the hemisphere in which a continent is located and determine whether the sentence is true or false.
- Write a paragraph with a topic sentence, concluding sentence, and details that incorporate key vocabulary.
- Proofread a partner's paragraph.

### Materials

flash cards from lesson 1, world maps, writing supports (BLM 15, BLM 16)

### Key Vocabulary

Same as in Lesson 1

### Introduce the Lesson

Start the class by reviewing the content and language objectives. Explain that students will be putting their knowledge to use today by writing a paragraph, but first they'll warm up by doing a writing and partner listening activity that will review the key vocabulary and content that they have been studying.

### Develop Understandings

Model the activity by telling students that you will dictate three sentences, two of which are true and one false. Their job will be to decide which one is false. Afterward, they will write their own sentences, which they will dictate to a partner. (This activity combines Partner Listening Dictation in Chapter 3 with Find the Fib in the *99 Ideas* book [Vogt & Echevarria, 2008], p. 186.) Tell students they can either listen to your sentences while looking at a world map, or they can challenge themselves by using only their powers of visualization.

Dictate the following sentences:

1. North America is in the Western hemisphere.
2. Europe is south of the Equator.
3. South America is west of the Prime Meridian.

When you say "go," have each student hold up one, two, or three fingers to indicate which sentence is the false one.

### Practice

Have students look at a map to write their own sentences. Display these sentence frames for them to choose from:

- _____ is in the _____ hemisphere.
- _____ is _____ of the Equator.
- _____ is _____ of the Prime Meridian.

*(continued)*

After a few minutes, have student pairs take turns dictating their sentences to each other. If they disagree on the answers, they should refer to the world map. Have them repeat the process with several other partners. This can also be done as an Inside-Outside Circle (see *99 Ideas*, p. 110).

### Apply

Display the vocabulary flash cards. Tell students the time has come to share their knowledge about maps and globes by writing a paragraph using the key vocabulary. Remind students to write a topic sentence and a concluding sentence about the topic, with the details in between.

This can be a differentiated assignment:

- Highly proficient students can write the paragraph without support.
- Intermediate level students can be given the topic and concluding sentences, with a few key words to include for details. (See BLM 15.)
- Students in the early-writing stage can be given the paragraph as a cloze activity. (See BLM 16.)

After students have written their paragraphs, they should practice reading them aloud for fluency, and then exchange them with a partner. The partner can proofread the paragraph for errors, unless you are using this as a formal assessment.

### Wrap Up

Review the content and language objectives. Students can finish their paragraphs for homework if necessary.

# SIOP® LESSON PLAN 5: *Latitude and Longitude*

**Developed by Robin Liten-Tejada**

# THINK-ALOUD, LESSON 5

- Now that students have a solid understanding of the functions of the Equator and Prime Meridian and the division of the Earth into hemispheres, I will extend the unit to introduce the students to latitude and longitude. We'll use the same floor map that we used in Lesson 2.

(This is an optional extension lesson for fourth and fifth graders. Third graders may learn only to read a letter-number grid, but the same process can be followed.)

### Content Objective

**SWBAT:**
- Locate specific places on the map or globe using lines of latitude and longitude.

### Language Objectives

**SWBAT:**
- Listen to a description of a location by latitude and longitude and identify the location on a map.
- Correctly pronounce and write a location's latitude and longitude following this structure:

  The _____ is located at _____° _____ latitude, _____° _____ longitude.
- Dictate locations described by latitude and longitude to a partner.
- Read a location described by latitude and longitude and identify the location on a map.

### Materials

masking tape, electrical tape in two colors, sentence strips, compass rose, index cards, file folders, flash cards from Lesson 1, three blank flash cards, blank sentence strips, reference world maps or globes

*(continued)*

# SIOP® LESSON PLAN 5: *Latitude and Longitude* (continued)

### Key Vocabulary

latitude, longitude, degrees

### Prior to Class

Use masking tape to create lines of latitude and longitude on the floor map created for Lesson 2. Label index cards to represent the lines of latitude, counting by 20s (i.e., 0°, 20°, 40°, 60°, 80°) and be sure to write N or S following the degree, for example, "60° N." You will have four lines above the Equator and four below. Then label lines of longitude, counting by 40s (i.e., 0°, 40°, 80°, 120°, 160°) and be sure to write E or W following the degree. You will have four lines to the east and four to the west. If you're able to bend the tape (see Planning Point) so that the longitude lines begin and end at the same points (representing the North and South Poles), that would be ideal. You will also need the vocabulary flash cards from the previous lesson, and three additional cards for:

- latitude
- longitude
- degrees

Also make four sentence strips for locations on the floor map, such as:

- 60° N lat, 120° E long
- 20° S lat, 40° W long
- 40° N lat, 0° long
- 0° lat, 160° E long

### Introduce the Lesson

Start the lesson with students by reviewing today's content and language objectives. Remind students about the activity that opened the unit: locating a ship that needed help in the middle of the ocean. Discuss the difficulty students had in finding the exact location and reflect on the ideas students had that would have made it easier. Explain that the system of imaginary lines circling the globe, called **lines of latitude** and **lines of longitude,** helps us find the exact location of any place on Earth. Tell students they will revisit their floor map to learn about latitude and longitude.

### Develop Understandings

Provide an activity for students to experience latitude and longitude.

**Label the Map**
Have the students gather around the floor map. Quickly label the Equator, Prime Meridian, and the four hemispheres. Refer to the compass rose, which should also be on the floor in view of the students.

Direct students' attention to the lines. Show the flash cards for the "Lines of Latitude" and "Lines of Longitude," and have students identify them on the grid. Introduce the abbreviations "lat." and "long." Hold up the card for "parallel," and explain that lines of latitude run parallel to the Equator, meaning they never intersect. If your vertical lines don't begin and end at the "North and South Poles," explain that your grid is only a portion of the map, and show a world map or globe to make sure that students understand that lines of longitude begin and end at the North and South Poles.

Explain that each line represents a number, called a "degree," that measures the distance relative to the Equator or Prime Meridian. Explain that since the Equator and Prime Meridian are the starting points, they are 0°. Explain that lines of latitude are also labeled "North" or "South" (or N or S) according to their location relative to the Equator, and lines of longitude are labeled "East" or "West" (or E or W) according to their location relative to the Prime Meridian. Label the Equator and Prime Meridian with 0°. Show students the index cards as you label the rest of the lines on the floor.

**Use the Map**
Put a book on the map at a location that matches one of your sentence strips. Show students the sentence strip and teach them how to say the location—for example, "60° N latitude, 120° E longitude." Have

*(continued)*

everyone repeat the location after you. Discuss what two hemispheres the book is in and how you can tell relative to the Equator and Prime Meridian. Place the book in the other places that match your sentence strips and have the students identify the location. After they guess, be sure to show them the location written on your strip to provide the visual reinforcement, and have everyone repeat the proper pronunciation after you.

One at a time, call out several locations and have a student stand in that spot. Ask for volunteers to stand in different places, giving students several minutes to think about how to say the location; then have them turn and tell a partner before reviewing all the locations together.

### Practice and Apply

**Speaking and Writing Practice**

Distribute to students copies of a world map that has several locations marked. Have students work with partners to practice properly reading the locations and then writing them.

**Listening Application**

Tell students to imagine the same situation as took place in the first lesson. A ship is in trouble somewhere in an ocean. Without showing the students, mark a spot on your map. Dictate that location to the students by providing the latitude and longitude. For example, say "The ship is located at 40° W latitude, 20° N longitude."

Have students mark that location on their world maps. Just like in the first lesson, have them compare their locations with a partner to see if they agree, and then show them yours to see who had it correct. Hopefully, most students were able to locate the "ship" this time!

Again, have students divide into pairs and give each pair a file folder to set up between them to block their partner's view of their map. Once again, tell students to imagine that an earthquake has occurred, or a plane has gone down, or any other situation where someone needs help somewhere on Earth. Have each student mark a small X on their map, and then have students take turns dictating their locations to their partners and then comparing their marks to see if they agree. For the dictation, they should use the sentence:

- The _____ is located at _____ ° _____ latitude, _____ ° _____ longitude.

Finally, have the pairs compare their marks to see if they agree.

Afterward, ask students to compare the results of this dictation with their first effort in Lesson 1.

### Wrap Up

Review the content and language objectives. Conduct a quick self-assessment for students to indicate the degree to which they met their objectives using Oral Number 1–3 for Self-Assessment (see Chapter 3).

For an informal assessment, have students complete a Tickets Out or write in their journals:

- Lines of latitude and longitude are important because _____

### Extensions

- Students can use an atlas or globe to find the latitude and longitude for the capital cities of all the countries represented in the class.
- To bring in a writing connection, students can write a process paragraph on finding a location using latitude and longitude, using the transition words "First, then, next, finally."
- There are many online geography games available if you Google "geography games." An appropriate one to practice latitude and longitude can be found at: http://www.kidsgeo.com/geography-games/latitude-longitude-map-game.php
- Discovery Education has several video clips that review the content covered in this unit. Two possibilities are:
  - "Using Maps and Globes"
  - "Understanding and Using Maps and Globes"

The website is: http://streaming.discoveryeducation.com/

## PLANNING POINT

- If the tape does not stretch and bend, you can use several smaller pieces to create a curved line.

# SIOP® LESSON PLAN 6: *Map and Globe Terms Review*

**Developed by Robin Liten-Tejada**

## THINK-ALOUD, LESSON 6

● Before we conclude the unit, it is important to give students an opportunity to review and reinforce the key vocabulary. Reviewing through an interactive game format is more engaging for the students. Numbered Heads Together with Movement is an excellent strategy for this purpose. Following the game, the students can play Concentration using the vocabulary cards. They can also use the cards for word sorts.

### Content Objective

**SWBAT:**
● Identify key terms related to locations on a map.

### Language Objectives

**SWBAT:**
● Listen to definitions and determine the correct vocabulary words.
● Read definitions and determine the correct vocabulary words.
● Collaborate politely with classmates.

### Materials

flash cards from Lessons 1 and 5, vocabulary word and definition cards (BLM 17)

### Key Vocabulary

Same as in Lessons 1 and 5

### Introduce the Lesson

Start the lesson by reading the content and language objectives. Ask students to tell a partner what they think they will learn today.

### Develop Understandings

Display all the key vocabulary word flash cards. Tell students the time has come for a final review. Have them look over the words and think to themselves which ones they feel they absolutely know the definitions for, and which ones they might still be unsure of. If possible, give students some time to review the words in their notebooks. Keep the words displayed for the game.

### Practice

Tell students they will play Numbered Heads Together with Movement. Teach or remind students of the instructions for the technique (see Chapter 3).

1. Divide students into groups of four. Have each student select a different number between 1–4. Each student should have a piece of paper on which to write answers.

2. Divide the board into the number of groups present, or place sheets of poster paper around the room if board space is not available.

3. Dictate a definition to the class (see BLM 17). Have the students confer quietly with their group to decide on the answer. When they decide on an answer, everyone writes it down.

4. Choose a number 1, 2, 3, or 4 (see Planning Point). When you say "Go," all the students who have that number will walk to the board or poster paper, carrying their answers with them. When everyone is in place, say "Write," and have the students write the answers at their locations. This is not a race! Students do not need to run, and should not start writing until you have directed them to do so.

5. Give a point to each team that has the correct answer, but keep the competition friendly. There should be no prize for winning, as that creates hard feelings. Remind students that the point here is to review and to help everyone learn.

6. After the game, have students reflect again on which words they knew and which they need to review further.

### Apply

To provide more vocabulary review, copy BLM 17 on card stock and cut up the cards. Student pairs can play Concentration. Have pairs place all the cards face down; then one partner selects two. If the cards selected match, having the correct definition and term, the player gets to keep the cards. If not, both cards should be turned back over. The trick is to remember where the cards are as the game progresses. The student with the most pairs at the end wins.

Students may also use the cards to quiz each other. Divide the cards into two random stacks that students hold in their hands, as in a card game. A student can read one of her cards to her partner, and the partner can select the corresponding card from her hand, if she thinks she has it. Once a match is made, the cards are set aside.

Students can sort the cards as well, matching the terms and definitions.

### Wrap Up

Close the lesson by reviewing the content and language objectives. Students are now ready for a formal assessment of both the content and academic language.

### Extension

Students can create a picture dictionary of the vocabulary learned in this unit.

## PLANNING POINT

- When calling numbers for Numbered Heads Together, it's best if you have the numbers written on cards or sticks that you can pull at random.

# Concluding Thoughts

When students reach the upper elementary grades, they are ready for more skill development, but still need concrete experiences to understand the social studies concepts well. The hands-on activities and physical movement in this unit provide that real-life support as students build their comprehension of the functions of maps and globes. The lessons involve a variety of language objectives, ensuring that students practice all four language domains. The Reader's Theater, for example, is an appropriate structure for upper elementary students to practice reading and speaking, working on pronunciation and intonation as well. Differentiation of tasks has been carefully planned out for classes with mixed English proficiency levels.

We hope this unit gave you new ideas for incorporating meaningful activities and attention to language development in your social studies lessons. We encourage you to read Chapters 5, 7, and 8 for additional units. Even if you currently teach in grades 3–5, you will find interesting SIOP® social studies and history lessons and effective integration of the new techniques in these other sample units.

# SIOP® U.S. History Unit: Grades 6–8

### By John Seidlitz and Deborah Short

## Introduction

You will find in this chapter a complete U.S. history unit, with lesson plans and hand-outs for middle school students. The chapter opens with a detailed discussion of the thinking process that went into the unit design by one of our SIOP® history educators, John Seidlitz. He offers his insights for planning this unit on the causes of the American Revolution. As you read this unit, you will see how several of the techniques from Chapters 2 and 3 are incorporated into the lessons, as well as how the activities in the unit lesson plans map onto the components and features of the SIOP® Model (found in Appendix A). If you have not yet read Chapter 4 about SIOP® unit and lesson design for English learners, please read it for overview of the planning process and a discussion of the lesson plan format used in this chapter and Chapter 8.

You will notice that there are teacher Think-Alouds and Planning Points in many of the lessons. The teacher Think-Alouds, identified with thought bubble icons, are questions that John asked himself or decisions he made during the SIOP® unit planning process. The Planning Points, identified with a flash drive icon, highlight or identify resources that support the implementation of the lessons.

In the following section, John Seidlitz explains how he planned the U.S. history unit, *Causes of the American Revolution.* You'll see that he first identified the main topic and the appropriate social studies and English language proficiency standards (ELPS) for Texas, where he taught. Then he established the overarching and topical understandings students should develop as a result of the lessons.

The chapter then continues with the detailed lesson plans for the units. The student handouts are included as blackline masters (BLMs) in Appendix D.

# Causes of the American Revolution

## Unit Overview, Grades 6–8

I taught eighth grade U.S. History, which covered 1492 to 1865, in a low-income district in Texas that was predominately Hispanic. I had heterogeneous classes and was responsible for the sheltered social studies instruction. I had some beginning English learners (ELs), but most of my students scored at the advanced or advanced high level on our Texas proficiency system. Sometimes I had classes with a mix of native English speakers and ELs.

At the time, English learners had three years of testing exemption within our accountability system. After the third full year of instruction, their scores would count for our state social studies test (Texas Assessment of Knowledge and Skills, or TAKS), which was given in eighth grade. My students at advanced levels faced this challenge because most had been in our schools for the three years, yet they were not yet fully proficient in English. Another challenge our ELs faced was that they had to pass the eleventh grade TAKS in order to graduate. One third of that test covered material learned in eighth grade. This placed a special burden on me as their eighth grade social studies teacher. It was important to our school as a whole and to the students as individuals that they become successful in social studies. Because of this, I always placed a very strong emphasis on vocabulary and tried to adhere to our state standards, the Texas Essential Knowledge and Skills (TEKS), when planning units and lessons.

The unit presented in this chapter is about the causes of the American Revolution. Although there were many causes, the economic roots of the conflict are strongly emphasized in the TEKS. I chose the following as the overarching and topical understandings for the unit to pull the state standards together around a central idea.

- **Overarching Understanding:** Economic changes can lead to political changes that can cause violent conflict.
- **Topical Understanding:** The economic changes following the French and Indian War led to new political understandings that ultimately led to the American Revolution.

Here are the TEKS that I addressed in the lessons:

4(A)    Analyze causes of the American Revolution, including mercantilism and British economic policies following the French and Indian War;

5(B)    Summarize arguments regarding protective tariffs and taxation;

30(B)   Analyze information by identifying cause-and-effect relationships and . . . making generalizations and predictions;

30(D)  Identify points of view from the historical context surrounding an event and the frame of reference which influenced the participants;

30(E)  Support a point of view on a social studies issue or event.

I noticed in our standards that students were expected not only to identify the causes of the American Revolution but also to *analyze* them. I wanted to select language objectives that would let the students articulate their analyses of the economic roots of colonial frustration with the British Parliament. In Texas, we have cross-curricular student expectations for language development called the ELPS (English Language Proficiency Standards). They are designed to be integrated into content instruction for our ELs. I use them as a basis for my language objectives. In planning, I therefore chose the following standards:

2(C)  Learn new language structures, expressions, and basic and academic vocabulary heard during classroom instruction and interactions;

3(C)  Speak using a variety of grammatical structures, sentence lengths, sentence types, and connecting words with increasing accuracy and ease as more English is acquired;

3(D)  Speak using grade-level content area vocabulary in context to internalize new English words and build academic language proficiency;

3(F)  Ask and give information ranging from using a very limited bank of high-frequency, high-need, concrete vocabulary, including key words and expressions needed for basic communication in academic and social contexts, to using abstract and content-based vocabulary during extended speaking assignments.

Drawing from these lists of standards, I created the content and language objectives for each of the lessons shown in Figure 7.1.

Because I have classes with mixed proficiency levels, I have to scaffold language practice and differentiate instruction from time to time. For example, in a class with a significant

**FIGURE 7.1**  *Unit Content and Language Objectives*

| Lesson | Content Objectives | Language Objectives |
|---|---|---|
| 1 | Students will identify the ways British mercantilist policies caused frustration for the American colonists. | Students will express points of view on mercantilism using a variety of sentence structures. |
| 2 | Students will identify ways in which the British policies following the French and Indian War led to colonial dissatisfaction. | Students will ask for and give information about British policies following the French and Indian War. |
| 3 | Students will explain the various acts of the British Parliament that were protested by the American colonists. | Students will conduct a learning styles debate about the conflict between the British Parliament and the Continental Congress. |
| 4 | Students will explain the importance of the Boston Massacre. | Students will dramatize the events of the Boston Massacre and use new vocabulary. |

number of beginners, I sometimes homogeneously group them and simplify stems, questions, and vocabulary. I then work with them separately. This route provides an opportunity for them to practice oral language and get feedback from me before sharing with the whole class. At other times, I make sure beginner ELs are heterogeneously grouped with more advanced students, who can help them prepare at least one response during activities that require sentence construction and reporting out. It can also be helpful to provide a bank of choices for these students to fill in the stems.

# Grades 6–8 Unit

The unit that John wrote follows. In Texas, this topic is taught in eighth grade. The lessons have been designed for 55-minute periods, and the entire unit may last 5 to 6 days. As you read these lessons, notice how John has incorporated a great deal of student–student interaction supported by appropriate language frames for oral and written discourse. John understands the importance of academic vocabulary development and so he has students keep a vocabulary section in their notebooks to record and practice using key terms. He points out,

> "Some essential high frequency vocabulary may be necessary for beginning and intermediate ELs to be able to participate in activities. These words may not be listed on the word wall. I often provide ELs a simplified English text or a native language resource (such as a chapter summary or Spanish glossary) in advance so that they can have some key concepts and essential vocabulary clarified before the lesson."

## SIOP® LESSON PLAN 1: *Mercantilism*

**Developed by John Seidlitz**

| | | |
|---|---|---|
| **Grade:** 8 | | |
| **Subject:** U.S. History | | **Date:** |

| Activities | Review & Check for Understanding |
|---|---|

**Content Objective:** Students will identify the ways British mercantilist policies caused frustration for the American colonists.

**Language Objective:** Students will express points of view on mercantilism using a variety of sentence structures.

**Vocabulary:** mercantilism, triangular trade, favorable balance of trade, protectionist, tariff, imperialism

**Visuals, Materials & Texts:** Sections of textbook discussing causes of mercantilism in the British Empire, sticky notes or index cards, word list posted on board (see Planning Point 1)

| *Activities* | *Review & Check for Understanding* |
|---|---|
| **Activating Prior Knowledge**<br>Review the objectives of the day, and discuss the terms *mercantilist policies* and *point of view* with students.<br><br>*Think–Pair–Share:*<br>Begin by reviewing the motives of the three major European powers—France, Spain, and England—for settling North America. Have students look at the following sentence starters. Give them two minutes to be able to respond to a partner (see Think-Aloud 1) using the starters:<br><br>• *The French colonized the central part of North America and Canada because . . .* | <br><br><br><br><br><br><br><br><br>Listen to students' responses during the discussion and give feedback. Make sure they include economic motivation as part of the discussion of each group's motivation for colonization.<br><br>*(continued)* |

# SIOP® LESSON PLAN 1: *Mercantilism* (continued)

| Activities | Review & Check for Understanding |
|---|---|
| • *The Spanish colonized the southern part of North America and South America because . . .*<br>• *The English colonized the Eastern seaboard because . . .*<br><br>After pairs talk, randomly select students to respond.<br><br>After reviewing the motives for colonization, ask the students to discuss the following questions with their partner:<br><br>• *If you were the King of England, what fears would you have about the French and Spanish?*<br>• *What might you decide to do as a result of those fears?*<br><br>Encourage students to use these stems:<br><br>• *I'm afraid the French might . . .*<br>• *To protect myself from the French I will . . .* | List responses from students, both fears and actions. If needed, model a suggestion, such as not allowing the colonies to trade with the French or building up British financial and military power. |
| **Building Vocabulary and Concept Knowledge**<br><br>*Predicting Definitions*<br>Have students look at the list of words on the board—*mercantilism, triangular trade, favorable balance of trade, protectionist, tariff, imperialism*—and work with a partner to predict definitions (procedures in Chapter 2). Have students explain the reasons for their prediction. For example, students might say, "I think *mercantilism* has to do with stores because the word looks a little like *merchant*." Or "I think *imperialism* means something to do with kings because I see *imperial*." Record student predictions on the board. | Randomly select students to share their predictions of the word meanings. |
| *Partner Reading*<br>Assign the section of the textbook about mercantilism to students to read aloud in groups of two or three. When they come to one of the words listed on the board, they should discuss whether the meaning the class predicted for the word was accurate. If it is not accurate, they should try to clarify or correct the definition from the context. If they still can't clarify the meaning, they should make another prediction. | Circulate and listen while students read and predict meanings. Help struggling groups use context clues to more effectively predict the meanings of the terms. |
| *Summary Frame*<br>After reading the passage, have each group use the following frame to summarize the lesson and then write individually in their journals:<br><br>• Mercantilism is _____ .<br>• It developed because _____ .<br>• Empires that favored mercantilism tried to _____ .<br>• One problem with pursuing mercantilist policies might be _____ .<br>• Colonists might not like mercantilist policies because _____ . | Observe student responses. Clarify any misconceptions in class discussion. |

*(continued)*

**Structured Conversation and Writing**

*Take a Stand*

Students consider their points of view regarding mercantilism and prepare to take a position on whether they think it would be better to pursue mercantilist policies. Positions include not allowing colonists to trade with other colonies, trying to increase the nation's supply of gold (thus taking some gold out of circulation), and taxing goods from other countries. They must write a response to one of the following stems on a sticky note or index card:

- *I believe the empire should continue to pursue mercantilist policies because . . .*
  or
- *I believe the empire should not pursue mercantilist policies because . . .*

When all students have written responses, have those who agreed to pursue the policies stand. Ask students who agree with the first statement to read their response. Then ask the students who disagree to stand. Call on a student and have him or her use the following frame:

- *I respectfully disagree with _____ because . . .*

Continue the discussion until a variety of viewpoints have been shared.

Close the lesson by reviewing the language and content objectives and asking quick questions about the vocabulary words.

Observe written responses. You can homogeneously group beginners and help them craft a response.

Listen to students' responses and clarify misconceptions.

Collect students' responses and check for understanding.

# PLANNING POINT 1

- List these words on the board prior to class: *mercantilism, triangular trade, favorable balance of trade, protectionist, tariff, imperialism.*

# THINK-ALOUD 1

- Make sure newcomer ELs are heterogeneously paired with more advanced students who can help them prepare at least one response.

# SIOP® LESSON PLAN 2: *The Effects of the French and Indian War*

**Developed by John Seidlitz**

**Grade:** 8
**Subject:** U.S. History                                    **Date:**

| | |
|---|---|
| **Content Objective:** Students will identify ways in which the British policies after the French and Indian War led to colonial dissatisfaction. | **Language Objective:** Students will ask for and give information about British policies following the French and Indian War. |
| **Vocabulary:** Appalachian Mountains, Proclamation of 1763, expansion, revenue, debt, frontier, Treaty of 1763 | **Visuals, Materials & Texts:** Sections of the textbook discussing the effects of the French and Indian War, anticipation reaction guide (BLM 18), scoring rubric (Figure 7.2) |

*(continued)*

# SIOP® LESSON PLAN 2: *The Effects of the French and Indian War* (continued)

| Activities | Review & Check for Understanding |
|---|---|
| **Activating Prior Knowledge**<br><br>*Anticipation/Reaction Guide*<br>Distribute the anticipation reaction guide (BLM 18). Have students scan the guide for any unfamiliar words. Explain the meaning of unfamiliar terms, especially those in the vocabulary list above. After all unfamiliar terms have been explained, have the students work with a partner to predict whether each statement listed on the guide is true or false. Selected students share their answers and their reasoning with the class. Have one student read the objectives aloud and ask others to paraphrase them. | Listen to students' responses during the discussion and give feedback. Students should be able to justify their predictions even if their answers are incorrect.<br><br>Be sure to review all key vocabulary terms before students do the partner reading activity. |
| **Building Vocabulary and Concept Knowledge**<br><br>*Partner Reading*<br>Student partners read the text, discussing the effects of the French and Indian War. While reading or afterward, the pairs check to see if their anticipation guide statements are true or false. | Look at students' responses. Assist students who have questions in using the text as a guide to identifying correct responses. |
| Students share their answers with the class using the frame:<br><br>• *We thought the statement* _____ *was true/false because . . . We found out we were correct/incorrect because . . .* | Randomly select students to share their frames. Write a few responses on the board. |
| *Cause-Effect Chart*<br>Students should work in small groups (see Planning Point 1) to create a cause-effect chart, listing three actions that the Parliament undertook in the left column, and three reasons the colonists reacted angrily in the right. The list of British actions might include: raising domestic taxes, passing tariffs, limiting trade, limiting westward immigration. Students should use the following frame to discuss the effects of the French and Indian War on the American colonists.<br><br>• *The British Parliament* _____. *This made the colonists angry because* _____. | |
| Have students record three sentences following this frame about the causes and effects in their notebooks. | Observe written responses. |
| **Structured Conversation and Writing**<br><br>*Letters to the Editor*<br>Students each write an editorial from the point of view of a colonist. Roles could include merchants, soldiers, teachers, fathers, and mothers. Each letter should begin:<br><br>    *Dear Editor, I'm frustrated with what our Parliament has been doing since the war. For example, . . .* | Collect students' editorials. Use the assessment rubric to score their work (see Figure 7.2).<br><br>Check for understanding the objectives of the day using Oral Number 1–3 for Self-Assessment (procedures in Chapter 3). Students can hold up fingers to indicate their response:<br><br>    1 = I didn't meet the objective.<br>    2 = I didn't meet the objective, but I made progress.<br>    3 = I met the objective. |

# PLANNING POINT 1

- You can preassign groups so beginners and intermediate-level students have support from more advanced learners. Or you can homogeneously group EL beginners and help them craft the sentences here and the editorial.

**FIGURE 7.2** *Letter to the Editor Rubric*

| CATEGORY | Above Standards (25 pts) | Meets Standards (20 pts) | Below Standards (10 pts) | Minimal to No Effort (0 pts) | Score |
|---|---|---|---|---|---|
| **Format** | Student follows all instructions. Letter reflects historical writing from the era. | Student follows all directions. | Student follows some but not all directions. | Student does not follow directions. | |
| **Historical Accuracy** | Factual information is accurate and relevant to argument. | Factual information is accurate. | Some factual information is missing or inaccurate. | Factual information is inaccurate. | |
| **Writing Style** | Writing style engages the reader. Student uses transitional and connecting words effectively. | Student uses transitional and connecting words effectively. | Writing style is stilted. Sentences are brief without transitional and connecting words to link ideas. | Letter is only 1–2 sentences long. Sentences are brief. | |
| **Support for Argument** | Student forms a coherent argument and successfully advocates for a position. | Student clearly describes a position. | Student offers a vague or weak position without support. | Student does not clearly identify or argue for a position. | |

# SIOP® LESSON PLAN 3: *Controversial Acts of Parliament*

## Developed by John Seidlitz

**Grade:** 8
**Subject:** U.S. History                                          **Date:** (See Planning Point 1.)

| | |
|---|---|
| **Content Objective:** Students will explain the various acts of the British Parliament that were protested by the American colonists. | **Language Objective:** Students will conduct a learning styles debate about the conflict between the British Parliament and the Continental Congress. |
| **Vocabulary:** mercantilism, French and Indian War, policies, Parliament, Continental Congress | **Visuals, Materials & Texts:** Sections of the textbook discussing causes of the American Revolution, sentence starters posted on board, markers, chart paper, T-chart (BLM 19) |

| Activities | Review & Check for Understanding |
|---|---|
| **Activating Prior Knowledge** *Review Sentence Starters* Students will review colonial viewpoints about the French and Indian War. Pose the following essential question to the class: <br><br> - *What was the significance of the French and Indian War?* | |

*(continued)*

*Causes of the American Revolution*

# SIOP® LESSON PLAN 3: *Controversial Acts of Parliament*

*(continued)*

| *Activities* | *Review & Check for Understanding* |
|---|---|
| Have students choose two of the following stems to discuss what they remember about the war. (See Think-Aloud 2.) | |
| • *Yesterday we talked about . . .* | |
| • *The French and Indian War was between . . .* | |
| • *The colonists were angry with Parliament after the French and Indian War because . . .* | Circulate and read students' responses. |
| • *I do/do not disagree with position of the colonists because . . .* | |
| Ask students first to respond in writing in their notebooks. After completing scaffolded sentence starters, they should discuss with a partner. | Circulate and listen to students during discussion. |
| **Building Vocabulary and Concept Knowledge** | |
| *Vocabulary Scan* | |
| Introduce the objectives for the day. Have students in groups of three or four scan the section of their textbook that discusses acts of Parliament that angered the American colonists and look for unfamiliar terms. Remind students to work from the end of the text forward for the vocabulary scan (procedures in Chapter 2). After discussing terms, each group's recorder writes the unfamiliar terms on its white board. After a few minutes, the teacher asks them to report out, records the terms on the board, and provides a short, written definition for each. (See Think-Aloud 3.) Key definitions can also be provided to ELs in their native language as needed. Have students write the words in the vocabulary section of their journals. | Use the Group Response with a White Board technique to collect and discuss new terms (procedures in Chapter 3). |
| *Partner Reading* | |
| Have students read text aloud in groups of two or three, alternating turns by paragraph. After each paragraph, the listening student(s) respond(s) with one of the following frames: | Circulate and listen to students during reading and discussion. Newcomers may opt out from reading aloud. |
| • *One Act of Parliament mentioned was . . .* or | |
| • *Parliament's action resulted in . . .* | |
| *T-Chart* | |
| The class fills out a T-chart with the following column headings: | Randomly select students to talk about what they read. Orally scaffold for beginning ELs by repeating sentence starters and by allowing time to practice reading answers to a partner. |
| 1. The British Parliament believed the colonists should be loyal and grateful because . . . | |
| 2. The colonists believed the British Parliament did not respect their rights as Englishmen because . . . | |
| Each student can create this T-chart in his/her notebook or use BLM 19. Model the task by eliciting ideas from the class to complete at least two ideas per column. | |

*(continued)*

**Structured Conversation and Writing**

*Learning Styles Debate*

Divide the class into two teams—the Parliament and the Colonists—for the Learning Styles Debate (procedures in Chapter 3). Parliament will argue that the colonists should be loyal and grateful to the British king. The colonists will argue that the British should respect their rights as Englishmen, or expect a revolt. Each team will subdivide into four groups with different responsibilities. Students should choose a group based on their interest or learning style, but aim for at least two students per group.

- Group One: Write a short letter to the editor of a local newspaper.
- Group Two: Make a list of talking points for an oral debate and practice defending them.
- Group Three: Create a political cartoon showing the team's point of view.
- Group Four: Write a chant illustrating either why the colonists should be loyal or why the Parliament was disrespectful.

Each group then presents to the class. First, have each Group Four perform the chants, one viewpoint, and then the other. Second, have each Group Three explain its political cartoon. Third, have each Group One read the letter to editor aloud. Fourth, have each Group Two read its talking points to the other group and respond to other point of view. (See Think-Aloud 4.)

*One-Sentence Summaries*

Students write a sentence stating which point of view they found valid after the debate.

- I would have supported _____ because . . .

Circulate, listen, and look while students prepare their work.

Review the objectives and vocabulary. Have students exchange sentences, and randomly call on some students to read their partner's sentence aloud.

---

## PLANNING POINT 1

- This lesson will last two class periods. Be sure to review the objectives at the end of the first period and remind students about them at the start of the second.

## THINK-ALOUD 1

- Students have been studying events leading up to the Revolutionary War. This lesson pulls together their knowledge in creative ways. In earlier units and lessons, students have already learned how to write letters to the editor, draw political cartoons, organize key points for a speech, and write chants. Here they apply these activities to a lesson that looks at events from different points of view.

## THINK-ALOUD 2

- One way I can differentiate for language proficiency is through the task, but I can also do so through the supports. I wrote these Differentiated Sentence Starters (procedures in Chapter 2) so the linguistic challenge would increase from the first to last and so I can encourage more advanced students to respond to the more challenging ones.

## THINK-ALOUD 3

● I want to make sure students learn key terms. If they do not select all of the following terms during this activity, I will add them: *representation, motive, corruption, duties, impressment,* and *legislation.*

## THINK-ALOUD 4

● Because each Group Two will have to "think on its feet" to respond to the other Group Two's talking points during the presentation, I have them perform last. This way, they will have heard other arguments and positions. It helps if some advanced students are in this group, but I do not preset the groups because the main purpose of Learning Styles Debate is to allow student selection of task according to interest.

## SIOP® LESSON PLAN 4: *Boston Massacre*

### Developed by John Seidlitz

| Grade: 8 | |
| --- | --- |
| Subject: U.S. History | Date: (Planning Point 1) |

| | |
| --- | --- |
| **Content Objective:** Students will explain the importance of the Boston Massacre event. | **Language Objective:** Students will dramatize the events of the Boston Massacre and use new vocabulary. |
| **Vocabulary:** Townshend Acts, impressment, sentry, mob, civilian, massacre | **Visuals, Materials & Texts:** Sections of the textbook discussing the causes of American Revolution, markers, chart paper, props for prop box (see Planning Point 2) |

| *Activities* | *Review & Check for Understanding* |
| --- | --- |
| **Activating Prior Knowledge**<br><br>*Think–Pair–Share*<br>Give partners two minutes to prepare responses to the following frame:<br><br>● *Colonists were angry with the British Parliament because* . . .<br><br>After pairs talk, randomly select students to respond. As they report out, create a bulleted list of the reasons the colonists were angry. Prompt students to explain the reasons and to elaborate as needed.<br><br>Go over the objectives, and have students look at the verbs to predict what they will do today. Preview today's lesson: They will be studying an event that greatly increased frustration and tension between the colonists and the British Parliament.<br><br>*KWL*<br>Some students may have some familiarity with the Boston Massacre. Create a class KWL chart (We Know, We Want to know, We Learned) and ask the students to think of one thing they know about the Boston Massacre. List their ideas in the "Know" column. Ask students to think of | Review students' responses. Emphasize that there were several issues: tariffs, trade restrictions, domestic taxes, settlement restrictions, and more.<br><br><br><br><br>Use a response signal (thumbs up) to make sure all students have a question before randomly selecting a student to respond when discussing the "We Want to know" column.<br><br>*(continued)* |

questions they have about the Boston Massacre and record their questions in the "We Want to know" column.

**Building Vocabulary and Concept Knowledge**

*Vocabulary Scan*

Have students conduct another vocabulary scan, working backward from the end of the section of the textbook discussing the Boston Massacre, looking for unfamiliar terms (procedures in Chapter 2). List all unfamiliar terms on the board and briefly define them. Have students write the words in the vocabulary section of their journals. Be sure to include the following words: *Townshend Acts, impressment, sentry, mob, civilian, massacre*

*Prop Box Improvisation*

Have students form groups of four or five to conduct a Prop Box Improvisation (procedures in Chapter 2). Each group will read the passage about the Boston Massacre and prepare a dramatic representation of the events. They will have access to a box of props they can use during their presentations. They may not practice with the props, but they can use them during their dramatization. (See Think-Aloud 1.) Each student must speak at least once during the presentation and each student must use at least one prop. All dramatizations must include all of the vocabulary: *Townshend Acts, impressment, sentry, mob, civilian, massacre.*

Have student groups perform. (See Planning Point 3.) After each dramatization, the students in the audience will discuss the skit using one of the following frames:

- *They demonstrated _____ using . . .*
- *They showed _____ with . . .*
- *I think they were trying to show _____ using . . .*
- *They represented . . .*

**Structured Conversation and Writing**

Revisit the KWL chart. Which questions were answered? Write the responses in the "We Learned" column. What other significant facts were learned about the Boston Massacre? Add responses also to the "We Learned" column.

*Differentiated Tickets Out*

Students select one of the following prompts to generate a Differentiated Tickets Out card (procedures in Chapter 3).

1. Complete this sentence:
   - *The Events of the Boston Massacre will probably cause _____ because _____.*

2. Create a cause-effect chart about the Boston Massacre and colonists' reactions.

3. Sketch a picture of the result of the Boston Massacre.

Use a response signal to make sure all students have at least one word they want to discuss the meaning of before beginning to create the list.

Circulate and monitor the practice.

Observe the skits. Make sure all students have a chance to orally respond to the other students' skits at least once during the presentation of the dramatizations.

Point out any unanswered questions and discuss possible ways to find answers.

Review Tickets Out, checking to see if students are able to predict an increase in tension on both sides as a result of the event.

Review the objectives.

## PLANNING POINT 1

- This lesson will last two class periods. Be sure to review the objectives at the end of the first period and remind students about them at the start of the second period.

## PLANNING POINT 2

- Prop box suggestions include feathers, rope, binoculars, sunglasses, canteen, fake swords and rifles (plastic or cut out of poster board), scarves, artificial flowers, crosses, colored cloth fabric, markers, construction paper, bandanas, cane, crown, and costume jewelry.

## THINK-ALOUD 1

- Although the students want to play with the prop, I have found the practice to be un-ruly. Students are more likely to engage in off-task behavior. Instead, I let them select their props and keep them in mind as they practice their skits. This way, too, there are enough props for all groups.

## PLANNING POINT 3

- The performances usually occur on the second day of this two-day lesson.

# Concluding Thoughts

Most of us remember what middle school students are like in class. Sometimes they can sit quietly and focus, and sometimes they just need to move around and interact with peers. This unit gives students multiple opportunities to be active, but carefully channels their energy and enthusiasm into learning situations. The lessons include a great deal of higher-order thinking tasks, ramping up the cognitive rigor of the subject. Yet the tasks and associated language frames are scaffolded so students are brought from guided to independent practice. And they are fun—tapping into student creativity through drama, art and music. The lessons expose students to different historical perspectives as well—an overarching goal of most history curricula.

We hope this unit gave you new ideas for incorporating meaningful activities and attention to language development in your history and social studies lessons. We encourage you to read Chapters 5, 6, and 8 for additional units. Even if the grades you currently teach are in middle school, you will find interesting SIOP® lessons and effective integration of the new techniques in these other sample units.

# SIOP® Global History Unit: Grades 9–12

### By John Seidlitz and Deborah Short

## Introduction

This chapter showcases a complete Global History unit, with lesson plans and handouts for high school students.[1] The chapter opens with a detailed discussion of the thinking process that went into the unit design by one of our SIOP® history educators, John Seidlitz. He offers his insights for planning this unit on policies aimed at containing the spread of communism after World War II. Although the unit is designed for high schoolers, we recognize that some states cover part of this material in their middle school standards. You should be able to adapt these lessons for those younger adolescent learners. As you read through these lessons, you will see how several of the techniques from Chapters 2 and 3

---

[1]This unit may also be used in a U.S. History course that covers the 20th century.

are incorporated into the lessons, as well as how the activities in the unit lesson plans map onto the components and features of the SIOP® Model (found in Appendix A). If you have not yet read Chapter 4 about SIOP® unit and lesson design for English learners, please read it for an overview of the planning process and a discussion of the lesson plan format used in this chapter and Chapter 7.

You will notice that there are teacher Think-Alouds and Planning Points in many of the lessons. The teacher Think-Alouds, identified with thought bubble icons, are questions that John asked himself or decisions he made during the SIOP® unit planning process. The Planning Points, identified with a flash drive icon, highlight or identify resources that support the implementation of the lessons.

In the following section, John Seidlitz explains how he planned the global history unit, *Containing Communism After WWII*. You'll see that he first identified the main topic and the appropriate social studies and English language proficiency standards (ELPS) for Texas, where he taught. Then he established the overarching and topical understandings students should develop as a result of the lessons.

The chapter continues with the detailed lesson plans for the units. The student handouts are included as blackline masters (BLMs) in Appendix D.

# *Containing Communism After World War II*

## Unit Overview, Grades 9–12

I taught history in San Antonio, Texas for a number of years. I had a very diverse population of students, most of whom were Hispanic and came from low-income backgrounds. Although one-fourth of my students were classified as English learners, most of them were at intermediate or advanced levels of fluency. I did have a few newcomer English learners every year, which of course posed a particular challenge. My school did not have a newcomer center, so these students were usually integrated into my classes upon enrollment.

I was classified as the "sheltered history" teacher on my campus, so I taught English learners in heterogeneous classes that contained EL and native English speakers together. I used specialized techniques to help them be successful with the curriculum. I used the SIOP® Model to plan all of my lessons because it helped me to focus on exactly what I needed to do to help my English learners understand the main concepts and at the same time develop their academic English skills. I found the SIOP® Model to be helpful, not just for my ELs, but for a lot of my students who struggled to strengthen their academic language skills.

In this chapter, I'll describe my process for planning a unit on the Cold War, with emphasis on efforts to contain communism. When I plan a unit, I always determine first the state standards, the Texas Essential Knowledge and Skills (TEKS), that I will include in the unit. In Texas, we have a standardized test in social studies that the high school students must pass in order to graduate. They are usually tested in eleventh grade. I always try to make sure that I teach all standards that are included on the test to a mastery level in the course. The TEKS for this unit are

5(A) Analyze causes of significant issues such as the Red Scare.

6(D) Describe the U.S. responses to Soviet aggression after WWII, including the Truman Doctrine, the Marshall Plan, the North Atlantic Treaty Organization, and the Berlin Air Lift.

24(C)  Explain and apply different methods that historians use to interpret the past, including the use of primary and secondary sources, points of view, frames of reference, and historical context.

24(G)  Support a point of view on a social studies issue or event.

Two of the standards address specific social studies information, and two focus on social studies skills. I like to start with the specific information I have to teach for a unit and then look for an overarching theme, or "big idea," to organize and integrate the information. This helps me keep history from becoming simply a list of events and people to memorize. I try to choose a theme that has relevance beyond the specific unit. In this way, I can make connections between what we are learning in history and the students' specific background experiences and often, present-day events.

The key facts or events that will have to be included are *The Red Scare, The Truman Doctrine, The Marshall Plan, The Formation of NATO,* and *The Berlin Air Lift.* At this point in the school year, we have already covered how fears of external aggression affect domestic and foreign policy. We looked at this when we reviewed both the Spanish-American War and the United States' involvement in World War I and World War II. I decided to use this knowledge as the link to the new topic. The overarching theme would thus be:

> The actions taken by groups are often the result of fears of
> external aggression, expressed through a variety of means.

Students could relate to this personally, because they often deal with fears of aggression and responses of others who fear them. This unit would be an example of the broader theme in this way:

> The United States responded to fears of communism and
> Soviet expansionism by enacting a policy of containment.

I planned to organize my lessons around this concept.

The next step for me is to divide the unit into specific content objectives, derived from the state standards. I choose objectives that will enable my students to master the standards, but also support the broader concept I'm teaching. The standards for this unit included the skills of identifying point of view and frame of reference, in this case "how groups respond to fears of aggression," so my objectives should provide opportunities for students to practice those skills. I decided on the following content objectives, one for each lesson in the unit:

- Students will be able to identify American fears of communism before the second World War.
- Students will be able to explain the purpose of the Marshall Plan.
- Students will be able to interpret how the Truman Doctrine reflected American fears of communism.
- Students will be able to explain the motivation of Western European countries and the United States in forming NATO.
- Students will be able to evaluate Soviet motivations for limiting access to Berlin and American motivations for its response.

After the content objectives are set, I develop the language objectives. I use our state English Language Proficiency Standards (ELPS) as a base. These are similar to the ESL or ELP standards you find in other states. I try to pick standards that not only support the social studies skills I'm teaching, but also provide the language practice my students will need to be successful in these lessons. It was helpful for me to take the time to really understand our state ELP standards and spend some time at the beginning of the year considering how I would include them throughout the year in instruction. The standards keep me thinking about the variety of language skills I need to include related to reading, writing, listening, and speaking, and language learning strategies. Figure 8.1 shows the standards I chose and the language objective I wrote based on the standard.

Now that I have my language objectives, I'm ready to start planning my lessons. Here's a map of my unit so far:

- **Overarching Understanding:** The actions taken by groups are often the results of fears of external aggression through a variety of military and diplomatic means.

- **Topical Understanding:** The United States responded to fears of communism and Soviet expansionism by enacting a policy of containment.

**FIGURE 8.1** *ELPS and Unit Language Objectives*

| ELPS | Language Objectives |
| --- | --- |
| 4(F) Use visual and contextual support and support from peers and teachers to read grade-appropriate content area text, enhance and confirm understanding, and develop vocabulary, grasp of language structures, and background knowledge needed to comprehend increasingly challenging language. | Students will be able to use visual and textual information to make inferences from text. |
| 1(D) Speak using learning strategies such as requesting assistance, employing non-verbal cues, and using synonyms and circumlocution. | Students will be able to express agreement and disagreement with the Marshall Plan. |
| 3(D) Speak using grade-level content area vocabulary in context to internalize new English words and build academic language proficiency. | Students will be able to use specific vocabulary and persuasive language to defend or oppose the formation of NATO orally. |
| 4(K) Demonstrate English comprehension and expand reading skills by employing analytical skills such as evaluating written information and performing critical analyses commensurate with content area and grade-level needs. | Students will be able to cite evidence from text to formulate an argument. |
| 5(F) Write using a variety of grade-appropriate sentence lengths, patterns, and connecting words to combine phrases, clauses, and sentences in increasingly accurate ways as more English is acquired. | Students will be able to write about the Berlin airlift using transitional and connecting words. |

## Lesson Topics

### Red Scare Review

- *Content Objective:* Students will be able to identify American fears of communism before the second World War.

- *Language Objective:* Students will be able to use visual and textual information to make inferences from text.

## Marshall Plan

- *Content Objective:* Students will be able to explain the purpose of the Marshall Plan.
- *Language Objective:* Students will be able to express agreement and disagreement with the Marshall Plan.

## Truman Doctrine

- *Content Objective:* Students will be able to interpret how the Truman Doctrine reflected American fears of communism and Soviet aggression.
- *Language Objective:* Students will be able to use specific vocabulary and persuasive language to defend or oppose the formation of NATO orally.

## Formation of NATO

- *Content Objective:* Students will be able to describe the motivation of Western European countries and the United States in forming NATO.
- *Language Objective:* Students will be able to cite evidence from the text to formulate an argument.

## Berlin Airlift

- *Content Objective:* Students will evaluate Soviet motivations for limiting access to Berlin and American motivations for its response.
- *Language Objective:* Students will be able to write a letter about the Berlin Airlift using transition and connecting words.

One of the first things to consider is how I will make sure my students have enough background knowledge and vocabulary to participate in the lesson activities in a meaningful way. This is challenging because of the diverse students I have. Some of my English learners have partial familiarity with U.S. and world history, while others have very little background. I always begin my lessons with activities that either refer to lessons previously taught or tap into what students already know about a topic. It helps to have a class discussion about the topic or connection. Over the years, I have found it is extremely important for my English learners that I teach at least some of the key vocabulary early in the lesson. To do this, I include visuals and provide opportunities for students to ask classmates for clarification.

Another way I help build and activate background is by checking the materials and ancillaries that are available with our textbook. The majority of my English learners are Spanish speaking, and fortunately, our textbook includes Spanish chapter summaries, key vocabulary, and section and chapter reviews. I choose specific resources that will help build background in my Spanish-speaking students and make these available before I teach the lesson. I have speakers of other languages from time to time, too. One year, I had two Arabic-speaking students and one Chinese student who were at the beginning and intermediate levels of fluency. Of course, resources are more limited for these language groups, but I try to at least provide Wikipedia articles in students' native languages about the topic we are discussing. This can be done by finding an appropriate article and then clicking on the language tab on the left of the Web page, when translations are available.

Before presenting the entire unit, let me walk you through one lesson's planning process. The objectives in my first lesson, as you saw above, are about identifying American fears of communism before World War II and using visual and textual information to make inferences. Since my main theme explores responses to perceived aggression, I decided it would be a good idea to start the unit by tapping into what students remembered from a previous lesson. Looking through the *99 Ideas* book (Vogt & Echevarria, 2008), I realized that using white boards and having a small group discussion might be helpful because of the varying background levels of the students. We had already discussed the Palmer Raids, which were conducted by the Department of Justice and the INS in the 1920s on suspected radical leftists and immigrants. I thought we could start here as an entry point for discussing American fear of the Soviets before World War II.

The first step would be to find out what students remembered about the Palmer Raids and then process that material in pairs. We would use the Group Response with White Board activity (see Chapter 3), which allows students to work with partners and put their ideas down on a white board. The lack of permanence with the white board—the ability to erase and change ideas—makes it a worthwhile tool to use with high schoolers. They tend not to like to take risks with their answers or look foolish in front of peers, so the group response with a white board is less intimidating.

After discussing the Palmer Raids, I would have the students read the textbook section discussing the Red Scare using the Adapted Chunk and Chew approach (see Chapter 3). I almost always use some type of shared or group reading activity to process the textbook, primary sources, and other secondary sources we read in class. It is very difficult for newcomers and intermediate level students to process the textbook, even with adequate background knowledge about the topic. Shared reading allows some flexibility and time to ask questions of native language and English-speaking peers. I often provide stems such as "Can you repeat that . . ." and "Can you help me understand . . ." for the students to help them feel more comfortable requesting assistance from other students in small groups.

After reading the textbook, students should have enough background schema to participate in an activity in which we analyze cartoons representing American fears of communism during the Red Scare. Interpreting these cartoons gives students a chance to practice using the language they encountered in the textbook and provides a visual to help them understand a particular point of view. Reviewing their analyses gives me a chance to clarify misconceptions and make sure students understand the key ideas. The discussion following this activity allows me to emphasize the theme we're focusing on in this unit: "How we respond to fears of aggression." I conclude the lesson by having the students do an activity called Differentiated Tickets Out (see Chapter 3). This activity is ideal for classrooms like mine, where students have a variety of levels of language proficiency. They can summarize their learning visually or in writing at varying degrees of complexity. They also have some choice in the task, which is always valuable when working with teenagers.

In the following pages, you can see how the unit plays out. The lessons require a high level of critical thinking, reading, writing, and discussing, but along the way, tasks are scaffolded for all students. This unit promotes the academic literacy skills needed by eleventh graders in a supportive yet comprehensive manner.

· · · · · · · · · · · · · · · · · · · · · · · · · · · · · · · · · · · · · · · · · · · · · · · · · · · · · · · · · · · · ·

**147**

# SIOP® LESSON PLAN 1: *Red Scare*

## Developed by John Seidlitz

**Grade:** 11
**Subject:** Global History                          **Date:** (See Planning Point 1)

| | |
|---|---|
| **Content Objective:** Students will be able to identify American fears of communism before the second World War. | **Language Objective:** Students will be able to use visual and textual information to make inferences from text. |
| **Vocabulary:** communism, containment, Red Scare, isolationism, expansionism, policy, diplomacy, aggression | **Visuals, Materials & Texts:** Sections of the textbook (see Think-Aloud 1) discussing causes of the Red Scare, legal-sized paper, political cartoons related to the Red Scare found at: http://newman.baruch.cuny.edu/digital/redscare/default.htm (see Planning Point 2), notes/text about the Palmer Raids[2] (from a prior lesson) for review. |

| *Activities* | *Review & Check for Understanding* |
|---|---|
| **Activating Prior Knowledge** | |
| *Group Response with White Board* | |
| Ask students to silently scan their notes that were taken about the Palmer Raids. Then have the students form pairs, with each pair sharing one white board (procedures in Chapter 3). Provide stems, and have the partners write the conclusion to each stem on their white boards. When all students have a response, ask one partner to hold up his or her board so all students can see it. Then ask the students to share out, making sure all the various responses are read aloud. | Review white boards for appropriate ideas and give feedback as needed. |
| Stems: | |
| ● *The Palmer Raids were . . .* | |
| ● *They took place . . .* | |
| ● *They were significant because . . .* | |
| ● *People feared communism and anarchism because . . .* | |
| **Building Vocabulary and Concept Knowledge** | |
| *Predicting Definitions* | |
| Post key words on the board. Have students predict or identify the meanings with a partner (procedures in Chapter 2). Review words with the class and confirm and clarify meanings. Have students record the words in their notebooks. | Circulate and listen to student responses |
| *Chunk and Chew Review* | |
| Have students read the textbook section discussing the Red Scare in groups of three, rotating the reader for this Adapted Chunk and Chew (procedures in Chapter 3). Every two or three paragraphs, the reader rotates. Students may "pass" if | |

*(continued)*

---

[2]The Palmer Raids were raids conducted by the U.S. Department of Justice and the Immigration and Naturalization Service in the 1920s on suspected radical leftists and immigrants. The point for students is that anti-communism did not begin with the Soviet Union's actions after World War II. The Palmer Raids were known as the first Red Scare. McCarthyism in the 1950s would later be known as the second Red Scare.

# SIOP® LESSON PLAN 1: *Red Scare* *(continued)*

| Activities | Review & Check for Understanding |
|---|---|

they do not wish to read, but must respond with the stems about what is read. Before each rotation, have the other students summarize the section orally using any of the following stems:

- *You read about . . .*
- *_____ happened because . . .*
- *_____ is significant because . . .*
- *_____ reminds me of . . .*
- *I wonder why . . .*

**Structured Conversation and Writing**

*Cartoon Analysis*

Have students form pairs, partners A and B. Give each pair one legal-sized piece of paper and a political cartoon related to the Red Scare, such as those found at: http://newman.baruch.cuny.edu/digital/redscare/default.htm

Student pairs should tape the cartoon to the legal-sized paper. They then label the important items they see in the cartoon. At the bottom of the page, have the students write a description and interpretation of the cartoon using at least one of these stems:

- *This cartoon portrays a fear of communism. It is . . .*
- *The illustrator was trying to show fears of communism by . . .*

Afterward, have the students participate in two rotations. In the first rotation, all A's stand and move to a new partner B. (B's remain seated.) A's discuss their cartoon interpretation with new B's and vice versa. A's return to their first partner and both students discuss what they learned from the new pairing. Then, give a signal to begin a second rotation, where B's move to a new partner A and repeat the process. (See Think-Aloud 2.)

*Think–Pair–Share Discussion*

- Pose this question to the class:
- "What fears of aggression do we have today in the U.S., and how are we responding to them?"
- Have students think about it, discuss with a partner, and then facilitate a whole class discussion.

*Differentiated Tickets Out*

Wrap up the lesson with Differentiated Tickets Out (procedures in Chapter 3). Post on the wall or board the following list:

1. Draw and label a stick figure drawing representing what we discussed today.

Observe the discussions and interpretations of the cartoons, provide feedback, and clarify misconceptions.

Allow students to share ideas without too much teacher explanation, except to clear up misconceptions or factual inaccuracies.

*(continued)*

2. Write a short rhyme/rap describing what we discussed today.

3. Finish the sentence "What we learned about today reminds me of_____ because . . ."

4. Draw a graphic organizer—Venn diagram, timeline, T-chart, or flow chart—representing what we discussed today.

Give the students a choice to complete any of these on one half sheet of paper. (See Think-Aloud 3.)

Collect and assess Tickets Out. Review the objectives for the day.

## PLANNING POINT 1

● This lesson may take two days.

## PLANNING POINT 2

● This website gives viewers permission to use these political cartoons for personal or non-commercial purposes, so they may be used in classrooms. My recommendations are at the following web pages:

http://newman.baruch.cuny.edu/digital/redscare/HTMLCODE/CHRON/RS017.HTM

http://newman.baruch.cuny.edu/digital/redscare/HTMLCODE/CHRON/RS018.HTM

http://newman.baruch.cuny.edu/digital/redscare/HTMLCODE/CHRON/RS015.HTM

http://newman.baruch.cuny.edu/digital/redscare/HTMLCODE/CHRON/RS071.HTM

## THINK-ALOUD 1

● I think it is important to teach the students how to use textbooks, and so I design activities that scaffold the reading process. They will need these skills when they are no longer in sheltered classes.

## THINK-ALOUD 2

● It is not necessary to have a different cartoon for each pair, although having some variety is preferred. When the rotations take place, the new pairs may have the same or different cartoons. Students can still have interesting conversations as they describe their interpretations of the cartoon(s).

## THINK-ALOUD 3

● I find that my high school students are more responsive to classroom tasks when I provide choices for them. By selecting one option over another, they are more invested in the task than if I assign it.

# SIOP® LESSON PLAN 2: *The Marshall Plan*

### Developed by John Seidlitz

**Grade:** 11
**Subject:** Global History                                      **Date:**

| | |
|---|---|
| **Content Objective:** Students will be able to explain the purpose of the Marshall Plan. | **Language Objective:** Students will be able to express agreement and disagreement with the Marshall Plan. |
| **Vocabulary:** Marshall Plan, Western Europe, Eastern Europe, state department, recovery, Yalta Conference | **Visuals, Materials & Texts:** Sections of the textbook discussing the Marshall Plan, posted options for Go to Your Corner activity (see choices in Activities section below), map showing nations that participated in Marshall Plan, pictures of WWII devastation in German cities (see Planning Point 1) |

| *Activities* | *Review & Check for Understanding* |
|---|---|
| **Activating Prior Knowledge** | |

*Go to Your Corner*

Post the following choices in four corners of the room. (See Planning Point 2.)

1. He's a good person who has lots of money and just wants to help out.

2. He's trying to impress someone else because it's important that people think he's good.

3. He wants everyone in the neighborhood to like him because he owns a business and can afford the loss.

4. He's afraid that if he doesn't give me the money, someone else will, and then I'll resent him for not helping out.

Read the following scenario to the students:

"A tornado has wiped out your neighborhood. You go home to inspect the damage, and there's a man writing out checks to people whose houses were destroyed. He offers you a check that will be enough to repair your home. He says there are no strings attached and nothing you have to do for it. Why did he give you the money?"

Tell students to move to the corner they think best represents their point of view and discuss their opinions.

Listen to students' conversations in the corners, and give feedback.

Ask one or more group members to summarize the discussion.

Explain to the students that after World War II, the United States gave money to Western Europe. Show the images of devastation to illustrate why Europe needed money. Tell students they will be reading about the plan—its design and implementation. Later they will choose which analogy they think best represents the reason the United States gave the money to Western Europe. Each student will decide whether he or she would have supported the plan.

*(continued)*

### Building Vocabulary and Concept Knowledge

*Vocabulary Scan*

Prior to reading the text, ask students to scan the section discussing the Marshall Plan backward (procedures in Chapter 2). Have students call out any unfamiliar words, and provide short definitions for the terms. Make sure to discuss the terms listed under key vocabulary if the students do not give these terms.

Ask students the meanings of low-frequency academic vocabulary not mentioned. Re-explain the purpose of scanning and expand the list as necessary. Circulate while students copy the terms in the vocabulary section of their notebooks.

*Insert Method*

Have students read the textbook section discussing the Marshall Plan with a partner. As they read, they should put a check mark (✓) by things they already know, a question mark (?) by facts or concepts they find confusing, an exclamation mark (!) by things that are unusual or surprising, and a plus sign (+) by ideas or concepts that are new. (See Planning Point 3.)

Circulate and listen to students' conversations. Ask beginning and intermediate students to summarize the material. Make sure beginning and intermediate students have access to native language resources on this topic (e.g., Wikipedia, textbook ancillaries).

Afterward, have partners join another pair and share their understandings and questions. Next, the small groups should discuss:

- Why did the United States give $13 billion to Western Europe after the War?

### Structured Conversation and Writing

*Take a Stand*

Have students return to their seats and complete the following sentence stem in their notebooks:

- *The main reason the United States created and implemented the Marshall Plan was . . .*

Select one student to begin and report his or her reason. If other students agree with that student, they will stand. If they do not, they remain seated. Call on those who agree or disagree to speak using the stems below. After a few students have spoken, open up discussion for a non-standing student to share and repeat the process.

Circulate and glance at students' responses. Make sure all students have written a response before beginning the discussion.

- *I respectfully disagree with _____ because . . .*
- *I agree with _____ because . . .*

*Tickets Out:*

Review the objectives with the students. Have them complete the following sentence on a piece of paper:

Collect and assess Tickets Out.

- *I support/do not support the Marshall Plan because . . .*

---

## PLANNING POINT 1

- Students will have a better understanding of the need for the Marshall Plan if they are provided with visuals. If available, use photos of the destruction and devastation in Europe from World War II in the textbook or on the Internet, such as at the following

sites: http://www.telegraph.co.uk/news/worldnews/europe/germany/2279721/
Nazi-photos-reveal-devastation-of-WWII-Allied-bombing-raids-on-Germany.html. A
map of countries that participated in the Marshall Plan may be in the textbook or at
such sites as: http://www.loc.gov/exhibits/marshall/images/wholemap.jpg.

## PLANNING POINT 2

- If possible, post these before class begins. Or have a student do it while you are taking roll. The Go to Your Corner activity is described in more detail in the *99 Ideas*
book (Vogt & Echevarria, 2008), p. 32.

## PLANNING POINT 3

- The Insert Method is described in more detail in the *99 Ideas* book (Vogt & Echevarria,
2008), p. 33.

## SIOP® LESSON PLAN 3: *The Truman Doctrine*

### Developed by John Seidlitz

**Grade:** 11
**Subject:** Global History

**Date:**

| Activities | Review & Check for Understanding |
|---|---|

**Content Objective:** Students will be able to interpret how the Truman Doctrine reflected American
fears of communism and Soviet aggression.

**Vocabulary:** Truman Doctrine, containment, foreign policy, totalitarian, Iron Curtain

**Language Objective:** Students will be able to cite
evidence from the text to formulate an oral argument.

**Visuals, Materials & Texts:** Sections of the textbook discussing the Truman Doctrine, Truman's
speech to Congress (BLMs 20 and 21), argumentation chart (BLM 22), map showing Warsaw Pact
(Eastern bloc) and NATO member (Western bloc)
countries (See Planning Point 1), signs for "Strongly
Agree," "Agree," "Disagree," "Strongly Disagree"

---

| Activities | Review & Check for Understanding |
|---|---|

**Activating Prior Knowledge**
Review the objectives for the lesson. Depending on
your students' knowledge, you may need to preteach
the concepts of "bully" and "communism."

*Value Line*
Post signs labeled "Strongly Agree," "Agree,"
"Disagree," and "Strongly Disagree" in a continuum across one of the walls or the board in the
classroom for the Value Line activity (see p. 94 in
*99 Ideas*). Read the first of the following series of
statements, and ask students to decide their level
of agreement or disagreement. Choose five students to demonstrate their opinions by asking
them to walk to the sign (or any point along the
continuum) that best represents their view. After
each student moves, the rest of the class members
point (or move, if desired) toward the locations

Make sure all students have made a choice before
having the five students share their points of view.
Select students at a variety of levels of background knowledge and proficiency to share, as
this topic involves familiar social language.

*(continued)*

that best represent their views. Have some of the five students explain why they selected that spot, especially if there are differences in opinion. Repeat for all statements.

1. If someone smaller than me were in a fight with a bully, I would jump in to help the smaller person.

2. If a bully picks on anybody, it's a threat to everybody's safety.

3. If others are fighting, it's not my business. I should leave them alone.

4. If a communist nation tries to make other nations communist, it can be compared with a bully.

Afterward remind students about the earlier lesson on the Red Scare. Discuss how the Soviet Union expanded into Eastern Europe and that Turkey and Greece had growing communist movements; also show students the map of Eastern Bloc and Western Bloc countries. Pose this question to the students:

- *Imagine you are in Congress. You have heard intelligence reports stating that the Soviet Union is expanding into Turkey and Greece. How do you respond?*

Facilitate this discussion, and prompt students to explain their opinions or provide evidence.

Have a class discussion about this as preparation for the reading.

### Building Vocabulary and Concept Knowledge

*Vocabulary Scan*

Prior to reading the text, ask students to scan the adapted version of Truman's speech to Congress in 1947 requesting aid to Greece and Turkey (see BLM 20). (See Think-Aloud 1.) Have students call out any unfamiliar words, and provide short definitions of the terms for the students (procedures in Chapter 2). Make sure to discuss the terms listed under key vocabulary if the students do not identify these terms. As with all primary sources, the class may need more time to do the scan of the speech than they would with a textbook. Divide the section up by paragraphs and have groups of students scan different sections to get a longer list of unfamiliar terms.

Make sure all students have highlighted at least one term before beginning.

Afterward, students should record words in their vocabulary notebooks.

*Argument Frames*

Have students read the text of Truman's speech with a partner. Ask them to fill out the attached Argumentation Chart in groups of three (BLM 22). Each student must fill out his or her own chart individually, although the groups may work together.

Circulate and observe students' responses. Make sure students at lower levels of proficiency are able to participate in the discussion that follows. Engage students in dialog to determine their opinions about Truman's request.

### Structured Conversation and Writing

*Sharing Frames*

Have each student decide whether he or she agrees or disagrees with the decision to send aid to Turkey and Greece. Pair up each student with another

Circulate and listen to student responses. Engage students in discussion, when appropriate.

*(continued)*

## SIOP® LESSON PLAN 3: *The Truman Doctrine* *(continued)*

| Activities | Review & Check for Understanding |
|---|---|
| student from a different group, and have them share their decisions and reasons. They may use their charts as a reference during the discussion.<br><br>Bring the class back together. Discuss with the students the concept of the Truman Doctrine—that the United States should support governments that opposed communism throughout the world. This practice began with Greece and Turkey, but continued with other countries throughout the Cold War.<br><br>*Whip Around, Pass Option*<br>Post the following outcome sentence starters:<br><br>• *I found out that the United States developed the Truman Doctrine because* . . .<br>• *I was surprised that Greece/Turkey* . . .<br>• *I think Truman was right/wrong because* . . .<br>• *I am still wondering why/how* . . .<br><br>Quickly "whip around" the room, giving each student a chance to answer, or take the option of saying "Pass." | Collect the Argumentation Charts. Review the objectives. |

## PLANNING POINT 1

- A map like this is often found in textbooks. Similar maps can be found on the Internet too. Sites like this one offer interactive maps (http://www.the-map-as-history. com/demos/tome04/index.php).

## THINK-ALOUD 1

- I use the adapted version (BLM 20) so students focus more on the key words. The original (BLM 21) is more difficult. However, if my class includes native English speakers or transitional ELs, I might give the original to some students during this step as an additional challenge.

## SIOP® LESSON PLAN 4: *The Formation of NATO*

**Developed by John Seidlitz**

**Grade:** 11
**Subject:** Global History

**Date:**

**Content Objective:** Students will be able to explain the motivation of Western European countries and the United States to form the NATO alliance.

**Language Objective:** Students will be able to use specific vocabulary and persuasive language to orally defend or oppose the formation of NATO.

**Vocabulary:** Alliance, Berlin Blockade, aggression, Warsaw Pact

**Visuals, Materials & Texts:** Sections of the textbook discussing the formation of NATO, map showing NATO countries (see Planning Point 1), NATO Pro-Con T-chart (BLM 23)

*(continued)*

| Activities | Review & Check for Understanding: |
|---|---|

### Activating Prior Knowledge
Review the objectives for the lesson.

*Oral Number 1–3 for Self-Assessment*
Read the following terms aloud in order to review vocabulary and ideas relevant to today's lesson. Have students rate their knowledge of each term on a scale of one to three (procedures in Chapter 3). One finger indicates no knowledge, two some familiarity, and three, you could explain what the term means to someone else. When students are unfamiliar with a term, either explain the term, have other students explain the term, or have them clarify the meaning in small groups:

Observe students' responses. During student-to-student interaction, engage students who lack some background knowledge in conversation about the terms.

| | |
|---|---|
| alliance | communism |
| blockade | capitalism |
| aggression | totalitarianism |
| Iron Curtain | Soviet Union |
| Marshall Plan | Warsaw Pact |
| Red Scare | |

Explain to students that today they will be discussing the Cold War alliances that were formed in response to fears of Soviet aggression after World War II.

### Building Vocabulary and Concept Knowledge

*QtA (Question the Author)*
Have students read their textbook section discussing the NATO Alliance in groups of three. Rotate readers, with students having the option to pass. After the reader reads, the other students (and the reader) respond orally to the presentation of information in the section using the following stems:

Ask students the meaning of low-frequency academic vocabulary not mentioned. Re-explain the purpose of scanning and expand the list as necessary.

- *This is about . . .*
- *The textbook author found this event significant because . . .*
- *The textbook author probably believed/did not believe . . .*
- *The textbook author probably supported/did not support . . .*
- *The pictures included on this page illustrate . . .*
- *The pictures included were selected by the textbook writers to show . . .*

Circulate and listen to students' conversations. Ask beginning and intermediate students to summarize material.

After each group finishes, discuss the following with the class.

- Why was NATO formed?
- Why was the Warsaw Pact formed?
- Do you think students in the former Soviet Union would read history the same way?
- Would the writers of Soviet textbooks have chosen different pictures or a different way to tell the story?
- Why or why not?

Facilitate this discussion, probing students to justify their opinions.

*(continued)*

## SIOP® LESSON PLAN 4: *The Formation of NATO* (continued)

| Activities | Review & Check for Understanding |
|---|---|
| **Structured Conversation and Writing**<br><br>*Conga Line*<br>Have students create a NATO Pro-Con T-chart in their notebooks (or use BLM 23) with the following headings:<br><br>● *Western Europe and the U.S. must form an alliance because . . .*<br><br>● *Western Europe and the U.S. must not form an alliance because . . .*<br><br>Have students start filling in their charts, adding two or three points in each column. Then complete the T-chart as a whole class. | Remind students to provide reasons for their positions. |
| Students then form two groups for a Conga Line (see Think-Aloud 1). One group is in favor of the alliance; the other is not. One group forms a long line. The second group forms a second line, facing the first, with about 2 feet distance between the lines. Each student should now face a partner. Line 1 members begin and share their opinions about the NATO Alliance with their Line 2 partners. Line 2 members listen and then give feedback and share their positions. At the signal, students in Line 1 move one step to the right to meet a new partner. The student at the far right end of Line 1 walks down to the other end of Line 1 to get a new partner. The process repeats. If desired, do this a third and fourth time and have the lines switch positions, so students defend the alternate position now. | Circulate and listen to students' conversations. Assist struggling students with using the chart to form sentences if they have trouble engaging in dialog. |
| *Tickets Out*<br>Have students respond to the following prompt on a note card:<br><br>● *Our textbooks probably show no/some bias related to the presentation of the Cold War because . . .* | Collect and assess Tickets Out. Review the objectives for the day. |

## PLANNING POINT 1

● Maps of Warsaw Pact and NATO countries are often found in textbooks. They can also be found on the Internet at sites such as http://www.the-map-as-history.com/demos/tome04/index.php

## THINK-ALOUD 1

● Depending on the layout of the room, I might do this activity as a Conga Line or an Inside-Outside Circle. In this way, it is more contained and I can observe the two groups easily. Another option is to Mingle and Match with students mingling randomly around the room, finding a nearby partner when I give the signal, and then discussing with their partner. Then they mingle again, find a new partner and repeat.

# SIOP® LESSON PLAN 5: *The Berlin Airlift*

**Developed by John Seidlitz**

**Grade:** 11
**Subject:** Global History                                      **Date:** (See Planning Point 1.)

**Content Objective:** Students will be able to evaluate Soviet motivations for limiting access to
Berlin and American motivations for its response.

**Language Objective:** Write about the Berlin
Airlift using transition and connecting words.

**Vocabulary:** Alliance, Berlin Blockade, aggression, Warsaw Pact, crisis, airlift, via

**Visuals, Materials & Texts:** Sections of the textbook discussing the Berlin Airlift, a map showing
the division of Europe after World War II, rubric
for letter (Figure 8.2)

| *Activities* | *Review & Check for Understanding* |
|---|---|

**Activating Prior Knowledge**

*Anticipation Guide*
Post the following sentences on the board. Ask
students to identify any unfamiliar words in the
sentences and explain, if needed. Have students
predict with a partner whether the statements
(posted on board) are true or false.

1. Communists controlled most of Eastern
   Europe after World War II. *True*

2. Berlin was in East Germany, but was controlled by Great Britain, France, the Soviet
   Union, and the United States. *True*

3. West Germany was part of the Communist
   Bloc and was under the control of the Soviet
   Union. *False*

Observe students' responses. During student-to-
student interaction, engage students who lack
some background in conversation.

Show students a map of the division of Europe
after World War II. Explain to the students that
East Germany was under the control of the Soviet
Union. Point out the location of Berlin and ask
students:

● *What problems do you think having a NATO-
allied city in a Warsaw Pact Country caused?*

Students can share answers with their partners and
should be ready to respond with the stem:

● *One problem might be . . .*

**Building Vocabulary and Concept Knowledge**

*Oh Yesterday + Year!*
Have students quickly make *Oh Yesterday after
World War II . . .* statements to review what they
have been studying in this unit (procedures in
Chapter 2). Give students time to think of a statement and share it with a peer. Then choose five or
six students to dramatically state their comment.

If necessary, give some ideas to beginners, with
key terms such as Red Scare, Marshall Plan, and
NATO alliance.

*Partner Reading*
Have students read the section of the textbook
about the Berlin Airlift with a partner. Ask them
to write four sentences in their notebooks that begin:

Heterogeneously group students, and allow students to opt out of reading if they are at early
levels of reading proficiency. Assist struggling
groups with forming sentences about each country.

*(continued)*

*Containing Communism After World War II*

## SIOP® LESSON PLAN 5: *The Berlin Airlift* (continued)

| Activities | Review & Check for Understanding |
|---|---|
| *The Soviet Union* . . . and four sentences that begin *The United States* . . . . For example:<br><br>● The Soviet Union<br>• controlled Eastern Europe.<br>• wanted to take control of West Berlin.<br>• blockaded all railway traffic into the city.<br>• was embarrassed by the success of the Berlin Airlift.<br><br>● The United States<br>• controlled part of West Berlin.<br>• wanted to break the Soviet Blockade.<br>• worked with France and Great Britain to supply the city with food via air.<br>• expanded military action in Western Europe as a result of increased fear of Soviet aggression.<br><br>Share and discuss answers with the class. Clarify understanding of the significance of the event. | |
| **Structured Conversation and Writing**<br><br>*Letter Writing*<br>Have each student write a letter from the point of view of a CIA analyst writing after the Soviets have begun to blockade West Berlin. Students will explain the Soviet actions in their letters to the U.S. President and recommend resupplying the city via air. Explain to the students the importance of connecting actions with outcomes in the letter. Review the following transitional and connecting words and phrases:<br><br>● _____ *due to* . . . , _____ *led to* . . . , _____ *contributed to* . . . , _____ *caused* . . .<br><br>● _____ *however* . . . ,<br><br>Students must use at least two of the phrases in their letters.<br>Read selected letters to the class. | Model for students how to use their notes to help construct their letters. Make sure students are able to successfully use the transitional phases and connecting words in their letters.<br><br><br><br><br>Collect and assess students' letters for content and language understanding using the rubric in Figure 8.2. |
| *Radio Broadcast* (See Planning Point 2.)<br>Reconnect to the general theme of fear of aggression. Choose one student to be the radio broadcaster. Ask other students to select the most significant reason they think Americans feared communism. Have each student choose a role as someone in the post–World War II era (name, occupation). Ask them to write one sentence:<br><br>● *I'm afraid of the Communists/Soviet Union because* . . .<br><br>The interviewer asks questions like:<br>● *Tell us who you are and what you do.*<br>● *Are you afraid of the Soviets? Why?*<br><br>Students should give brief responses, pretending to be the character they created. | Review the objectives for the day. |

## PLANNING POINT 1

- This lesson will last for two days.

## PLANNING POINT 2

- You may want to play a radio interview for the students from an audio file or podcast.

**FIGURE 8.2** *Rubric for Letter to the President*

| CATEGORY | *Above Standards (25 pts)* | *Meets Standards (20 pts)* | *Below Standards (10 pts)* | *Minimal to No Effort (0 pts)* | *Score* |
|---|---|---|---|---|---|
| **Format** | Student follows all instructions. Letter reflects appropriate formality. | Student follows all directions. | Student follows some but not all directions. | Student does not follow directions. | |
| **Historical Accuracy** | Factual information is accurate and relevant to argument. | Factual information is accurate. | Some factual information is missing or inaccurate. | Factual information is inaccurate. | |
| **Writing Style** | Writing style engages the reader. Student uses transitional and connecting words effectively. | Writing style is proficient. Student uses transitional and connecting words effectively. | Writing style is stilted. Sentences are brief without transitional and connecting words to link ideas. | Letter is only 1–2 sentences long. Sentences are brief. No transitional or connecting words. | |
| **Support for Argument** | Student forms coherent argument and successfully advocates for position. | Student clearly describes position. | Student offers vague or weak position without support. | Student does not clearly identify or argue for position. | |

# Concluding Thoughts

The United States became a superpower after World War II, and this unit helps students understand the events that led to that status. For high schoolers, knowledge of geopolitical relationships is critical for civic participation as they become adults. The topics in this unit are rather abstract and complicated, but John Seidlitz's lessons break down the information into accessible chunks and have the students talk about or write about their new understandings every step of the way. Moreover, the lessons provide the language scaffolds to enable all students to participate in this process. Together, the activities for content knowledge and language practice advance students' understanding and academic language skills.

We hope this unit gave you new ideas for incorporating meaningful activities and attention to language development in your history and social studies lessons. We encourage you to read Chapters 5, 6, and 7 for additional units. Even if you currently teach at the high school level, you will find interesting SIOP® lessons and effective integration of new techniques in these other sample units.

# chapter 9

# Pulling It All Together

As we planned this final chapter, we decided to share some of the things we have learned in the process of writing this book, related to our collaborations with our content contributors and our understandings of lesson and unit planning using the SIOP® Model. We also asked our contributors to share what they have learned, and we have included their thoughts and insights in the second half of this chapter. Together, we have learned to be better SIOP® teachers and professional developers.

## What We Have Learned

One important finding for all of us is the confirmation that becoming an effective SIOP® teacher is a process that takes time, reflection, practice, and commitment. Unlike many of the educational initiatives that we have all been involved in during our careers, the SIOP® Model is not about tweaking our teaching a little here and adding a little something there, while expecting immediate results in our students' academic achievement. Instead, the SIOP® Model is about purposeful planning, consistent attention to teaching the academic language and content of your discipline, and maintaining the belief that all students,

including English learners, can reach high academic standards while developing their English proficiency. We know from our SIOP® research studies that if teachers are high implementers of the model, their students' academic performance increases significantly (Center for Applied Linguistics, 2007; Echevarria & Richards, 2009; Short, Fidelman & Louguit, 2010).

We also have become even more aware that good teaching is about attention to detail. For example, as we were reading and editing the lesson and unit plans created by our contributors, from time to time we had to call or email and ask questions about the purpose of a particular handout, the steps to a process, or the application of an activity. This made us realize how important it is to use precise language with English learners, both in our speech and in the materials we prepare for them. Consistent labeling for classroom routines, procedures, and activities reduces ambiguity and confusion, and serves as additional scaffolding for ELs. How great it would be if all teachers across the school used the same lexicon for their activities! With the SIOP® Model and collaboration, it is possible to do just that. Then when students walk into any class and are told to prepare Cornell notes, for instance, they will know immediately what to do. Clear task explanations allow students to get down to work quickly and facilitate classroom management.

We also had to seriously consider the role of teachers as content experts. You know where you are going with a lesson, and what needs to be taught, learned, and assessed. Students, including English learners, don't have this insider information, and sometimes they are academically lost because they do not know what is expected of them, or what they are to do. Obviously, this is a primary function of the content and language objectives, to point the way and assist students in knowing what to expect. But when we make assumptions about what students know and can do, we may be basing those assumptions on what *we* know and what *we* can do. Being precise in your use of terms, and carefully explaining and modeling processes and procedures related to the content you are teaching will assist your English learners in becoming more successful in learning your content.

We also sharpened our skills in designing SIOP® lessons and units. Our contributors, for the most part, created and wrote the lessons based on their teaching experiences. Our role was to clarify, verify, elaborate, and expand—adding more ideas, differentiations, and the like. In doing this, we became even more aware of how challenging it is to write detailed SIOP® lesson and unit plans. Teachers new to the SIOP® Model often balk at the time and work it takes to write lessons, yet as we have mentioned previously, with practice, the amount of time and effort is diminished. The end goal needs to be kept in sight: the academic and language proficiency benefits for the English learners who will be productive members of our society in the future. Our contributors to the ELA book explained, "As we gained more experience and more practice using the SIOP® Model, it just became an internalized part of our natural teaching style. We're not denying that it was hard work and we experienced successes as well as failures along the way, but we realized that, like with anything in life, once you begin to reap the benefits of a challenging task, the challenges don't seem so immense" (Vogt, Echevarria & Short, 2010).

We also realized the value of working with others. While the three of us were used to working and writing together, adding our contributors into the mix was exciting. They offered new perspectives and many new ideas. It was fun (but hard work) to prepare these books with them. As one of our science contributors mentioned, "Collaboration was essential for me. It was difficult to sit alone and plan and put my thoughts into writing. The questions that my colleagues asked and answered led to more clearly planned lessons with a variety of objectives and techniques included." We firmly believe these books have been enhanced by collaboration.

Finally, we have learned from our contributors that experienced, knowledgeable, successful teachers who are well-versed in the SIOP® Model continue to grow and learn through the process of carefully planning and teaching effective and appropriate lessons for English learners. As one of the contributors to the math book explained, "Coming up with higher-order thinking questions (consistently) was difficult for me. Therefore, I know that I need additional professional development in this area. Self-awareness is the key to change. This project helped me identify some of my own weaknesses" (Echevarria, Vogt & Short, 2010).

In the section that follows, you will hear the voices of our SIOP® history and social studies specialists. They elaborate on what they learned during the process of working together to help write this book.

# What Our SIOP® History and Social Studies Contributors Have Learned

## Robin Liten-Tejada

My work with the SIOP® model has framed my 23-year career in teaching English language learners. I first began collaborating with Deborah Short and the Center for Applied Linguistics in 1991, participating in projects leading to my involvement in the development of SIOP®. Those years truly helped me refine my understanding of teaching and the components of effective instruction for language learners. I have often felt like an artist, pulling together all the pieces to create lessons that to me seemed like works of art; lessons that involve concrete background building activities, multiple opportunities for student interaction, explicitly teaching learning strategies, always incorporating opportunities to read, write, speak, and listen to the key academic vocabulary, and always cycling back to my content and language objectives.

In my current position as curriculum specialist, I conduct frequent professional development workshops on SIOP® strategies, and lead district- and school-wide training and coaching. This has allowed me the privilege of observing and collaborating with many teachers and has given me an appreciation of the struggles teachers face in implementing the Model. For many teachers, this framework represents a new way to consider teaching ELLs, and I have come to believe that it is best for teachers in this situation to take it slowly. I recommend choosing one or two components to work on for a period of time, to engage in peer observations and coaching for support, and to collaborate on lesson plans. I have repeatedly witnessed that once teachers "get it," there is no going back! I am touched by the passion teachers have for learning new ways to reach their language learners, and this inspires me to work even harder to provide support!

Working on this Social Studies book has provided another opportunity to delve deeper into the SIOP® materials that have been recently published. I enjoyed collaborating with teachers with whom I haven't worked previously to learn how they teach certain units, and to transform their lessons into SIOP® activities and units.

Finally, as always, I am eternally grateful for the professional growth opportunities that my collaboration with the SIOP® researchers has provided me over the years. Without a doubt, it has made me the teacher I am today.

## John Seidlitz

I remember the first time I was exposed to the SIOP® Model. I was really inspired by the strategies, techniques, and approaches for building content and language together. But when I looked at the eight components and thirty features, I wondered, "How can anyone have time to implement all of this in a lesson?" Writing these social studies lessons has helped me to finally find the answer to that question. My answer is, "Knowing how much this will benefit my students, how can I *not* take time to implement the SIOP® Model?"

I always knew that teaching social studies to ELs involved careful planning, but writing these plans for other educators to use really made me think about *how* I was planning. A lot of successful strategies that I understood implicitly became much clearer to me as I wrote explanations in the lessons.

Successful use of the SIOP® Model involves providing ELs with the academic language that gives them access to the most significant ideas we teach in social studies. This involves explicit teaching of language and learning strategies and making sure that the materials selected truly provide the kind of access that matters to kids. It has to happen in every lesson, every day. It's all about language. If we make sure kids have access to academic language, and learn academic language, they can truly understand the significant ideas we teach in our history and social studies classrooms.

# Final Thoughts

In closing, we would like to reiterate the importance of collaboration. For over fifteen years, we have collaborated about the SIOP® Model, with each other and with educators throughout the country and now throughout the world. We are convinced that these collaborations have resulted in a comprehensive model of instruction for English learners that is not only empirically validated, but is appropriate, essential, and *doable* for teachers. Yes, it takes time and effort to create, write, and then teach SIOP® lessons, but the results are well worth it.

Our overarching goal for this book, and for the other SIOP® books in the series, is to help you pull it all together as you create your SIOP® history, social studies, geography, civics, and economics lesson plans and units. These resources should further your confidence in how to effectively teach these subjects to your English learners. We hope that as you become a successful SIOP® teacher, you will find rewards in your students' growth in both the academic language and the conceptual knowledge of your course's standards and curriculum.

# appendix a: SIOP® Protocol and Component Overview
(Echevarria, Vogt, & Short, 2000; 2004; 2008)

The SIOP® Model was designed to help teachers systematically, consistently, and concurrently teach grade-level academic content and academic language to English learners (ELs). Teachers have found it effective with both ELs and native-English speaking students who are still developing academic literacy. The model consists of eight components and 30 features. The following brief overview is offered to remind you of the preparation and actions teachers should undertake in order to deliver effective SIOP® instruction.

## Lesson Preparation

The focus for each SIOP® social studies lesson is the content and language objectives. We suggest that the objectives be linked to curriculum standards and the academic language students need for success in social studies. Your goal is to help students gain important experience with key grade-level content and skills as they progress toward fluency in English. Hopefully, you now post and discuss the objectives with students each day, even if one period continues a lesson from a previous day, so that students know what they are expected to learn and/or be able to do by the end of that lesson. When you provide a road map at the start of each lesson, students focus on what is important and take an active part in their learning process.

The Lesson Preparation component also advocates for supplementary materials (e.g., visuals, multimedia, adapted or bilingual texts, study guides) because grade-level texts are often difficult for many English learners to comprehend. Graphics or illustrations may be used to make content meaningful—the final feature of the component. It is important to remember that meaningful activities provide access to the key concepts in your social studies lessons; this is much more important than just providing "fun" activities that students readily enjoy. Certainly, "fun" is good, but "meaningful" and "effective" are better. You will also want to plan tasks and projects for students so they have structured opportunities for oral interaction throughout your lessons.

## Building Background

In SIOP® lessons, you are expected to connect new concepts with students' personal experiences and past learning. As you prepare ELs for social studies lessons, you may at times have to build background knowledge because many English learners either have not been studying in U.S. schools or are unfamiliar with American culture. At other times, you may need to activate your students' prior knowledge in order to find out what they already know, to identify misinformation, or to discover when you need to fill in gaps.

The SIOP® Model places importance on building a broad vocabulary base for students. We need to increase vocabulary instruction across the curriculum so our students will become effective readers, writers, speakers, and listeners—and historians. As a social studies teacher, you already explicitly teach key vocabulary. Go even further for your ELs by helping them develop word learning strategies such as using context clues, word parts (e.g., affixes), visual aids (e.g., illustrations), and cognates (a word related in meaning and form to a word in another language). Then be sure to design lesson activities that give students multiple opportunities to use new social studies vocabulary both orally and in writing, such as those found in this book and in *99 Ideas and Activities for Teaching with the SIOP® Model* (Vogt & Echevarria, 2008). In order to move words from receptive knowledge to expressive use, vocabulary needs reinforcement through different learning modes.

## Comprehensible Input

If you present information in a way that students cannot understand, such as an explanation that is spoken too rapidly, or texts that are far above students' reading levels with no visuals or graphic organizers to assist them, many students—including English learners—will be unable to learn the necessary content. Instead, modify "traditional" instruction with a variety of ESL methods and SIOP® techniques so your students can comprehend the lesson's key concepts. These techniques include, among others:

- Teacher talk appropriate to student proficiency levels (e.g., simple sentences, slower speech)
- Demonstrations and modeling (e.g., modeling how to complete a task or problem)
- Gestures, pantomime, and movement
- Role-plays, improvisation, and simulations
- Visuals, such as pictures, real objects, illustrations, charts, and graphic organizers
- Restatement, paraphrasing, repetition, and written records of key points on the board, screen, or chart paper
- Previews and reviews of important information (perhaps in the native language, if possible and as appropriate)
- Hands-on, experiential, and discovery activities

Remember, too, that academic tasks must be explained clearly, both orally and in writing for students. You cannot assume English learners know how to do an assignment because it is a regular routine for the rest of your students. Talk through the procedures and use models and examples of good products and appropriate participation, so students know the steps they should take and can envision the desired result.

When you are dealing with complicated and abstract concepts, it can be particularly difficult to convey information to less proficient students. You can boost the comprehensibility of what you're teaching through native language support, if possible. Supplementary materials (e.g., adapted texts or CDs) in a student's primary language may be used to introduce a new topic, and native language tutoring (if available) can help students check their understanding.

## Strategies

This component addresses student learning strategies, teacher-scaffolded instruction, and higher-order thinking skills. By explicitly teaching cognitive and metacognitive learning strategies, you help equip students for academic learning both inside and outside the SIOP® classroom. You should capitalize on the cognitive and metacognitive strategies students already use in their first language because those will transfer to the new language.

As a SIOP® teacher, you must frequently scaffold instruction so students can be successful with their academic tasks. You want to support their efforts at their current performance level, but also move them to a higher level of understanding and accomplishment. When students master a skill or task, you remove the supports you provided and add new ones for the next level. Your goal, of course, is for English learners to be able to work independently. They often achieve this independence one step at a time.

You need to ask your ELs a range of questions, some of which should require critical thinking. It is easy to ask simple, factual questions, and sometimes we fall into that trap with beginning English speakers. We must go beyond questions that can be answered with a one- or two-word response, and instead, ask questions and create projects or tasks that require students to think more critically and apply their language skills in a more extended way. Remember this important adage: "Just because ELs don't speak English proficiently doesn't mean they can't *think*."

### Interaction

We know that students learn through interaction with one another and with their teachers. They need oral language practice to help develop and deepen their content knowledge and support their second language skills. Clearly, you are the main role model for appropriate English usage, word choice, intonation, fluency, and the like, but do not discount the value of student–student interaction. In pairs and small groups, English learners practice new language structures and vocabulary that you have taught as well as important language functions, such as asking for clarification, confirming interpretations, elaborating on one's own or another's idea, and evaluating opinions.

Don't forget that sometimes the interaction patterns expected in an American classroom differ from students' cultural norms and prior schooling experiences. You will want to be sensitive to sociocultural differences and work with students to help them become competent in the culture you have established in your classroom, while respecting their values.

### Practice & Application

Practice and application of new material is essential for all learners. Our research on the SIOP® Model found that lessons with hands-on, visual, and other kinesthetic tasks benefit ELs because students practice the language and content knowledge through multiple modalities. As a SIOP® social studies teacher, you want to make sure your lessons include a variety of activities that encourage students to apply both the social studies content and the English language skills they are learning.

### Lesson Delivery

If you have delivered a successful SIOP® lesson, that means that the planning you did worked—the content and language objectives were met, the pacing was appropriate, and the students had a high level of engagement. We know that lesson preparation is crucial to effective delivery, but so are classroom management skills. We encourage you to set routines, make sure students know the lesson objectives so they can stay on track, and introduce (and revisit) meaningful activities that appeal to students. Don't waste time, but be mindful of student understanding so that you don't move a lesson too swiftly for students to grasp the key information.

### Review & Assessment

Each SIOP® social studies lesson needs time for review and assessment. You will do your English learners a disservice if you spend the last five minutes teaching a new concept rather than reviewing what they have learned so far. Revisit key vocabulary and concepts with your students to wrap up each lesson. Check on student comprehension frequently throughout the lesson period so you know whether additional explanations or reteaching are needed. When you assess students, be sure to provide multiple measures for students to demonstrate their understanding of the content. Assessments should look at the range of language and content development, including measures of vocabulary, comprehension skills, and content concepts.

## WHY IS THE SIOP® MODEL NEEDED NOW?

We all are aware of the changing demographics in our U.S. school systems. English learners are the fastest growing subgroup of students and have been for the past two decades. According to the U.S. Department of Education in 2006, English learners numbered 5.4 million in U.S. elementary and secondary schools, about 12% of the student population, and they are expected to comprise about 25% of that population by 2025. In several states, this percentage has already been exceeded. The educational reform movement, and the No Child Left Behind (NCLB) Act in particular, has had a direct impact on English learners. States have implemented standards-based instruction and high-stakes testing, but in many content classes, little or no accommodation is made for the specific language development needs of English learners; this raises a significant barrier to ELs' success because they are expected to achieve high academic standards in English. In many states, ELs are required to pass end-of-grade tests in order to be promoted and/or exit exams in order to graduate.

Unfortunately, teacher development has not kept pace with the EL growth rate. Far too few teachers receive an undergraduate education that includes coursework in English as a second language (ESL) methodologies, which can be applied in content classes through sheltered instruction, and in second language acquisition theory, which can help teachers understand what students should be able to accomplish in a second language according to their proficiency levels, prior schooling, and sociocultural backgrounds. At the end of 2008, only four states—Arizona, California, Florida, and New York—required some undergraduate coursework in these areas for all teacher candidates.

Some teachers receive inservice training in working with ELs from their schools or districts, but it is rarely sufficient for the task they confront. Teachers are expected to teach ELs the new language, English, so the ELs can attain a high degree of proficiency, and in addition, instruct them in all the topics of the different grade-level content courses (more often than not taught in English). A survey conducted by Zehler and colleagues (2003) in 2002 found that approximately 43% of elementary and secondary teachers had ELs in their classrooms, yet only 11% were certified in bilingual education and only 18% in English as a second language. In the five years prior to the survey, teachers who worked with three or more ELs had received on average four hours of inservice training in how to serve them—hardly enough to reach a satisfactory level of confidence and competence.

Even teachers who have received university preparation in teaching English learners report limited opportunities for additional professional development. In a recent survey that sampled teachers in 22 small, medium, and large districts in California, the researchers found that during the previous five years, "forty-three percent of teachers with 50 percent or more English learners in their classrooms had received no more than one inservice that focused on the instruction of English learners" (Gandara, Maxwell-Jolly & Driscoll, 2005, p. 13). Fifty percent of the teachers with somewhat fewer students (26%–50% English learners in their classes) had received either no such inservice or only one. The result of this paucity of professional development is that ELs sit in classes with teachers and other staff who lack expertise in second language acquisition, multicultural awareness, and effective, research-based classroom practices.

It is not surprising, then, that ELs have experienced persistent underachievement on high-stakes tests and other accountability measures. On nearly every state and national assessment, ELs lag behind their native-English speaking peers and demonstrate significant achievement gaps (Kindler, 2002; Kober, et al., 2006; Lee, Grigg & Dion, 2007; Lee, Grigg & Donahue, 2007). In addition to having underqualified teachers, ELs are also more likely to be enrolled in poor, majority-minority schools that have fewer resources and teachers with less experience and fewer credentials than those serving English-proficient students (Cosentino de Cohen, Deterding & Clewell, 2005).

Lower performance on assessments is also the result of education policy. Although research has shown that it takes several years of instruction to become proficient in English (four to nine years, depending on a student's literacy level in the native language and prior schooling) (Collier, 1987; Cummins, 2006; Genesee, Lindholm-Leary, Saunders, & Christian, 2006), current NCLB policy forces schools to test ELs in reading after one year of U.S. schooling in grades 3–8 and one grade in high school. English learners are supposed to take the tests in mathematics and science from the start. Adding to the disconnect between research and policy is the fact that these tests have been designed for native English speakers, rendering them neither valid nor reliable for ELs (AERA, APA, & NCME, 2000). By definition, an English learner is **not** proficient in English; as most of these state assessments are in English, the majority of ELs score poorly on them and are unable to demonstrate their real level of understanding of the subject matter.

Even though it is hard to turn around education policy, teachers, schools, districts, and universities do have opportunities to enact changes in professional development and program design. With this book we hope to help social studies and history teachers grow professionally and develop appropriate skills for working with English learners. There are many approaches and numerous combinations of techniques that can be applied to the delivery of sheltered content instruction. Currently, however, the SIOP® Model is the only scientifically validated model of sheltered instruction for English learners, and it has a growing research base (Center for Applied Linguistics, 2007; Echevarria, Richards, Canges & Francis, 2009; Echevarria & Short, in press; Echevarria, Short & Powers, 2006; Short & Richards, 2008). The SIOP® Model is distinct from other approaches in that it offers a field-tested protocol for systematic lesson planning, delivery, and assessment, making its application for teaching English learners transparent for both preservice candidates preparing to be teachers and practicing teachers engaged in staff development. Further, it provides a framework for organizing the instructional practices essential for sound sheltered content instruction.

## THE SIOP® MODEL COMPONENTS AND FEATURES

### Lesson Preparation

1. **Content objectives** clearly defined, displayed and reviewed with students
2. **Language objectives** clearly defined, displayed and reviewed with students
3. **Content concepts** appropriate for age and educational background level of students
4. **Supplementary materials** used to a high degree, making the lesson clear and meaningful (e.g., computer programs, graphs, models, visuals)
5. **Adaptation of content** (e.g., text, assignment) to all levels of student proficiency
6. **Meaningful activities** that integrate lesson concepts (e.g., interviews, letter writing, simulations, models) with language practice opportunities for reading, writing, listening, and/or speaking

### Building Background

7. **Concepts explicitly linked to students' background experiences**
8. **Links explicitly made between past learning and new concepts**

9. **Key vocabulary emphasized** (e.g., introduced, written, repeated, and highlighted for students to see)

## Comprehensible Input

10. **Speech appropriate** for students' proficiency levels (e.g., slower rate, enunciation, and simple sentence structure for beginners)

11. **Clear explanation of academic tasks**

12. **A variety of techniques** used to make content concepts clear (e.g., modeling, visuals, hands-on activities, demonstrations, gestures, body language)

## Strategies

13. Ample opportunities provided for students to use **learning strategies**

14. **Scaffolding techniques** consistently used, assisting and supporting student understanding (e.g., think-alouds)

15. A variety of **questions or tasks that promote higher-order thinking skills** (e.g., literal, analytical, and interpretive questions)

## Interaction

16. Frequent opportunities for **interaction** and discussion between teacher / student and among students, which **encourage elaborated responses** about lesson concepts

17. **Grouping configurations** support language and content objectives of the lesson

18. Sufficient **wait time for student responses** consistently provided

19. Ample opportunities for students to **clarify key concepts in Ll** as needed with aide, peer, or L1 text

## Practice & Application

20. **Hands-on materials and / or manipulatives** provided for students **to practice** using new content knowledge

21. Activities provided for students to **apply content and language knowledge** in the classroom

22. Activities integrate **all language skills** (i.e., reading, writing, listening, and speaking)

## Lesson Delivery

23. **Content objectives** clearly supported by lesson delivery

24. **Language objectives** clearly supported by lesson delivery

25. **Students engaged** approximately 90% to 100% of the period

26. **Pacing** of the lesson appropriate to students' ability levels

## Review & Assessment

27. Comprehensive **review of key vocabulary**

28. Comprehensive **review of key content concepts**

29. Regular **feedback** provided to students on their output (e.g., language, content, work)

30. **Assessment of student comprehension and learning** of all lesson objectives (e.g., spot checking, group response) throughout the lesson

# appendix b: Academic Social Studies and History Vocabulary Based on Sample State Standards

*Academic Social Studies and History Vocabulary Based on Sample State Standards*
*Grade Band: K–2*

| Historical & Social Sciences Analysis | Geography | History | Government | Civic Education | Economy | General Academic |
|---|---|---|---|---|---|---|
| artworks | Africa | America the Beautiful | Congress | bald eagle | buyer | because |
| cause and effect | Antarctica | American | education | citizen | consumer | cause |
| century | Arctic | American Indians | Election Day | citizenship | economy | characteristic |
| current events | Arctic Ocean | American legends | government | courage | exchange | communicate |
| date | Atlantic Ocean | biography | Governor | fair play | goods | compare |
| decade | Asia | calendar | institutions | flag | manufacture | describe |
| diaries | Australia | ceremony | law | good sportsmanship | market | different |
| documentary | city | culture | military force | heroism | money | discuss |
| fact | bay | community | nation | honesty | producers | draw |
| fiction | behind | customs | President | individual responsibility | production | effect |
| future | Canada | daily lives | transport | local community | seller | explain |
| generation | cardinal directions | Declaration of Independence | treaty | national | services | feature |
| globe | community center | documents | Vice President | patriotism | trade | label |
| historical figure | compass rose | early times | Washington, DC | Pledge of Allegiance | | locate |
| legend | continents | folklore | | respect | | migrate |
| letters | country | holiday | | rights | | model |
| location | desert | immigrants | | Statue of Liberty | | organize |
| map | environment | individual action | | symbols | | pattern |
| map skills | Europe | interviews | | U.S. Constitution | | position |
| order | far | oral histories | | | | question |
| past | fire station | photographs | | | | relationship |
| physical characteristics | forest | Pilgrims | | | | similar |
| present | Great Lakes | Star Spangled Banner | | | | trace |
| primary source | home | Thanksgiving | | | | |

*(continued)*

*Grade Band: K–2 (continued)*

| Historical & Social Sciences Analysis | Geography | History | Government | Civic Education | Economy | General Academic |
|---|---|---|---|---|---|---|
| report | hospital | town | | | | |
| sequence | in front of | traditions | | | | |
| timeline | Indian Ocean | village | | | | |
| year | lake | | | | | |
| | left | | | | | |
| | legend | | | | | |
| | map symbols | | | | | |
| | Mexico | | | | | |
| | near | | | | | |
| | neighborhood | | | | | |
| | North America | | | | | |
| | oceans | | | | | |
| | Pacific Ocean | | | | | |
| | physical environment | | | | | |
| | place of worship | | | | | |
| | police station | | | | | |
| | river | | | | | |
| | rural | | | | | |
| | scale | | | | | |
| | school | | | | | |
| | shelter | | | | | |
| | South America | | | | | |
| | state | | | | | |
| | suburban | | | | | |
| | transportation | | | | | |
| | United States of America | | | | | |
| | urban | | | | | |

Academic Social Studies and History Vocabulary Based on Sample State Standards
Grade Band: 3–5 (builds on K–2 Academic Vocabulary)

| Historical & Social Sciences Analysis | Geography | U.S. History | Government | Civic Education | World History | Economy | General Academic |
|---|---|---|---|---|---|---|---|
| artifacts | Atlantic trade routes | abolitionist | American Revolution | American dream | accomplishments of explorers | capital resources | achievement |
| bias | border | agricultural economy | Articles of Confederation | American ideals | Ancient China | consumption | aims |
| chronological sequence | capital | American Indian nations | Bill of Rights | civic involvement | Ancient Greece | costs and benefits | apply |
| consequences | geographical features | cooperation and conflict | direct democracy | responsibilities | dynasty | human resources | conflict |
| documentary sources | charts | annexation | Cabinet | civic life | Ancient Rome | economic choices | argument |
| eyewitness accounts | climate | British colonial period | city council | leadership | Athens | economics | as a result |
| historical accounts | coastal area | broken treaties | Confederacy | national pride | Aztec | economy of the local region | assimilation |
| journal | coordinate grid system | Civil War | Congress | non-violent protest | circumnavigate | entrepreneurship | chronological |
| of the time/era | delta | cliff dwellers | constitutional democracy | private property | civilizations | expenses | claimed by |
| period | distance | colonists | Declaration of Independence | privileges | conquistadors | free-market economic system | compare |
| perspective | equator | colonization | diplomacy | public property | Counter Reformation | human capital | comparison |
| point of view | geography | cultural | executive branch | rights | emperor | income | connect |
| problem-solving | hemisphere | desert Southwest | federal system of government | voting | empire | natural resources | contrast |
| secondary sources | human geography | early land and sea routes | first and second Continental Congresses | | fountain of youth | | contribution |
| social practices | human movement | European settlements | fundamental principles | | global | | control |
| viewpoint | International Date Line | expedition | House of Representatives | | Great Zimbabwe | | cultural |

(continued)

*Grade Band: 3–5 (builds on K–2 Academic Vocabulary) (continued)*

| Historical & Social Sciences Analysis | Geography | U.S. History | Government | Civic Education | World History | Economy | General Academic |
|---|---|---|---|---|---|---|---|
| | landforms | exploration | individual liberty | | hunter-gatherer economy | | cycle |
| | latitude | explorers | judicial branch | | Inca | | defeat |
| | longitude | federal and state governments | land policies | | key European expeditions | | define |
| | mountain pass | folklore traditions | legislative branch | | kingdom | | details |
| | mountain range | founding of the colonies | local government | | Magellan | | development |
| | navigation | French and Indian War | mayor | | Mali | | diagrams |
| North Pole | New World | Great Depression | military force | | Marco Polo | | difference |
| | North Pole | growth of towns and cities | national landmarks | | Mayan | | distinguish |
| | peninsula | immigration | political, religious, and economic ideas and interests | | Northwest passage | | diversity |
| | physical environment | impact and economic hardship of war | powers of federal, state, local governments | | Protestant Reformation | | encroachment |
| | physical geography | internal migration | President | | | | evaluate |
| | physical map | inventions | representative assemblies | | silk route | | examine |
| | plateau | Lewis and Clark | representative democracy | | Sparta | | function |
| | political map | Loyalist | role of citizens | | trade | | goals |
| | population | massacres | rule of law | | | | identify |
| | population density | Mexican-American War | Senate | | | | if - then |
| | prime meridian | migration | sovereign American Indian tribes | | | | impact |

| Historical & Social Sciences Analysis | Geography | U.S. History | Government | Civic Education | World History | Economy | General Academic |
|---|---|---|---|---|---|---|---|
| | regional | military battles | state government | | | | influence |
| | relief map | nomadic nations of the Great Plains | Supreme Court | | | | interpret |
| | resources | original 13 colonies | three branches of government | | | | justify |
| | savannas | overland trails | tribal council | | | | negotiation |
| South Pole | South Pole | Parliament | unified nation | | | | obstacles |
| | state capital | Patriot | U.S. Capitol | | | | opinion |
| | transportation | pre-Columbian settlements | | | | | outcome |
| | Tropic of Cancer | proponents and opponents of slavery | | | | | permanent |
| | Tropic of Capricorn | protests | | | | | political |
| | valleys | Pueblo people | | | | | prior to |
| | vegetation | religious beliefs | | | | | quantity |
| | wildlife | religious traditions | | | | | resemble |
| | | reservation | | | | | role |
| | | resistance of Indian nations | | | | | sequential order |
| | | routes of early explorers | | | | | significance |
| | | settlement | | | | | similarity |
| | | slavery | | | | | social |
| | | states and territories | | | | | summarize |
| | | state's rights | | | | | temporary |
| | | systems of government | | | | | |

(continued)

Grade Band: 3–5 (builds on K–2 Academic Vocabulary)  (continued)

| Historical & Social Sciences Analysis | Geography | U.S. History | Government | Civic Education | World History | Economy | General Academic |
|---|---|---|---|---|---|---|---|
| | | territory | | | | | |
| | | Tory | | | | | |
| | | Trail of Tears | | | | | |
| | | Treaty of Paris | | | | | |
| | | tribal constitutions | | | | | |
| | | Underground Railroad | | | | | |
| | | Vietnam War | | | | | |
| | | woodland peoples | | | | | |
| | | World War I | | | | | |
| | | World War II | | | | | |

*Note:* In many states, the grade 4 curriculum focuses on individual state histories. Academic vocabulary for these specific curricula are not included here.

These examples of academic vocabulary are not all inclusive. Individual names of countries, leaders, and other historical figures may not be included.

Academic Social Studies and History Vocabulary Based on *Sample State Standards*
Grade Band: 6–8 (builds on K–5 Academic Vocabulary)

| Historical & Social Sciences Analysis | Geography | U.S. History | Government | Civic Education | World History | Economics | General Academic |
|---|---|---|---|---|---|---|---|
| author's perspectives | boundaries constituting the North and South | abolition of slavery | checks and balances | authority | agricultural revolution | agrarian economy | action |
| correlation in historical events | cartography | agricultural and industrial development | citizenship | civic duty | Alexander the Great | banking | advantage |
| credibility of primary and secondary sources | climates of world regions | amendments to the Constitution | democratic forms of government | civil disobedience | archeological studies | business expansion | alternative |
| disintegration of empires | development of city-states | American constitutional democracy | democratic practices | constraints | Aztec, Mayan and Incan empires | capitalism | approach |
| distinguish essential from incidental | emergence | American political institutions | dictatorship | discrimination | beliefs and practices of Brahmanism | child labor | assess |
| distinguish fact from opinion | encounter | American Revolution | elected officials | free press | beliefs of Judaism | common market | attribute |
| distinguish relevant from irrelevant | Eurasian land mass | Articles of Confederation | federalism | function of elections | bubonic plague | contracts | challenge |
| draw sound conclusions | global threats | Bill of Rights | feudalism | interest groups | Buddha | cotton-producing states | circumstances |
| economic and political issues | major river systems | black Americans | foundation of political order | law-making process | Byzantine Empire | credit | cite |
| frame questions | Meso-American and Andean civilizations | changing boundaries of the United States | government of the Roman Republic | political parties | capitalism | depression | consequences |
| growth of economic systems | Niger River | civic republicanism | legal | political process | caste system | economic problems | consideration |
| historical continuity | physical features | Civil War | oligarchy |  | Catholic Church | industrialization | contrary to |
| historical migration of people | topography | classical liberal principles | policy |  | civilizations of Mesopotamia, Egypt, and Kush | interstate commerce | criteria |
| historical narratives | transfer | Compromise of 1850 | principles |  | class structures | labor movement | detect |
| interpretations of history | transformation | conflicting interpretations of state and federal authority | security |  | Confucius | land grants | differentiate |

*(continued)*

Grade Band: 6–8 (builds on K–5 Academic Vocabulary) (continued)

| Historical & Social Sciences Analysis | Geography | U.S. History | Government | Civic Education | World History | Economics | General Academic |
|---|---|---|---|---|---|---|---|
| long and short-term causal relations | urbanization | constitutional amendment | self-government | | Constantine | market economy | disadvantage |
| physical and cultural features | vegetative zones | Constitutional Convention | tyranny | | cottage industry | overland trade | distinguish |
| role of chance, oversight, and error in history | voyages of discovery | domestic resistance movements | veto power | | Crusades | social and economic patterns | domination |
| sources | waterways | dual sovereignty | | | domestication of plants and animals | strikes and protests | dynamic |
| verifiable and unverifiable information | | economic incentives | | | economic surplus | subsidies | established |
| | | Emancipation Proclamation | | | Egyptian art and architecture | surplus | evidence |
| | | emergence of two political party systems | | | Egyptian trade | tariffs | except |
| | | federal Indian policy | | | emergence of cities | | excerpt |
| | | federalism | | | English Bill of Rights | | expansion |
| | | Federalist Papers | | | Enlightenment | | external |
| | | free Blacks | | | evolution of language | | factors |
| | | free public education | | | geographic, political, economic, religious, and social structures | | however |
| | | Freedmen's Bureau | | | Greek mythology | | impose |
| | | Gettysburg Address | | | Hammurabi's Code | | in addition |
| | | Great Awakening | | | Han Dynasty | | in conclusion |

| Historical & Social Sciences Analysis | Geography | U.S. History | Government | Civic Education | World History | Economics | General Academic |
|---|---|---|---|---|---|---|---|
| | | industrialization | | | human modifications of the physical environment | | innovation |
| | | integration | | | intellectual, linguistic, religious and philosophical influences | | internal |
| | | "Jim Crow" laws | | | Islamic scholarship | | isolation |
| | | land-grant system | | | Japanese Buddhism | | link |
| | | majority rule | | | Julius Caesar | | major |
| | | Manifest Destiny | | | Magna Carta | | minor |
| | | Mayflower Compact | | | medieval | | neutral |
| | | Mexican–American War | | | Mediterranean | | occurrence |
| | | Missouri Compromise | | | mercantilism | | oppose |
| | | nationalism | | | Meso–American achievements | | outline |
| | | Northwest Ordinance | | | Middle Ages | | participation |
| | | pioneer women | | | missionaries | | practical |
| | | policy of Indian removal | | | monotheistic religion | | reject |
| | | Populism | | | moral and ethical traditions | | relevant |
| | | racial segregation | | | Nile Valley | | response |
| | | Reconstruction | | | origins of Christianity | | stable |
| | | religious freedom | | | Paleolithic era | | support |
| | | religious persecution | | | Persian and Peloponnesian Wars | | tension |

*(continued)*

Grade Band: 6–8 (builds on K–5 Academic Vocabulary) (continued)

| Historical & Social Sciences Analysis | Geography | U.S. History | Government | Civic Education | World History | Economics | General Academic |
|---|---|---|---|---|---|---|---|
| | | rights | | | Persian Empire | | therefore |
| | | separate but equal | | | polytheistic religion | | trend |
| | | separation of powers | | | Qin Dynasty | | unless |
| | | significance of famous speeches | | | Queen Hatshepsut | | |
| | | slavery | | | Ramses the Great | | |
| | | state constitutions | | | regional commerce | | |
| | | States' Rights Doctrine | | | religious beliefs | | |
| | | suffrage movement | | | Renaissance | | |
| | | technological developments | | | rise of military society | | |
| | | territorial acquisitions | | | Roman Republic | | |
| | | Texas War for Independence | | | scientific method | | |
| | | transcendentalism and individualism | | | Scientific Revolution | | |
| | | Underground Railroad | | | social and political order | | |
| | | War of 1812 | | | trans-Saharan caravan trade | | |
| | | wave of immigration | | | values, social customs, and traditions | | |
| | | westward expansion | | | warfare | | |
| | | | | | Western Civilization | | |

*Academic Social Studies and History Vocabulary Based on Sample State Standards*
*Grade Band: 9–12 (builds on K–8 Academic Vocabulary)*

| Historical & Social Sciences Analysis | Geography | U.S. History | Government | Civic Education | World History | Economics | General Academic |
|---|---|---|---|---|---|---|---|
| analyze authors' use of evidence | border disputes | atomic bomb | advise and consent | campaign advertising | Allied Powers | basic economic indicators | adjustment |
| analyze changes | climate change | Bay of Pigs | bipartisanship | civil liberties | anthropology | blue collar | analogy |
| analyze different political systems across time | ecological tourism | Civil Rights movement | constitutional issues | election campaigns | archaeology | collective bargaining | contemporary |
| analyze issues and consequences of alternative actions | conservation | Berlin blockade | communism | due process | apartheid | bonds | association |
| analyze legislation and court cases | deforestation | changing roles of women in society | constitutional amendments | economic rights | appeasement | cartels | complexity |
| construct and test hypotheses | encroachment | constitutional crisis | electoral college | free speech | Axis Powers | corporate mergers | contributes to |
| distinguish between sound generalizations and misleading oversimplifications | global warming | Cuban Missile Crisis | executive order | freedom of assembly | Berlin Wall | cost-benefit analyses | crisis |
| distinguish valid arguments from fallacious arguments | land trusts | domestic policy speeches | fascism | freedom of religion | Cold War | domestic and international competition | cumulative |
| employ information from primary and secondary sources | natural resource management | emergence of capitalism | filibuster | fundamental values and principles of civil society | Communist Party | economic principles | derive |
| evaluate consequences of past events and decisions | reforestation | Enlightenment | foreign policy | individual's legal obligations | Cultural Revolution | effects of free trade | framework |
| evaluate major debates among historians | sea level rise | federal versus state authority | formation of public policy | lobbyists | diplomacy | effects of technological developments on the economy | fraudulent |
| geopolitical, cultural, military, and economic significance | shifting geographic and political borders | Federalist Papers | free and responsible press | obligations of civic-mindedness | economic and military power shifts | emerging economies | friction |
| human costs of the war | underdeveloped countries | Harlem Renaissance | governmental agencies | political process | espionage | exchange rates | furthermore |

*(continued)*

Grade Band: 9–12 (builds on K–8 Academic Vocabulary) (continued)

| Historical & Social Sciences Analysis | Geography | U.S. History | Government | Civic Education | World History | Economics | General Academic |
|---|---|---|---|---|---|---|---|
| identify bias and prejudice in historical interpretations | renewable and nonrenewable natural resources | Hiroshima and Nagasaki | landmark U.S. Supreme Court decisions | polling | European Union | federal budget | generalization |
| information, technological, and communications revolutions | | Industrial Revolution | majority rule | primaries | excavations | Federal Reserve | implication |
| interpret past events in terms of present-day norms and values | | industrialization | nongovernmental agencies | process of naturalization | feudalism | fiscal | inconsistent |
| methods of research | | International Declaration of Human Rights | opposition | reciprocity between rights and obligations | fossils | fluctuation | inference |
| nation-building | | Korean War | organization and jurisdictions of federal, state, and local courts | registered voter | French Revolution | foreign exchange | justify |
| New Imperialism | | Latin American policies | Parliamentary system | religious diversity | genocide | functions of the financial markets | moreover |
| nonintervention | | Marshall Plan | partisan | voting rights | Greco-Roman views | gains in consumption and production efficiency from trade | negotiations |
| patterns of domestic and international migration | | mass production | pocket veto | | Holocaust | global economy | nevertheless |
| perceptions | | McCarthyism | political cartoon | | Humanism | Great Depression | options |
| social change | | media influence | political systems in contemporary society | | Inquisition | income gap | paradigm |
| | | NATO | processes of lawmaking | | Iron Curtain | investment | perspective |
| | | nuclear powers | referendum | | Judeo-Christian views | issues of international trade | retrospective |

| Historical & Social Sciences Analysis | Geography | U.S. History | Government | Civic Education | World History | Economics | General Academic |
|---|---|---|---|---|---|---|---|
| | | Open Door policy | regulatory committees | | League of Nations | labor | resolve |
| | | Populism | roles of broadcast, print, and electronic media | | Marshall Plan | labor market | series |
| | | Progressive movement | scope of presidential power | | Nazism | marginal benefit | skeptical |
| | | relations between the United States and Mexico | Senate confirmation | | Organization of American States | market economy | stabilize |
| | | religious intolerance | totalitarian governments | | Russian Revolution | monetary and nonmonetary incentives | symbolize |
| | | religious liberty | | | samurai | monetary issues | synthesis |
| | | Romanticism | | | shogun | national debt | uncertainty |
| | | rural to urban migration | | | socialism | New Deal economic policies | verify |
| | | scientific and technological changes | | | Soviet Union | opportunity cost | |
| | | secession | | | Truman Doctrine | partnership | |
| | | Social Darwinism | | | United Nations | postindustrial economy | |
| | | Social Democracy | | | Western political ideas of the rule of law | price controls | |
| | | Space Age | | | Western political thought | profit | |
| | | Spanish–American War | | | World Bank | recession | |
| | | Super Powers | | | World Court | recovery | |

(continued)

Grade Band: 9–12 (builds on K–8 Academic Vocabulary) (continued)

| Historical & Social Sciences Analysis | Geography | U.S. History | Government | Civic Education | World History | Economics | General Academic |
|---|---|---|---|---|---|---|---|
| | | technological change | | | | redistribution of wealth | |
| | | terrorism | | | | revenue streams | |
| | | The Great Society | | | | scarcity | |
| | | Truman Doctrine | | | | service sector | |
| | | unalienable natural rights | | | | sources of revenue | |
| | | U.S. Middle East policy | | | | Social Security | |
| | | Utopianism | | | | stock market | |
| | | Voting Rights Act | | | | stocks | |
| | | wartime strategy | | | | taxation | |
| | | Watergate scandal | | | | the law of supply and demand | |
| | | Women's liberation | | | | trade restrictions | |
| | | | | | | trusts | |
| | | | | | | unemployment | |
| | | | | | | Wall Street | |
| | | | | | | welfare | |
| | | | | | | white collar | |
| | | | | | | working class | |

*Note*: Some states focus on individual state histories in one of the middle grades. Academic vocabulary for these specific curricula are not included here.

These examples of academic vocabulary are not intended to be all-inclusive. Many individual names of countries, leaders, and other historical figures are not included.

# appendix c: List of Activities and Techniques by Social Science Subject Area and Grade Level

The activities and techniques in Chapters 2 and 3 can be used across the social science disciplines and across multiple grade levels. This list of the activities and techniques shows the featured classroom applications in those chapters, organized by social science subject area and grade level.

**Lesson Preparation**

| | | |
|---|---|---|
| Building Language Objectives from Content Objectives | Geography | Grade 6 |
| Differentiating Sentence Starters | U.S. History | Grade 8 |

**Building Background**

| | | |
|---|---|---|
| Concrete Personal Experiences | U.S. History | Grade 5 |
| Post a Connection | Social Studies | Grade 2 |
| Oh Yesterday + Year! | U.S. History | Grade 7 |
| Predict Definitions | VA History | Grade 4 |
| Vocabulary Scan | World History | Grade 10 |

**Comprehensible Input**

| | | |
|---|---|---|
| Prop Box Improv | TX History | Grade 7 |
| Listen for Information | Social Studies | Grade 1 |
| Move It! | U.S. Government | Grade 9 |

**Strategies**

| | | |
|---|---|---|
| Highlight Key Information | Social Studies | Grade 5 |
| Cut and Match Answers | Social Studies | Grade 3 |
| Expert/Novice | World History | Grade 10 |

**Interaction**

| | | |
|---|---|---|
| Structured Conversations | Social Studies | Grade 2 |
| Learning Styles Debate | U.S. History | Grade 8 |
| You Are There | Economics | Grade 12 |

**Practice & Application**

| | | |
|---|---|---|
| Reader's Theater | Social Studies | Grade 6 |
| Living Diorama | Social Studies | Kindergarten |
| Partner Listening Dictation | U.S. Government | Grade 11 |
| Go Graphic – One Step Further | Geography | Grade 9 |

**Lesson Delivery**

| | | |
|---|---|---|
| Group Response with a Whiteboard | World History | Grade 11 |
| Chunk and Chew Review | Ancient Civilizations | Grade 7 |
| Stand Up/Sit Down | U.S. Government | Grade 12 |

**Review & Assessment**

| | | |
|---|---|---|
| Oral Number 1-3 for Self-Assessment | Social Studies | Grade 1 |
| Self-Assessment Rubrics | Social Studies | Grade 3 |
| Number Wheels | Civics | Grade 12 |
| Whip Around, Pass Option | Social Studies | Kindergarten |
| Numbered Heads Together with Movement | Social Studies | Grade 4 |
| Differentiated Tickets Out | U.S. History | Grade 11 |

# appendix d: Blackline Masters

BLM 1      My Personal Timeline     188

BLM 2      My Personal Timeline Sentences     189

BLM 3      My Life in the Past and Present (Venn Diagram)     190

BLM 4      My Life in the Past and Present Activity Sheet     191

BLM 5      How Can We Tell That This Is from the Past?     192

BLM 6      Is It Past or Present? (images)     193

BLM 7      Is It Past or Present? (chart)     195

BLM 8      Is It Past or Present? Bingo     198

BLM 9      Instructions for Making a Flipbook     199

BLM 10    Can You Label the World Map?     200

BLM 11    What's My Hemisphere? (short answer)     201

BLM 12    What's My Hemisphere? (multiple choice)     202

BLM 13    Reader's Theater Script: Maps and Globes     203

BLM 14    Reader's Theater Rubric: Maps and Globes     204

BLM 15    Understanding Maps and Globes (paragraph)     205

BLM 16    Understanding Maps and Globes (word bank)     206

BLM 17    Vocabulary Word and Definition Cards     207

BLM 18    Anticipation/Reaction Guide: The Effects of the French and Indian War     211

BLM 19    British versus Colonist Points of View     212

BLM 20    Truman Doctrine Speech—Adapted Text     213

BLM 21    Truman Doctrine Speech—Original Text     214

BLM 22    Argumentation Chart for Truman Doctrine     218

BLM 23    NATO Pro–Con Chart     219

## My Personal Timeline (model for poster)

On a large sheet of paper, chart paper, or poster board, draw a timeline similar to this on which the teacher and students will arrange their photographs in chronological order.

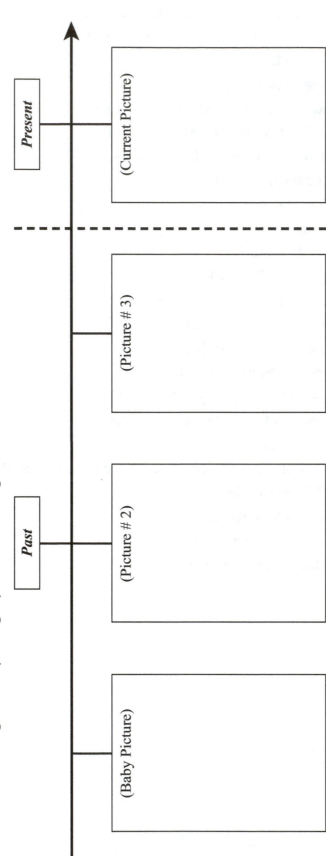

# My Personal Timeline Sentences

**Complete a sentence for each picture.**

When I was a baby, I _____

_____

_____.

When I was _____, I _____

_____

_____.

When I was _____, I _____

_____

_____.

Now I am _____, and I _____

_____

_____.

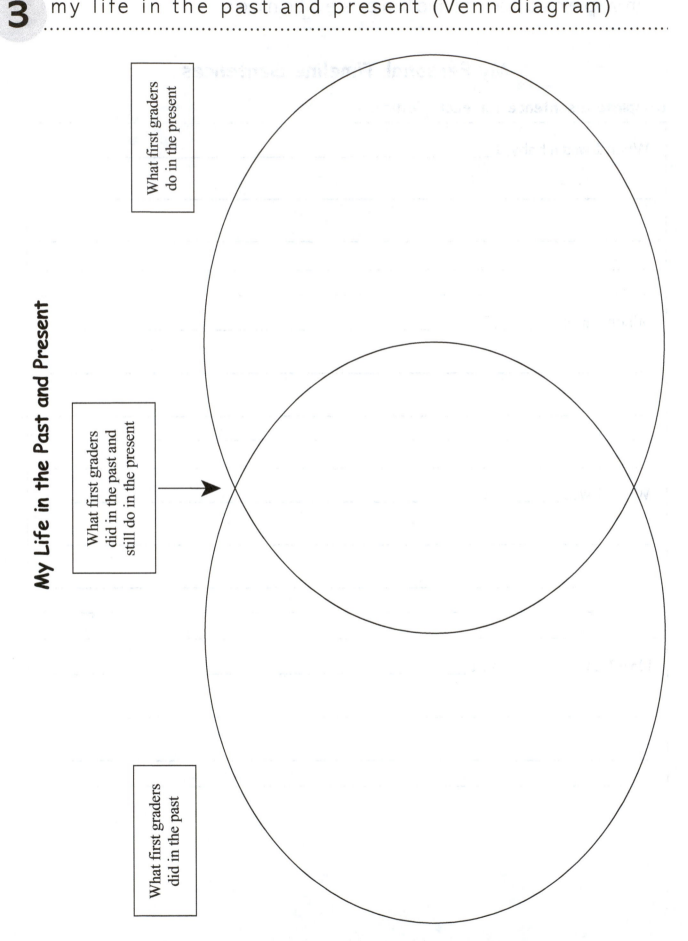

**My Life in the Past and Present**

What first graders do in the present

What first graders did in the past and still do in the present

What first graders did in the past

## My Life in the Past and Present

**Teacher Instructions:** Display this activity sheet, and read the titles with students. Be sure they understand the actions depicted. Distribute a set of cut-up squares to each group of students. Have groups categorize actions in a large Venn diagram: what students did in the past, what they do in the present, and what actions are the same in both time periods. There are three for each category (see Unit Guide in Chapter 5).

| play | drink from a glass | use the toilet |
|---|---|---|
| walk | listen to stories | crawl |
| drink from the bottle | use diapers | sleep |

## How Can We Tell That This Is From The Past?

*Source:* Free download from www.colonialwilliamsburg.org, The Official Site of Colonial Williamsburg.

Specific photo link: www.colonialwilliamsburg.org/media/downloads/wallpaper/800/dancers.jpg

## Is it Past or Present?

**Instructions to Teacher:** Cut apart the pictures on BLM 6. If desired, laminate the sheets before cutting. Give a complete set of pictures to each pair of students. Pairs will classify pictures as Past or Present in the appropriate category on BLM 7.

## 6 is it past or present? (images)

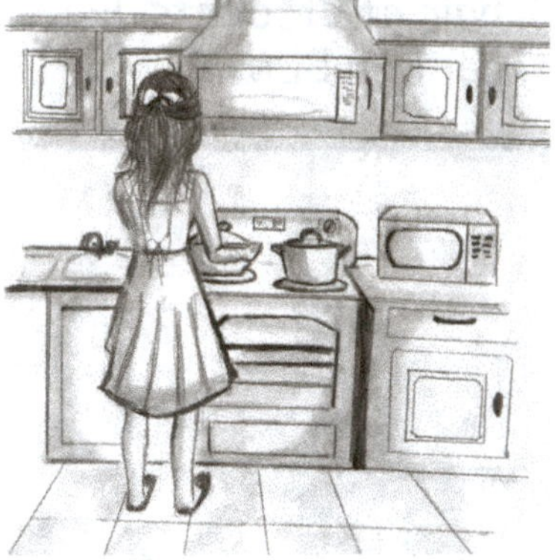

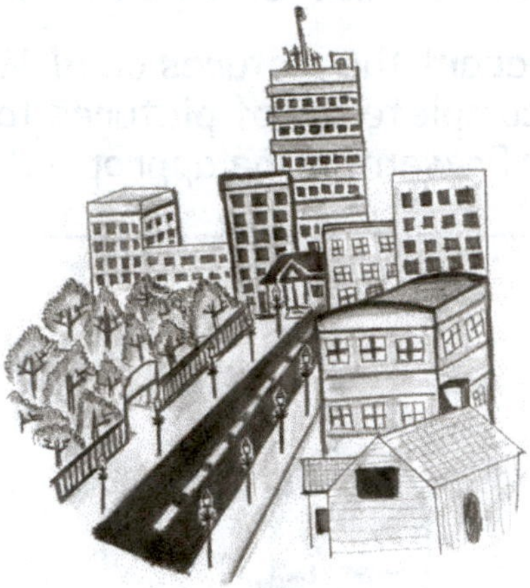

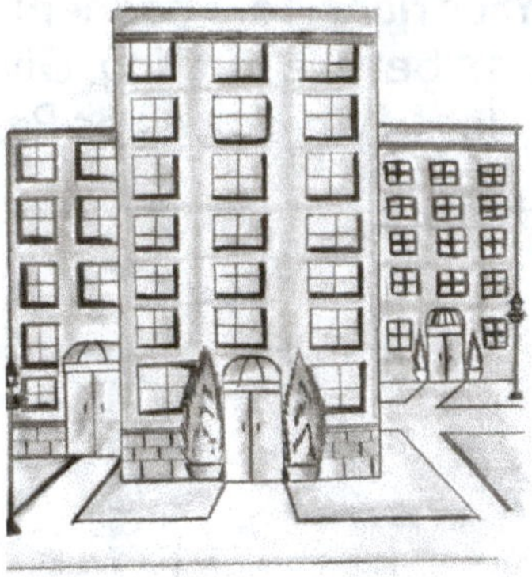

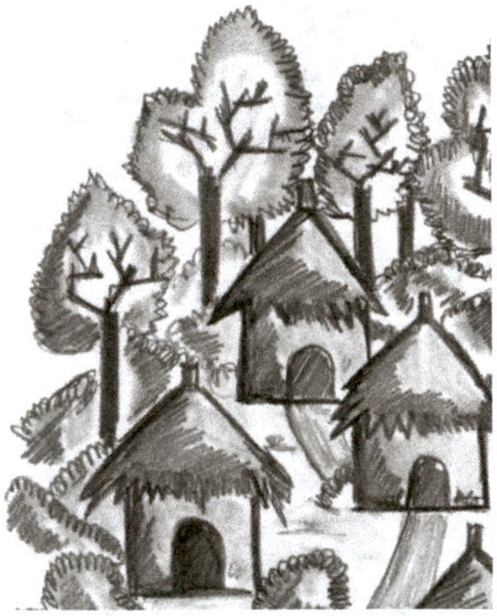

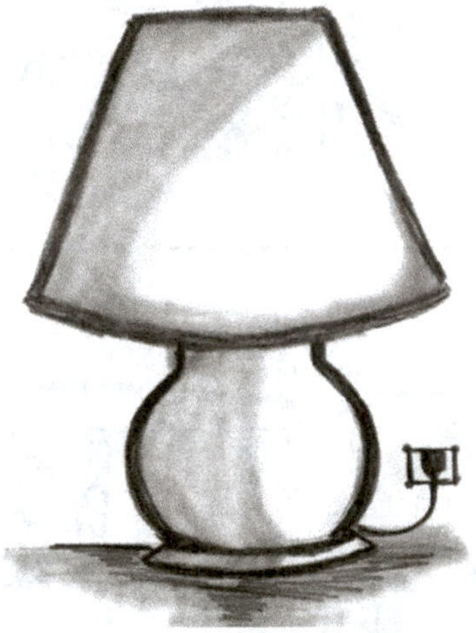

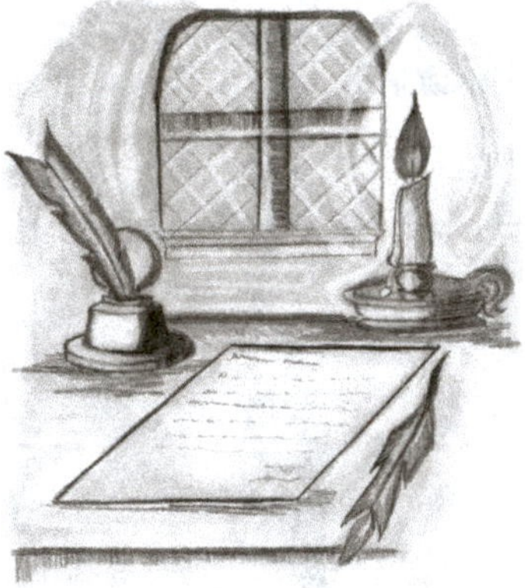

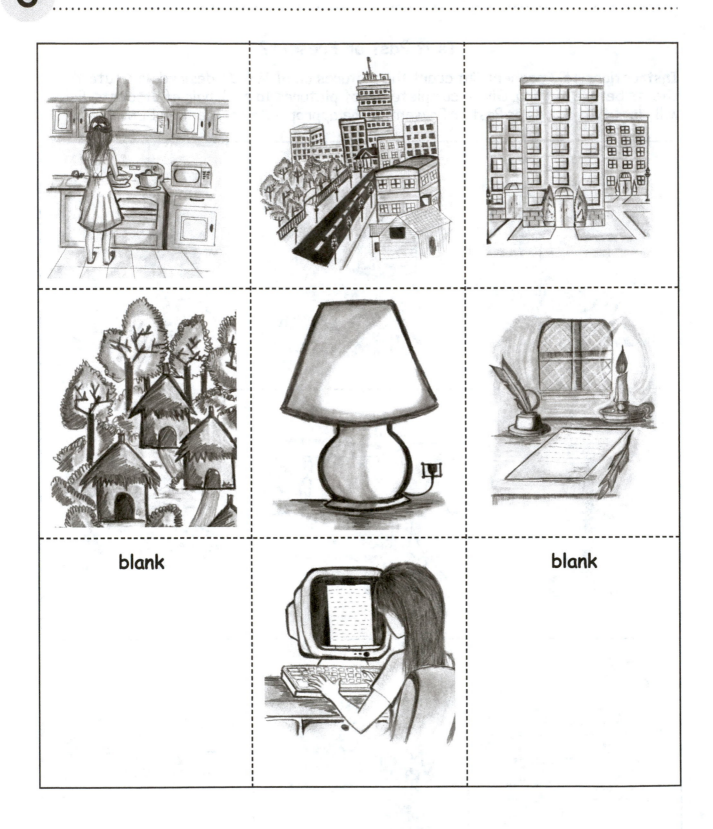

**blank**

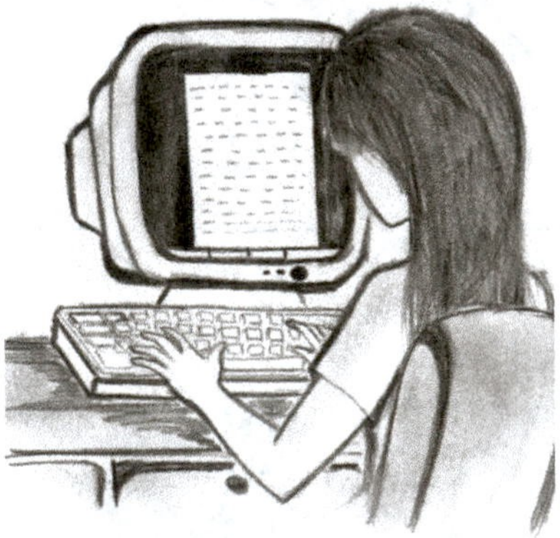

**blank**

## Is it Past or Present?

**Teacher Instructions:** Staple the three pages together. Have students work with partners to classify their pictures as "Past" or "Present" in the appropriate categories. They will explain their choices to their partners.

|  | Past | Present |
|---|---|---|
| Getting food |  |  |
| Cooking food |  |  |
| Getting clothes |  |  |

|  | Past | Present |
|---|---|---|
| Transportation |  |  |
| Writing a letter |  |  |
| Light |  |  |

| | Past | Present |
|---|---|---|
| Homes | | |
| Communities | | |

## Is it Past or Present? Bingo

Each student pair will select nine of their pictures and place one in each square. Refer to the Unit Guide in Chapter 5 for instructions.

## Instructions for Making a Flipbook

1. Place one sheet of 8$\frac{1}{2}$" x 11" paper or 9" x 12" construction paper on top of another sheet, with one sheet about an inch higher than the other.

2. Fold over, leaving about an inch for tabs.

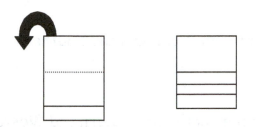

3. Fold in half vertically to create two columns (for "Past" and "Present").

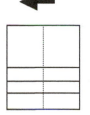

4. Fold over $\frac{1}{4}$" at the crease to create a strong edge, and staple along the edge.

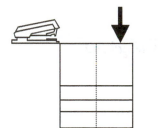

5. On the cover page, have students write the title "Past" on the left side and "Present" on the right side. They should choose three aspects of daily life to compare, or the teacher will select, if appropriate. Students will write a different aspect on each tab (e.g., Transportation, Homes, Food, Clothes, Community, or Family Life). Students will draw an illustration on the page corresponding to that tab to show an example from the past on one side and the present on the other side.

## Can You Label the World Map?

*Test your prior knowledge! Work with a partner to read the definitions. See how many of these you can find on the world map.*

1. hemisphere – half of the Earth

2. imaginary lines – lines that cannot be seen

3. Equator – imaginary line that divides the Earth into Northern and Southern Hemispheres

4. Prime Meridian – imaginary line that divides the Earth into Eastern and Western Hemispheres

5. Northern Hemisphere – area of the Earth north of the Equator

6. Southern Hemisphere – area of the Earth south of the Equator

7. Eastern Hemisphere – area of the Earth east of the Prime Meridian

8. Western Hemisphere – area of the Earth west of the Prime Meridian

9. parallel – lines that never intersect

10. lines of latitude – imaginary parallel lines that run east and west

11. lines of longitude – imaginary lines that run from the North Pole to the South Pole

**What's My Hemisphere?**

*Use a world map to answer these questions. Write complete sentences.*

1. Which continents does the Equator pass through?

2. Which continents does the Prime Meridian pass through?

3. Which ocean is located only in the Northern Hemisphere?

4. Which two oceans are located in all four hemispheres?

5. Which continents are in the Northern Hemisphere?

6. Which continents are in the Southern Hemisphere?

7. Which continents are in the Western Hemisphere?

8. Which continents are in the Eastern Hemisphere?

9. Which hemisphere would you prefer to live in? Why?

## What's My Hemisphere?

Use a world map to answer these questions. Circle the correct answers.

1. Which three continents does the Equator pass through?
   South America - North America - Africa - Asia

2. Which three continents does the Prime Meridian pass through?
   Europe - Africa - South America - Antarctica

3. Which ocean is located only in the Northern Hemisphere?
   Atlantic - Arctic

4. Which two oceans are located in all four hemispheres?
   Atlantic - Pacific - Indian - Arctic

5. Which five continents are in the Northern Hemisphere?
   North America – South America - Europe - Asia
   Africa - Australia - Antarctica

6. Which five continents are in the Southern Hemisphere?
   North America - South America - Europe - Asia
   Africa - Australia - Antarctica

7. Which four continents are in the Western Hemisphere?
   North America - South America - Europe - Asia
   Africa - Australia - Antarctica

8. Which five continents are in the Eastern Hemisphere?
   North America - South America - Europe - Asia
   Africa - Australia - Antarctica

9. Which hemisphere would you prefer to live in? Why?

## Reader's Theater Script: Maps and Globes

> **Roles:** Equator, Prime Meridian, Northern Hemisphere, Southern Hemisphere, Eastern Hemisphere, Western Hemisphere

**All:** We are important parts of maps and globes. We help you identify locations.

**Equator:** I'm the Equator. I circle the globe and divide the Earth into the Northern and Southern Hemispheres.

**Prime Meridian:** I'm the Prime Meridian. I run from the North Pole to the South Pole. I divide the Earth into the Eastern and Western Hemispheres.

**Equator and Prime Meridian:** We are imaginary lines. You can't really see us.

**Northern Hemisphere:** I'm the Northern Hemisphere. I'm the half of the Earth located north of the Equator. I have five continents.

**Southern Hemisphere:** I'm the Southern Hemisphere. I'm the half of the Earth located south of the Equator. I also have five continents.

**Northern and Southern Hemispheres:** We share South America, Africa, and Asia.

**Eastern Hemisphere:** I'm the Eastern Hemisphere. I'm the half of the Earth located east of the Prime Meridian. I have five continents.

**Western Hemisphere:** I'm the Western Hemisphere. I'm the half of the Earth located west of the Prime Meridian. I also have five continents.

**Eastern and Western Hemispheres:** We share Europe, Africa, and Antarctica.

**All:** We are important parts of maps and globes. We help you identify locations!

*Source:* © Robin Liten-Tejada, Arlington Public Schools, 2009. Used with permission.

## Reader's Theater: Maps and Globes Scoring Rubric

*Write the name of each student performing the same role as you are in the reader's theater. You will score only that person as you listen to each group's presentation.*

*Use the following points:*

*3 = excellent*
*2 = good*
*1 = tried but needs lots more practice*
*0 = not at all*

Role: _____

| Group | Student name | Correct pronunciation | Fluent speech | Energetic presentation | Total |
|---|---|---|---|---|---|
| 1 | | | | | |
| 2 | | | | | |
| 3 | | | | | |
| 4 | | | | | |

Comments:

*Source:* © Robin Liten-Tejada, Arlington Public Schools, 2009. Used with permission.

## Understanding Maps and Globes

*Fill in the details to complete this paragraph about maps and globes. Then copy it on a sheet of paper. Read your paragraph aloud several times to practice fluency. Exchange your paragraph with a partner to proofread.*

Maps and globes have imaginary lines that help us find our location. The Equator _____

_____. The Prime Meridian _____.

(What would you like to say about the hemispheres?) _____

_____

Knowing about the imaginary lines and the hemispheres helps us find our place on Earth.

## Understanding Maps and Globes

*Choose the correct words to complete this paragraph about maps and globes. Use each word one time. Then copy the paragraph on a sheet of paper. Read your paragraph aloud several times to practice fluency. Exchange your paragraph with a partner to proofread.*

**Vocabulary:** east - Meridian - imaginary - Prime - southern - lines - Equator - hemispheres - western - northern - South

Maps and globes have _____ lines that help us find our location.

The _____ divides the Earth into the Northern and _____

Hemispheres. The Equator runs from _____ to west around the middle of the

Earth. The Prime _____ divides the Earth into the Eastern and

_____ Hemispheres. The _____ Meridian begins and ends at the

North and _____ Poles. There are four _____ all together. The

United States is in the _____ and Western hemispheres. Knowing

about the imaginary _____ and the hemispheres helps us find our place

on the Earth.

**Vocabulary Word and Definition Cards**

| | |
|---|---|
| hemisphere | half of the Earth |
| imaginary lines | lines that cannot be seen |
| Equator | imaginary line that divides the Earth into Northern and Southern Hemispheres |
| Prime Meridian | imaginary line that divides the Earth into Eastern and Western Hemispheres |

| Northern Hemisphere | area of the Earth north of the Equator |
| Southern Hemisphere | area of the Earth south of the Equator |
| Eastern Hemisphere | area of the Earth east of the Prime Meridian |
| Western Hemisphere | area of the Earth west of the Prime Meridian |

| | |
|---|---|
| parallel | lines that never intersect |
| lines of latitude | imaginary lines that run east and west parallel to the Equator |
| lines of longitude | imaginary lines that run from the North Pole to the South Pole |
| seven continents | North America South America Europe Africa Asia Australia Antarctica |

| | |
|---|---|
| five oceans | Atlantic<br>Pacific<br>Indian<br>Arctic<br>Southern |
| The cardinal directions | north<br>south<br>east<br>west |
| The United States is located in these two hemispheres. | Northern Hemisphere<br><br>Western Hemisphere |
| 39° N latitude, 77° W longitude | The location of Washington DC, the capital of the United States. |

## Anticipation/Reaction Guide
## The Effects of the French and Indian War

Identify each of the following statements as true or false. Below each statement, write the reason you believe it to be true or false.

T  F  1.  The French and Indian War was fought between the French and Native Americans.

T  F  2.  The British and French pursuit of mercantilist foreign policies was the main cause of the French and Indian War.

T  F  3.  The French and Indian War is also called the Eight Years War.

T  F  4.  After the French and Indian War, the British lowered taxes on the colonists because Parliament was grateful that they were willing to defend the empire.

T  F  5.  After the Treaty of Paris was signed in 1763, the British ordered the colonists not to move west of the Appalachian Mountains, because they didn't want to have any more conflicts with the Native American tribes.

T  F  6.  The British were able to pay off their debt with the revenue they raised as a result of winning the war.

T  F  7.  The French and Indian War showed the colonists that they could work together well as a group.

**British versus Colonist Points of View**

| The British Parliament believed the colonists should be loyal and grateful because . . . | The colonists believed the British Parliament did not respect their rights as English subjects because . . . |
| --- | --- |
|  |  |

## Truman Doctrine Speech—Adapted Text

### PRESIDENT HARRY S. TRUMAN'S ADDRESS BEFORE A JOINT SESSION OF CONGRESS, MARCH 12, 1947
### (Adapted by John Seidlitz)

Mr. President, Mr. Speaker, Members of the Congress of the United States:

The gravity of the situation which confronts the world today necessitates my appearance before a joint session of the Congress. The foreign policy and the national security of this country are involved. The peoples of a number of countries of the world have recently had totalitarian regimes forced on them against their will.

The United States has received from the Greek Government an urgent appeal for financial and economic assistance.

The future of Turkey as an independent and economically sound state is clearly no less important to the freedom-loving peoples of the world than the future of Greece.

I am fully aware of the broad implications involved if the United States extends assistance to Greece and Turkey, and I shall discuss these implications with you at this time.

One of the primary objectives of the foreign policy of the United States is the creation of conditions in which we and other nations will be able to work out a way of life free from coercion.

This is a serious course upon which we embark.

I would not recommend it except that the alternative is much more serious.

The seeds of totalitarian regimes are nurtured by misery and want. They spread and grow in the evil soil of poverty and strife. They reach their full growth when the hope of a people for a better life has died. We must keep that hope alive.

The free peoples of the world look to us for support in maintaining their freedoms.

If we falter in our leadership, we may endanger the peace of the world—and we shall surely endanger the welfare of our own nation.

Great responsibilities have been placed upon us by the swift movement of events.

I am confident that the Congress will face these responsibilities squarely.

# Truman Doctrine Speech—Original Text

## PRESIDENT HARRY S. TRUMAN'S ADDRESS BEFORE A JOINT SESSION OF CONGRESS, MARCH 12, 1947[1]

Mr. President, Mr. Speaker, Members of the Congress of the United States:

The gravity of the situation which confronts the world today necessitates my appearance before a joint session of the Congress. The foreign policy and the national security of this country are involved.

One aspect of the present situation, which I wish to present to you at this time for your consideration and decision, concerns Greece and Turkey.

The United States has received from the Greek Government an urgent appeal for financial and economic assistance. Preliminary reports from the American Economic Mission now in Greece and reports from the American Ambassador in Greece corroborate the statement of the Greek Government that assistance is imperative if Greece is to survive as a free nation.

I do not believe that the American people and the Congress wish to turn a deaf ear to the appeal of the Greek Government.

When forces of liberation entered Greece they found that the retreating Germans had destroyed virtually all the railways, roads, port facilities, communications, and merchant marine. More than a thousand villages had been burned. Eighty-five per cent of the children were tubercular. Livestock, poultry, and draft animals had almost disappeared. Inflation had wiped out practically all savings.

As a result of these tragic conditions, a militant minority, exploiting human want and misery, was able to create political chaos which, until now, has made economic recovery impossible.

The very existence of the Greek state is today threatened by the terrorist activities of several thousand armed men, led by Communists, who defy the government's authority at a number of points, particularly along the northern boundaries. A Commission appointed by the United Nations security Council is at present investigating disturbed conditions in northern Greece and alleged border violations along the frontier between Greece on the one hand and Albania, Bulgaria, and Yugoslavia on the other.

Meanwhile, the Greek Government is unable to cope with the situation. The Greek army is small and poorly equipped. It needs supplies and equipment if it is to restore the authority of the government throughout Greek territory. Greece must have assistance if it is to become a self-supporting and self-respecting democracy.

The United States must supply that assistance. We have already extended to Greece certain types of relief and economic aid but these are inadequate.

There is no other country to which democratic Greece can turn.

---

[1]President Truman's speech to Congress is part of the public record. More information about this speech and the Truman Doctrine can be found at Harry S. Truman Library site (www.trumanlibrary.org) and the National Archives site (www.archives.org).

No other nation is willing and able to provide the necessary support for a democratic Greek government.

The British Government, which has been helping Greece, can give no further financial or economic aid after March 31. Great Britain finds itself under the necessity of reducing or liquidating its commitments in several parts of the world, including Greece.

We have considered how the United Nations might assist in this crisis. But the situation is an urgent one requiring immediate action and the United Nations and its related organizations are not in a position to extend help of the kind that is required.

It is important to note that the Greek Government has asked for our aid in utilizing effectively the financial and other assistance we may give to Greece, and in improving its public administration. It is of the utmost importance that we supervise the use of any funds made available to Greece; in such a manner that each dollar spent will count toward making Greece self-supporting, and will help to build an economy in which a healthy democracy can flourish.

Greece's neighbor, Turkey, also deserves our attention.

The future of Turkey as an independent and economically sound state is clearly no less important to the freedom-loving peoples of the world than the future of Greece. The circumstances in which Turkey finds itself today are considerably different from those of Greece. Turkey has been spared the disasters that have beset Greece. And during the war, the United States and Great Britain furnished Turkey with material aid.

Nevertheless, Turkey now needs our support.

Since the war Turkey has sought financial assistance from Great Britain and the United States for the purpose of effecting that modernization necessary for the maintenance of its national integrity.

That integrity is essential to the preservation of order in the Middle East.

The British government has informed us that, owing to its own difficulties can no longer extend financial or economic aid to Turkey.

As in the case of Greece, if Turkey is to have the assistance it needs, the United States must supply it. We are the only country able to provide that help.

I am fully aware of the broad implications involved if the United States extends assistance to Greece and Turkey, and I shall discuss these implications with you at this time.

One of the primary objectives of the foreign policy of the United States is the creation of conditions in which we and other nations will be able to work out a way of life free from coercion. This was a fundamental issue in the war with Germany and Japan. Our victory was won over countries which sought to impose their will, and their way of life, upon other nations.

To ensure the peaceful development of nations, free from coercion, the United States has taken a leading part in establishing the United Nations, The United Nations is designed to make possible lasting freedom and independence for all its members. We shall not realize our objectives, however, unless we are willing to help free peoples to maintain their free institutions and their national integrity against aggressive movements that seek to impose upon them totalitarian regimes. This is no more than a frank recognition that totalitarian regimes imposed on free peoples, by direct or indirect aggression, undermine the foundations of international peace and hence the security of the United States.

The peoples of a number of countries of the world have recently had totalitarian regimes forced upon them against their will. The Government of the United States has made frequent protests against coercion and intimidation, in violation of the Yalta agreement, in Poland, Rumania, and Bulgaria. I must also state that in a number of other countries there have been similar developments.

At the present moment in world history nearly every nation must choose between alternative ways of life. The choice is too often not a free one.

One way of life is based upon the will of the majority (*democracy*), and is distinguished by free institutions, representative government, free elections, guarantees of individual liberty, freedom of speech and religion, and freedom from political oppression.

The second way of life (*communism*) is based upon the will of a minority forcibly imposed upon the majority. It relies upon terror and oppression, a controlled press and radio; fixed elections, and the suppression of personal freedoms.

I believe that it must be the policy of the United States to support free peoples who are resisting attempted subjugation by armed minorities or by outside pressures.

I believe that we must assist free peoples to work out their own destinies in their own way.

I believe that our help should be primarily through economic and financial aid which is essential to economic stability and orderly political processes.

It is necessary only to glance at a map to realize that the survival and integrity of the Greek nation are of grave importance in a much wider situation. If Greece should fall under the control of an armed minority, the effect upon its neighbor, Turkey, would be immediate and serious. Confusion and disorder might well spread throughout the entire Middle East.

Moreover, the disappearance of Greece as an independent state would have a profound effect upon those countries in Europe whose peoples are struggling against great difficulties to maintain their freedoms and their independence while they repair the damages of war.

Should we fail to aid Greece and Turkey in this fateful hour, the effect will be far reaching to the West as well as to the East.

We must take immediate and resolute action.

I therefore ask the Congress to provide authority for assistance to Greece and Turkey in the amount of $400,000,000 for the period ending June 30, 1948. In requesting these funds, I have taken into consideration the maximum amount of relief assistance which would be furnished to Greece out of the $350,000,000 which I recently requested that the Congress authorize for the prevention of starvation and suffering in countries devastated by the war.

In addition to funds, I ask the Congress to authorize the detail of American civilian and military personnel to Greece and Turkey, at the request of those countries, to assist in the tasks of reconstruction, and for the purpose of supervising the use of such financial and material assistance as may be furnished. I recommend that authority also be provided for the instruction and training of selected Greek and Turkish personnel.

Finally, I ask that the Congress provide authority which will permit the speediest and most effective use, in terms of needed commodities, supplies, and equipment, of such funds as may be authorized.

If further funds, or further authority, should be needed for purposes indicated in this message, I shall not hesitate to bring the situation before the Congress. On this subject the Executive and Legislative branches of the Government must work together.

This is a serious course upon which we embark.

I would not recommend it except that the alternative is much more serious. The United States contributed $341,000,000,000 toward winning World War II. This is an investment in world freedom and world peace.

The assistance that I am recommending for Greece and Turkey amounts to little more than 1 tenth of 1 per cent of this investment. It is only common sense that we should safeguard this investment and make sure that it was not in vain.

The seeds of totalitarian regimes are nurtured by misery and want. They spread and grow in the evil soil of poverty and strife. They reach their full growth when the hope of a people for a better life has died. We must keep that hope alive.

The free peoples of the world look to us for support in maintaining their freedoms.

If we falter in our leadership, we may endanger the peace of the world—and we shall surely endanger the welfare of our own nation.

Great responsibilities have been placed upon us by the swift movement of events.

I am confident that the Congress will face these responsibilities squarely.

**Argumentation Chart for Truman Doctrine**

| Truman believes Congress should . . . | because . . . | He used persuasive words and phrases such as . . . | He might be right because . . . | He might be wrong because . . . |
|---|---|---|---|---|
| | | | | |

## NATO Pro–Con Chart

| Western Europe and the United States must form an alliance because . . . | Western Europe and the United States must not form an alliance because . . . |
| --- | --- |
|  |  |

# references

American Educational Research Association (AERA), American Psychological Association (APA), & National Council on Measurement in Education (NCME). (2000). Position statement of the American Educational Research Association concerning high-stakes testing in pre-K–12 education. *Educational Researcher, 29,* 24–25.

August, D., & Shanahan, T. (Eds.). (2006). *Developing literacy in second-language learners: A report of the National Literacy Panel on Language-Minority Children and Youth.* Mahwah, NJ: Erlbaum.

Aukerman, M. (2007). A culpable CALP: Rethinking the conversational/academic proficiency distinction in early literacy instruction. *The Reading Teacher, 60*(7), 626–635.

Bailey, A. L. (Ed.). (2007). *The language demands of school: Putting academic English to the test.* New Haven, CT: Yale University Press.

Bailey, A., & Butler, F. (2007). A conceptual framework of academic English language for broad application to education. In A. Bailey (Ed.), *The language demands of school: Putting academic English to the test* (pp. 68–102). New Haven, CT: Yale University Press.

Bartolomé, L. I. (1998). *The misteaching of academic discourses: The politics of language in the classroom.* Boulder, CO: Westview Press.

Baumann, J., Jones, L., & Seifert-Kessell, N. (1993). Using think-alouds to enhance children's comprehension monitoring abilities. *The Reading Teacher, 47*(3), 184–193.

Biancarosa, G., & Snow, C. (2004). *Reading next: A vision for action and research in middle and high school literacy.* Report to the Carnegie Corporation of New York. Washington, DC: Alliance for Excellent Education.

Buehl, D. (2009). *Strategies for interactive learning* (3rd ed.). Newark, DE: International Reading Association.

California Department of Education. (2008). Statewide Stanford 9 test results for reading: Number of students tested and percent scoring at or above the 50th percentile ranking. Retrieved April 1, 2009, from http://www.cde.ca.gov/dataquest/.

Castillo, M. (2008). *Reviewing objectives with English language learners.* Presented at SEI Seminar, Phoenix, AZ.

Cazden, C. (1976). How knowledge about language helps the classroom teacher—or does it? A personal account. *The Urban Review, 9,* 74–91.

Cazden, C. (1986). Classroom discourse. In M. D. Wittrock (Ed.), *Handbook of research on teaching* (3rd ed.) (pp. 432–463). New York, NY: Macmillan.

Cazden, C. (2001). *Classroom discourse: The language of teaching and learning* (2nd ed.). Portsmouth, NH: Heinemann.

Center for Applied Linguistics. (2007). *Academic literacy through sheltered instruction for secondary English language learners.* Final Report to the Carnegie Corporation of New York. Washington, DC: Center for Applied Linguistics.

Chamot, A. U., & O'Malley, J. M. (1994). *The CALLA handbook: Implementing the cognitive academic language learning approach.* Reading, MA: Addison-Wesley.

Cloud, N., Genesee, F., & Hamayan, E. (2009). *Literacy instruction for English language learners.* Portsmouth, NH: Heinemann.

Cloud, N., Lakin, J., Leininger, E., & Maxwell, L. (2010). *Teaching adolescent English language learners: Essential strategies for middle and high school.* Philadelphia: Caslon Publishing.

Coffin, C. (1997). Constructing and giving value to the past. In J. R. Martin & F. Christie (Eds.), *Genres and institutions: Social processes in the workplace and school* (pp. 196–230). London: Pinter Publishers.

Collier, V. (1987). Age and rate of acquisition of second language for academic purposes. *TESOL Quarterly, 21*(3), 617–641.

Cosentino de Cohen, C., Deterding, N., & Clewell, B. C. (2005). *Who's left behind? Immigrant children in high and low LEP schools.* Washington, DC: Urban Institute. Retrieved January 2, 2009 at http://www.urban.org/UploadedPDF/411231_whos_left_behind.pdf

Coxhead, A. (2000). A new academic word list. *TESOL Quarterly, 34*(2), 213–238.

Cummins, J. (1979). *Cognitive/academic language proficiency, linguistic interdependence, the optimum age questions, and some other matters.* Working Papers on Bilingualism, No. 19, 121–129. Toronto: Ontario Institute for Studies in Education.

Cummins, J. (2000). *Language, power, and pedagogy: Bilingual children in the crossfire.* Clevedon, UK: Multilingual Matters.

Cummins, J. (2006). How long does it take for an English language learner to become proficient in a second language? In E. Hamayan & R. Freeman (Eds.), *English language learners at school: A guide for administrators* (pp. 59–61). Philadelphia, PA: Caslon Publishing.

Deussen, T., Autio, E., Miller, B., Lockwood, A. T., & Stewart, V. (2008). *What teachers should know about instruction for English language learners.* Portland, OR: Northwest Regional Educational Laboratory.

Dutro, S., & Moran, C. (2003). Rethinking English language instruction: An architectural approach. In G. Garcia (Ed.), *English learners: Reaching the highest level of English literacy* (pp. 227–258). Newark, NJ: International Reading Association.

Echevarria, J. (1995). Interactive reading instruction: A comparison of proximal and distal effects of instructional conversations. *Exceptional Children, 61*(6), 536–552.

Echevarria, J., & Graves, A. (2007). *Sheltered content instruction: Teaching English language learners with diverse abilities* (3rd ed.). Boston, MA: Allyn & Bacon.

Echevarria, J., Richards, C., Canges, R., & Francis, D. (2009). *Using the SIOP® Model to promote the acquisition of language and science concepts.* Submitted for publication.

Echevarria, J., & Short, D. J. (in press). Programs and practices for effective sheltered content instruction. In D. Dolson & L. Burnham-Massey (Eds.), *Improving education for English learners: Research-based approaches.* Sacramento, CA: California Department of Education.

Echevarria, J., Short, D., & Powers, K. (2006). School reform and standards-based education: An instructional model for English language learners. *Journal of Educational Research, 99*(4), 195–211.

Echevarria, J., & Silver, J. (1995). *Instructional conversations: Understanding through discussion.* [Videotape]. National Center for Research on Cultural Diversity and Second Language Learning.

Echevarria, J., Vogt, M.E., & Short, D. J. (2008a). *Making content comprehensible for English learners: The SIOP® Model* (3rd ed.). Boston, MA: Allyn & Bacon.

Echevarria, J., Short, D., & Vogt, M.E. (2008b). *Implementing the SIOP® model through effective professional development and coaching.* Boston, MA: Pearson/Allyn & Bacon.

Echevarria, J., Vogt, M.E., & Short, D. (2010a). *Making content comprehensible for elementary English learners: The SIOP® model.* Boston, MA: Allyn & Bacon.

Echevarria, J., Vogt, M.E., & Short, D. (2010b). *Making content comprehensible for secondary English learners: The SIOP® model.* Boston, MA: Allyn & Bacon.

Echevarria, J., Vogt, M.E., & Short, D. (2010c). *The SIOP® model for teaching mathematics to English learners.* Boston, MA: Allyn & Bacon.

Fisher, D., & Frey, N. (2008). *Word wise & content rich: Five essential steps to teaching academic vocabulary.* Portsmouth, NH: Heinemann.

Flynt, E. S., & Brozo, W. G. (2008). Developing academic language: Got words? *The Reading Teacher, 61*(6), 500–502.

Gandara, P., Maxwell-Jolly, J., & Driscoll, A. (2005). *Listening to teachers of English language learners: A survey of California teachers' challenges, experiences, and professional development needs.* Santa Cruz, CA: The Center for the Future of Teaching and Learning.

Garcia, G., & Beltran, D. (2003). Revisioning the blueprint: Building for the academic success of English learners. In G. Garcia (Ed.), *English learners: Reaching the highest levels of English literacy.* Newark, DE: International Reading Association.

Garcia, G. E., & Godina, H. (2004). Addressing the literacy needs of adolescent English language learners. In T. Jetton & J. Dole (Eds.), *Adolescent literacy: Research and practice* (pp. 304–320). New York, NY: The Guildford Press.

Genesee, F., Lindholm-Leary, K., Saunders, W., & Christian, D. (2006). *Educating English language learners: A synthesis of research evidence.* New York, NY: Cambridge University Press.

Gersten, R., Baker, S. K., Shanahan, T., Linan-Thompson, S., Collins, P., & Scarcella, R. (2007). *Effective literacy and English language instruction for English learners in the elementary grades: A Practice Guide* (NCEE 2007-4011). Washington, DC: National Center for Education Evaluation and Regional Assistance, Institute of Education Sciences, U.S. Department of Education. Retrieved from http://ies.ed.gov/ncee.

Gibbons, P. (2003). Mediating language learning: Teacher interactions with ESL students in a content-based classroom. *TESOL Quarterly, 37*(2), 247–273.

Goldenberg, C. (2008). Teaching English language learners: What the research does—and does not—say. *The American Educator, 32*(2), 8–23.

Gottlieb, M., Katz, A., & Ernst-Slavit, G. (2009). *Paper to practice: Using the TESOL ELP standards in PreK–12 classrooms.* Alexandria, VA: Teachers of English to Speakers of Other Languages.

Graham, S., & Perin, D. (2007). *Writing next: Effective strategies to improve writing of adolescents in middle and high schools.* A report to the Carnegie Corporation of New York. Washington, DC: Alliance for Excellent Education.

Hall, D. (1979). *Ox-Cart Man.* New York: Viking Press.

Harmin, M. (1994). *Inspiring active learning: A handbook for teachers.* Alexandria, VA: Association for Supervision and Curriculum Development.

Hiebert, E. H. (2005). *Word Zones™: 5,586 most frequent words in written English.* Available at www.textproject.org.

Hiebert, E. H. (2005). *1,000 most frequent words in middle-grades and high school texts.* Available at www.textproject.org.

Hiebert, E. H., & Lubliner, S. (2008). The nature, learning, and instruction of general academic vocabulary. In S. J. Samuels & A. Farstrup (Eds.), *What research has to say about vocabulary* (pp. 106–129). Newark, DE: International Reading Association.

Kagan, S. (1994). *Cooperative learning*. San Clemente, CA: Kagan Publishing.

Kindler, A. (2002). *Survey of the states' limited English proficient students and available educational programs and services. 2000-01 summary report*. Washington, DC: National Clearinghouse for English Language Acquisition.

Kober, N., Zabala, D., Chudowsky, N., Chudowsky, V., Gayler, K., & McMurrer, J. (2006). *State high school exit exams: A challenging year*. Washington, DC: Center on Education Policy.

Krashen, S. (1985). *The input hypothesis: Issues and implications*. London: Longman.

Lee, J., Grigg, W., & Dion, P. (2007). *The nation's report card: Mathematics 2007*. (NCES 2007-494). U.S. Department of Education, Institute of Education Sciences, National Center for Education Statistics. Washington, DC: U.S. Government Printing Office.

Lee, J., Grigg, W., & Donahue, P. (2007). *The nation's report card: Reading 2007*. (NCES 2007-496). U.S. Department of Education, Institute of Education Sciences, National Center for Education Statistics. Washington, DC: U.S. Government Printing Office.

Lee, J., & Weiss, A. (2007). *The nation's report card: U.S. History 2006* (NCES 2007–474). U.S. Department of Education, National Center for Education Statistics. Washington, DC: U.S. Government Printing Office.

Lee, O. (2005). Science education with English language learners: Synthesis and research agenda. *Review of Educational Research, 75*(4), 491–530.

Lemke, J. (1990). *Talking science: Language, learning and values*. New York, NY: Ablex.

Lutkus, A., & Weiss, A. (2007). *The nation's report card: Civics 2006* (NCES 2007–476). U.S. Department of Education, National Center for Education Statistics. Washington, DC: U.S. Government Printing Office.

Marzano, R. J., & Pickering, D. J. (2005). *Building academic vocabulary for student achievement: Teacher's manual*. Alexandria, VA: Association for Supervision and Curriculum Development.

Marzano, R., Pickering, D., & Pollock, J. (2001) *Classroom instruction that works*. Alexandria, VA: Association for Supervision and Curriculum Development.

Mead, N., & Sandene, B. (2007). *The nation's report card: Economics 2006* (NCES 2007–475). U.S. Department of Education, National Center for Education Statistics. Washington, DC: U.S. Government Printing Office.

Mehan, H. (1979). *Learning lessons*. Cambridge, MA: Harvard University Press.

Meredith, K., Meredith, J., & Temple, C. (1997). The insert method. In *Reading and Writing for Critical Thinking (RWCT) workbook*. Newark, DE: International Reading Association.

Nagy, W., & Scott, J. (2000). Vocabulary processes. In M. Kamil, P. Mosenthal, P. D. Pearson, & R. Barr (Eds.), *Handbook of reading research*, Volume III (pp. 269–284). Mahwah, NJ: Erlbaum.

National Center for Education Statistics. (2002). Schools and staffing survey, 1999-2000: *Overview of the data for public, private, public charter, and Bureau of Indian Affairs elementary and secondary schools*. (NCES 2002-313). Washington, DC: U.S. Department of Education, National Center for Education Statistics.

National Institute of Child Health and Human Development (NICHD). (2000). *Report of the National Reading Panel, Teaching children to read: An evidence-based assessment of the scientific research literature on reading and its implications for reading instruction*. (NIH Publication No. 00-4769). Washington, DC: U.S. Department of Health and Human Services.

Oczkus, L. (2009). *Interactive think-aloud lessons: 25 surefire ways to engage students and improve comprehension*. New York: Scholastic, and Newark, DE: International Reading Association.

Parish, T., Merikel, A., Perez, M., Linquanti, R., Socias, M., Spain, M., Speroni, C., Esra, P., Brock, L., & Delancey, D. (2006). *Effects of the implementation of Proposition 227 on the education of English learners, K–12: Findings from a five-year evaluation*. Palo Alto, CA: American Institutes for Research.

Perryman, B., & Seidlitz, J. (2009). *Seven steps to an interactive classroom: Engaging all students in classroom conversation*. San Antonio, TX: Canter Press.

Reiss, J. (2008). *102 content strategies for English language learners*. Upper Saddle River, NJ: Pearson/Merrill Prentice Hall.

Rowe, M. B. (1996, September). Science, silence, and sanctions. *Science and Children, 34*(1), 34–37.

Saul, E. W. (2004). *Crossing borders in literacy and science instruction*. Newark, DE: International Reading Association/National Science Teachers Association.

Saunders, W., & Goldenberg, C. (In press). Research to guide English language development. In D. Dolson & L. Burnham-Massey (Eds.), *Improving education for English learners: Research-based approaches*. Sacramento, CA: California Department of Education.

Saunders, W., & Goldenberg, C. (1992). *The effects of instructional conversations on transitional students' concept development*. Revised version of paper presented at the annual meeting of the American Educational Research Association, San Francisco, CA.

Schleppegrell, M. (2004). *The language of schooling: A functional linguistics perspective.* Mahwah, NJ: Erlbaum.

Scott, J. A., Jamison-Noel, D., & Asselin, M. (2003). Vocabulary instruction throughout the day in twenty-three Canadian upper-elementary classrooms. *The Elementary School Journal, 103*, 269–286.

Seidlitz, J. (2008). *Navigating the ELPS: Using the new standards to improve instruction for English learners* (2nd ed.). San Antonio, TX: Canter Press.

Short, D. (2002). Language learning in sheltered social studies classes. *TESOL Journal, 11*(1), 18–24.

Short, D. (2009). *Sheltered instruction: Curriculum and lesson design.* Paper presented at the 31st Sanibel Leadership Conference, Sanibel, FL, June, 2009.

Short, D., Fidelman, C., & Louguit, M. (2009). *The effects of SIOP® Model instruction on the academic language development of English language learners.* Manuscript submitted for publication.

Short, D., & Fitzsimmons, S. (2007). *Double the work: Challenges and solutions to acquiring language and academic literacy for adolescent English language learners.* Report to Carnegie Corporation of New York. Washington, DC: Alliance for Excellent Education.

Short, D., & Hillyard, L. (2005). *SIOP® unit planner.* Unpublished manuscript. Washington, DC: Center for Applied Linguistics.

Short, D., Vogt, M.E., & Echevarria, J. (2011). *The SIOP® model for teaching science to English learners.* Boston: Allyn & Bacon.

Short, D., Vogt, M., & Echevarria, J. (2008). *The SIOP® model for administrators.* Boston, MA: Pearson/Allyn & Bacon.

Siegel, H. (2002). Multiculturalism, universalism, and science education: In search of common ground. *Science Education, 86*, 803–820.

Snow, C.E., Cancino, H., De Temple, J., & Schley, S. (1991). Giving formal definitions: A linguistic or metalinguistic skill? In E. Bialystok (Ed.), *Language processing and language awareness by bilingual children* (pp. 90–112). Cambridge: Cambridge University Press.

Stahl, S. A., & Nagy, W. E. (2006). *Teaching word meanings.* Mahwah, NJ: Erlbaum.

Suarez-Orozco, C., Suarez-Orozco, M. M., & Todorova, I. (2008). *Learning in a new land: Immigrant students in American society.* Cambridge, MA: Harvard University Press.

Teachers of English to Speakers of Other Languages, Inc. (2006). *PreK-12 English language proficiency standards.* Alexandria, VA: Author.

Tharp, R., & Gallimore, R. (1988). *Rousing minds to life: Teaching, learning and schooling in social context.* Cambridge, MA: Cambridge University Press.

U.S. Department of Education. (2006). *Building partnerships to help English language learners.* Fact sheet. Retrieved January 2, 2008 at http://www.ed.gov/nclb/methods/english/lepfactsheet.html.

Vogt, M.E., & Echevarria, J. (2008). *99 ideas and activities for teaching English learners with the SIOP® Model.* Boston, MA: Allyn & Bacon.

Vogt, M.E., Echevarria, J., & Short, D. (2010). *The SIOP® model for teaching English-language arts to English learners.* Boston, MA: Allyn & Bacon.

Walqui, A. (2006). Scaffolding instruction for English language learners: A conceptual framework. *The International Journal of Bilingual Education and Bilingualism, 9*(2), 159–180.

Watson, K., & Young, B. (1986). Discourse for learning in the classroom. *Language Arts, 63*(2), 126–133.

Wiggins, G., & McTighe, J. (2005). *Understanding by design* (2nd ed.). Boston: Merrill Education.

Zehler, A. M., Fleishman, H. L., Hopstock, P. J., Stephenson, T. G., Pendzik, M. L., & Sapru, S. (2003). *Descriptive study of services to LEP students and to LEP students with disabilities; Policy report: Summary of findings related to LEP and SpEd-LEP students.* Arlington, VA: Development Associates.

Zwiers, J. (2004). *Developing academic thinking skills in grades 6–12.* Newark, DE: International Reading Association.

Zwiers, J. (2008). *Building academic language: Essential practices for content classrooms.* San Francisco, CA: Jossey-Bass.

# index

Note: Page numbers followed by f refer to figures.

## A

academic language
  academic tasks and, 5
  in classroom discourse, 5–8, 12, 14–15
  common core (general), 5
  content-specific, 5
  defined, 3–4
  development opportunities, 6–7
  language-content-task framework and, 8–9, 9f
  in social studies/history, 3, 8–12
    grades K–2, 11, 171–172
    grades 3–5, 11, 173–176
    grades 6–8, 11, 177–180
    grades 9–12, 11, 181–184
    high frequency vocabulary, 9, 10f
  spectrum, 4–5, 4f
academic language instruction
  effective, 15–16
  explicit, 17
  research on, 15
academic literacy, need for, 2
academic proficiency, NAEP performance levels, 2–3, 3f
academic tasks
  general and specific, 5
  language-content-task framework for, 8–9, 9f
academic vocabulary
  elements, 16–17
  high frequency, 9, 10f
  learning, scaffolding techniques for, 17
academic writing, 7
activities, templates for, 187–219
American Educational Research Association (AERA), 169
American Psychological Association (APA), 169
analytical writing, 8
Anticipation/Reaction Guide template (Effects of the French and Indian War), 211
APA (American Psychological Association), 169
Asselin, M., 12
assessment. see self-assessment techniques
August, D., 7
Aukerman, M., 5
Autio, E., 15

## B

Bailey, A. L., 5
Baker, S. K., 4
Bartolomé, L. I., 15
Beltran, D., 7
blackline masters, for activities, 187–219
British versus Colonist Points of View activity template, 212
Brozo, W. G., 4
Buehl, D., 23

Building Background component, 30–31, 165–166, 169–170
  activities and techniques in, 185
    Concrete Personal Experiences, 31–33
    Oh Yesterday + Year!, 35–36
    Post a Connection, 34–35
    Predict Definitions, 36–37, 38f
    Vocabulary Scan, 38–40
    Whip Around, Pass Option, 76–77
  technology utilization in, 93
Butler, F., 5

## C

Can You Label the World Map? blackline master, 200
Canges, R., 169
Castillo, M., 90
Causes of the American Revolution U.S. history unit, grades 6–8, 129–131
  lesson plans, 131–140
Cazden, C., 5, 6, 17
Center for Applied Linguistics, 162, 169
Chamot, A. U., 4
Charlotte-Mecklenburg Schools, North Carolina, 85
Christian, D., 169
Chunk and Chew Review (technique), 66–68, 146, 185
civic education, word and phrase lists
  grades K–2, 171–172
  grades 3–5, 173–176
  grades 6–8, 177–180
  grades 9–12, 181–184
civics, NAEP performance levels, 2–3, 3f
classroom culture, learning opportunities and, 15
classroom discourse, 17–22
  academic language in, 5–8, 14–15
  enrichment techniques, 18–19
  turn-taking in, 18
Clewell, B. C., 169
clicker devices, 92–93
Clifton Public Schools, New Jersey, 85
Cloud, N., 7, 8, 23
Coffin, C., 9
collaboration, teachers and, 162–163
Collier, V., 169
Collins, P., 4
comments
  for enriching classroom talk, 18–19
  fortifying or justifying responses, 19
common core academic language, 5
Comparing the Past to the Present lesson plan, K–2 social studies unit, 104–106
comparison words, 17
Comprehensible Input component, 166, 170
  activities and techniques in, 185
    Listen for Information, 42–44

Move It!, 44–45
    Prop Box Improv, 40–42
  technology utilization in, 93
computer simulations, 92
Concrete Personal Experiences (technique), 31–33, 185
Connection, Making a (technique), 34–35, 185
consequences, comments considering, 19
Containing Communism After WWII global history unit, grades 9–12, 142–144
  lesson plans, 147–159
  lesson topics, 144–146
content objectives
  history units
    grades 6–8, 130f
    grades 9–12, 143, 144–145
  in lesson preparation, 28, 29f
  in SIOP® Model, 15–16
  social studies units
    grades K–2, 99
    grades 3–5, 114
content words, in SIOP® Model, 16
content-specific language, 5
  language-content-task framework and, 8–9, 9f
context, for learning new words, 17
conversational language
  academic language versus, 5
  in student-teacher interaction, 6, 19–20
  Turn and Talk example, 20–22
Conversations, Structured (technique), 53–54, 185
Cosentino de Cohen, C., 169
Coxhead, A., 9
Coxhead Academic Word List, 9
Cummins, J., 5, 169
Cut and Match Answers (activity), 47–49, 48f, 185

## D

Debate, Learning Styles (technique), 55–56, 185
Deterding, N., 169
Deussen, T., 15
Dictation, Partner Listening (technique), 62–63, 185
Differentiated Tickets Out (activity), 79–80, 146, 185
differentiation, defined, 27
Dion, P., 168
discussion, in academic language development, 17–22
Donahue, P., 168
Driscoll, A., 168
Dutro, S., 8

## E

Echevarria, J., 5, 16, 17, 18, 23, 84, 90, 94, 122, 146, 152, 162, 163, 165, 169

economics
  lesson techniques and activities,
    grade 12 application, 57–58
  NAEP performance levels, 2–3, 3f
  word and phrase lists
    grades K–2, 171–172
    grades 3–5, 173–176
    grades 6–8, 177–180
    grades 9–12, 181–184
ELA (English-language arts), teaching
    words and word parts in, 16
ELPS (English Language Proficiency
    Standards), 12, 130, 142, 144
  language objectives, 144f
ELs (English learners)
  academic language development and, 12,
    14–15
  history/social studies and, 3, 5
  and need for sheltered instruction, 168–169
  performance assessments, 168
  performance prediction, 5, 12
  reading instruction for, 7
  teacher expectations for, 15
  underachievement, 168–169
  word-level versus text-level skills
    disparity in, 7
English
  academic. see academic language
  as a second language. see ESL (English
    as a second language)
English Language Proficiency Standards
    (ELPS), 12, 130, 142, 144
  language objectives, 144f
English-language arts (ELA), teaching
    words and word parts in, 16
Ernst-Slavit, G., 12
ESL (English as a second language), 168
  word parts and, 16
ethical ramifications, comments
    considering, 19
evaluation, in student-teacher interaction, 6
Evans, E., 49
Expert/Novice (technique), 49–51, 185

**F**
factual writing, 7–8
feedback, in student-teacher interaction, 6
Fidelman, C., 162
Fisher, D., 23, 84
Fitzsimmons, S., 15
flipbook, instructions for making, 199
Flipping from the Past to Present lesson plan,
    grades K–2 social studies unit, 110–111
  flipbook instructions, 199
Flynt, E. S., 4
Francis, D., 169
Frey, N., 23, 84

**G**
Gallimore, R., 17
Gandara, P., 168
Garcia, G. E., 7
general academic language, 5
Genesee, F., 23, 169
geography
  lesson techniques and activities
    grade 6 application, 28
    grade 9 application, 63–64

maps and globes unit, grades 3–5,
    113–116
  lesson plans, 116–127
word and phrase lists
    grades K–2, 171–172
    grades 3–5, 173–176
    grades 6–8, 177–180
    grades 9–12, 181–184
Gersten, R., 4, 15
global history.
  unit-planning, grades 9–12, 142–144
  lesson plans, 147–159
  lesson topics, 144–146
Go Graphic – One Step Further Activity,
    63–64, 185
Goldenberg, C., 4, 5, 7, 15, 17, 20
Gottlieb, M., 12
government
  lesson techniques and activities
    grade 9 application, 45
    grade 11 application (sheltered), 62–63
    grade 12 application, 69–70, 74–75
  word and phrase lists
    grades K–2, 171–172
    grades 3–5, 173–176
    grades 6–8, 177–180
    grades 9–12, 181–184
Graham, S., 7
graphic organizers
  in Cut and Match Answers Activity,
    47–49, 48f
  in Go Graphic – One Step Further
    Activity, 63–64
Graves, A., 5
Grigg, W., 168
Group Response with White Board
    (technique), 65–66, 146, 185
group work, 14, 15
  discussion, 20
group-administered reviews, 92–93

**H**
Hall, D., 107
Hamayan, E., 23
Harmin, M., 76
Hiebert, E. H., 9
higher-order thinking questions,
    development of, 163
Highlighting, Key Information in Text
    (technique), 46–47, 185
Hillyard, L., 35, 88, 89
Himmel, J., 49
historical & social sciences analysis, word
    and phrase lists
    grades K–2, 171–172
    grades 3–5, 173–176
    grades 6–8, 177–180
    grades 9–12, 181–184
history
  lesson techniques and activities, 26–27.
    see also global history; U.S. history;
    world history; individual SIOP®
    components; individual techniques
    and activities
  NAEP performance levels, 2–3, 3f
  unit planning
    grades 6–8, 129–140
    grades 9–12, 142–159

word and phrase lists (grades K–2),
    171–172
How Can We Tell That This Is From the
    Past? blackline master, 192
How Do You Know It's From the Past?
    lesson plan, K–2 social studies
    unit, 107–108
  blackline master for, 192

**I**
indicators, model performance, 12
information
  Key, Highlighting in Text (technique),
    46–47, 185
  Listening for (technique), 42–44, 185
  Initiation-Response-Evaluation/Feedback
    (IRE/F) discourse pattern, 6, 18,
    20–22
Inspiration software, 92
instructional patterns, in classroom
    discourse, 18
instructional units. see SIOP® unit planning
Interaction component, 167, 170
  activities and techniques for, 185
    Cut and Match Answers, 47–49
    Expert/Novice, 49–51
    Learning Styles Debate, 55–56
    Living Diorama, 60–62
    Partner Listening Dictation, 62–63
    Structured Conversations, 53–54
    You Are There, 56–58
  features, 18
  technology utilization in, 93
interactive white boards, 91–92
IRE/F (Initiation-Response-
    Evaluation/Feedback) discourse
    pattern, 6, 18, 20–22
Is it Past or Present? (bingo game), 109
  blackline masters for, 193–198

**J**
Jamison-Noel, D., 12

**K**
Katz, A., 12
Kidspiration software, 92
Kindler, A., 168
Kober, N., 168
Krashen, S., 17

**L**
Lakin, J., 7
Language Learner software, 92
language objectives
  history units
    grades 6–8, 130f
    grades 9–12, 144f, 145
  in lesson preparation, 28, 29f, 185
  in SIOP® Model, 15–16
  social studies units
    grades K–2, 99–100
    grades 3–5, 114–115
language proficiency, national standards
    for, 12
language-content-task framework, academic
    task, 8–9, 9f
Latitude and Longitude lesson plan, grades
    3–5 social studies unit, 123–125

learning
new words, context for, 17
passive vs. group work, 12, 14
Learning Styles Debate (technique), 55–56, 185
Lee, J., 2, 168
Lee, O., 15
Leininger, E., 7
Lela Alston Elementary School, Phoenix, Arizona, 85
Lemke, J., 15
lesson. *see* SIOP® lessons
Lesson Delivery component, 167, 170
activities and techniques for, 185
Chunk and Chew Review, 66–68
Group Response with White Board, 65–66
Learning Styles Debate, 55–56
Living Diorama, 60–62
Stand Up/Sit Down, 68–70
technology utilization in, 93
Lesson Preparation component, 165, 169
activities and techniques for, 185
language and content objectives, 28, 29f
sentence starters, differentiating, 30–31
technology utilization in, 93
Linan-Thompson, S., 4
Lindholm-Leary, K., 169
listening techniques
listening for information, 42–44, 185
partner listening dictation, 62–63, 185
Liten-Tejada, R, 24, 52, 60, 94, 97, 98, 101, 103, 104, 107, 108, 110, 112, 113, 116, 118, 120, 122, 123, 126, 163
Living Diorama activity, 60–62, 185
Living in the Past and Present lesson plan, K–2 social studies unit, 108–110
bingo game, 109
blackline master for, 198
Lockwood, A. T., 15
Louguit, M., 162
Lutkus, A., 2

**M**
Map and Globes (lesson plans), grades 3–5 social studies unit
Reader's Theater, 120–122
script and scoring rubric for, 203–204
Student-Generated Writing, 122–123
blackline masters for, 205–206
Terms Review, 126–127
vocabulary/definition card templates for, 207–210
maps and globes
paragraph activity, 205
Reader's Theater activity
scoring rubric, 204
script, 203
word bank activity, 206
Marzano, R. J., 23, 39
Maxwell, L., 7
Maxwell-Jolly, J., 168
McTighe, J., 98
Mead, N., 2
Mehan, H., 6

Miller, B., 15
model performance indicators, 12
Moran, C., 8
Move It! Activity, 44–45, 185
multimedia tools, 92
My Life in the Past and Present lesson plan, K–2 social studies unit, 103–104
activity sheet, 191
Venn diagram, 105f
template, 190
My Personal Timeline lesson plan, in K–2 social studies unit
101–102, 189
poster template, 188
sentences template, 189

**N**
NAEP (National Assessment of Educational Progress), 2
Nagy, W. E., 17
National Assessment of Educational Progress (NAEP), 2
National Council on Measurement in Education (NCME), 169
National Institute of Child Health and Human Development (NICHD), 7
National Reading Panel, 7
NATO pro-con chart, 219
NCLB (No Child Left Behind) Act, 1, 168, 169
NCME (National Council on Measurement in Education), 169
news media, social sciences and, 2
NICHD (National Institute of Child Health and Human Development), 7
No Child Left Behind (NCLB) Act, 1, 168, 169
Number Wheels Activity, 73–75, 185
Numbered Heads Together With Movement Activity, 77–78, 185

**O**
observation, reporting on, 19
Oh Yesterday + Year! Activity, 35–36, 185
O'Malley, J. M., 4
open-ended questions, 18
oral discourse, in effective academic language instruction, 17–22
oral proficiency, 7
development, 12, 14
*The OxCart Man* (Hall), 107

**P**
Palmer Raids, 146, 147
Partner Listening Dictation (technique), 62–63, 185
passive learning, 12
Past and Present social studies unit, grades K–2, 98–100
lesson plans, 98–111
performance indicators, model, 12
Perin, D., 7
Perryman, B., 9, 10, 40, 41, 49
Personal Experiences, Concrete (technique), 31–33, 185
personal writing, 8
Pickering, D. J., 23, 39

Planning Points, for SIOP® lesson plans
global history unit, grades 9–12
lesson 1, 149
lesson 2, 151–152
lesson 3, 154
lesson 4, 156
lesson 5, 159
social studies unit, grades K–2
lesson 5, 110
lesson 6, 111
social studies unit, grades 3–5
lesson 2, 120
lesson 5, 125
lesson 6, 127
U. S. history unit, grades 6–8
lesson 1, 133
lesson 2, 135
lesson 3, 137
lesson 4, 140
points of view, comments appreciating, 19
Pollock, J., 39
polysemous words, 2
Post a Connection (technique), 34–35, 185
PowerPoint presentations, 91
Powers, K., 169
Practice & Application component, 167, 170
activities and techniques for, 185
Cut and Match Answers, 47–49
Go Graphic – One Step Further, 63–64
Learning Styles Debate, 55–56
Living Diorama, 60–62
Partner Listening Dictation, 62–63
Reader's Theater, 58–60
Structured Conversations, 53–54
technology utilization in, 93
Predict Definitions (technique), 36–37, 185
problem, reporting on, 19
process/function words, in SIOP® Model, 16
professional learning community (PLC), 25, 26
Prop Box Improv Activity, 40–42, 185

**Q**
questions/questioning
lesson development, 83–84
open-ended, 18
in student-teacher interaction, 6
Quickdraw Technique, example, 21, 22

**R**
Reader's Theater activity, 58–59, 60f, 185
Maps and Globes
scoring rubric, 204
script, 203
reading, components of, 7
reading comprehension, ELs and, 7
Reiss, J., 23
responses
comments fortifying or justifying, 19
Group, with White Board (technique), 65–66, 146, 185
in student-teacher interaction, 6
responsibility, gradual release of, 84–85, 84f
Review & Assessment component, 167, 170
activities and techniques for, 185
Differentiated Tickets Out, 79–80
Living Diorama, 60–62

Number Wheels, 73–75
Numbered Heads Together, 77–78
Oral Number 1–3 for Self-Assessment, 71–72
Self-Assessment Rubrics, 72–73, 72f, 102
Stand Up/Sit Down, 68–70
Whip Around, Pass Option, 76–77
technology utilization in, 93
Richards, C., 162, 169
rote memorization, 15
rubrics
    Letter to the Editor, 135f
    Letter to the President, 159f
    maps and globes Reader's Theater activity, 204
    self-assessment techniques, 72–73, 72f, 185
        example, 102

**S**

Sandene, B., 2
Saunders, W., 17, 20, 169
scaffolding techniques, 17
Scarcella, R., 4
Schleppegrell, M., 7
Scott, J., 17
Scott, J. A., 12
Seidlitz, J., 9, 10, 12, 14, 24, 40, 41, 52, 95, 128, 129, 131, 133, 135, 138, 141, 142, 147, 150, 152, 154, 157, 159, 163
self-assessment techniques
    numerical, 71–72
    rubrics, 72–73, 72f, 185
        example, 102
self-awareness, teacher, 163
sentence starters, differentiating, 30–31, 185
sentence stems
    high frequency academic vocabulary, 9, 10f
    Texas state social studies standards and tests, 13–14
SFL (systemic functional linguistics), 7–8
Shanahan, T., 4, 7
sheltered instruction
    EL need, 168–169
    observation protocol. see SIOP® entries
Short, D., 9, 15, 24, 52, 84, 86, 88, 89, 90, 94, 97, 112, 128, 141, 162, 163, 169
Short, D. J., 9, 16, 165, 169
signal words, 17
Silver, J., 18
SIOP® (Sheltered Instruction Observation Protocol), 165–170
    activities and techniques mapped to, 185
SIOP® lesson plans/planning, 87, 90–91, 91f
    formats, 93–95
        templates, 94f, 95f
    history units
        grades 6–8, 131–140
        grades 9–12, 147–159
    over time, 91, 92f
    social studies units
        grades K–2, 101–111
        grades 3–5, 116–127
    technology in, 91–93

SIOP® lessons
    planning questions, 83–84. see also SIOP® lesson plans/planning
    techniques and activities used in, 26–27. see also individual SIOP® components; individual techniques and activities
        history. see global history, U.S. history; world history
        social studies. see also specific content areas
        grade K application, 76–77
        grade 1 application, 43–44, 71–72
        grade 2 application, 34–35, 54
        grade 3 application, 48–49, 73
        grade 4 application, 78
        grade 5 application, 46–47
        grade 6 application, 59
SIOP® Model
    building background, 165–166, 169–170
    comprehensible input, 166, 170
    effective academic language teaching in, 15–22
        oral discourse, 17–22
        vocabulary, 16–17
    ELs and, 168–169
    goals, 162
    interaction in, 167, 170
    learning strategies in, 166–167, 170
    lesson delivery in, 167, 170
    lesson preparation in, 166, 169
    practice & application in, 167, 170
    purpose, 15
    review & assessment in, 167, 170
    strategies, 166
SIOP® Protocol, 165–170
    activities and techniques mapped to, 185
SIOP® unit planning
    history
        grades 6–8, 129–140
        grades 9–12, 142–159
    planner templates
        unit planner 1, 88f–89f
        unit planner 2, 87, 90f
    planning questions, 83–84
    social studies
        grades K–2, 98–100
        grades 3–5, 113–127
    steps in, 85–87, 86f
    student considerations in, 84–85, 84f
small-group discussion, 20
Snow, C. E., 5
social studies. see also specific content areas
    lesson techniques and activities, 26–27. see also individual SIOP® components; individual techniques and activities
        grade K application, 76–77
        grade 1 application, 43–44, 71–72
        grade 2 application, 34–35, 54
        grade 3 application, 48–49, 73
        grade 4 application, 78
        grade 5 application, 46–47
        grade 6 application, 59

NAEP performance levels, 2–3, 3f
news media and, 2
unit planning in, grades K–2, 98–111
    lesson plans, 101–111
Stahl, S. A., 17
Stand Up/Sit Down Activity, 68–70, 185
Stewart, V., 15
Strategies component, 166–167, 170
    activities and techniques in, 185
        Chunk and Chew Review, 66–68
        Cut and Match Answers, 47–49
        Expert/Novice, 49–51
        Highlight Key Information in Text, 46–47
    technology utilization in, 93
Structured Conversations (technique), 53–54, 185
student-teacher interaction, conversational language in, 6, 19–20
Suarez-Orosco, C., 12
Suarez-Orosco, M. M., 12
systemic functional linguistics (SFL), 7–8

**T**

TAKS (Texas Assessment of Knowledge and Skills), 129
teachers
    collaboration between, 162–163
    as content experts, 162
    effective, techniques used by, 18–19
    expectations for ELs, 15
    modeling writing, 7
    professional development deficits, 168
    self-awareness, 163
    in SIOP® unit design, 85
Teachers of English to Speakers of Other Languages, Inc. (TESOL), 12
technology, in SIOP® lesson planning, 91–93
    component examples, 93
    low-tech versus high-tech, 93
TEKS (Texas Essential Knowledge and Skills)
    global history unit, grades 9–12, 142–143
    U.S. history unit, grades 6–8, 129–130
templates, for activities, 187–219
TESOL (Teachers of English to Speakers of Other Languages, Inc.), 12
Texas Assessment of Knowledge and Skills (TAKS), 129
Texas Essential Knowledge and Skills (TEKS)
    global history unit, grades 9–12, 142–143
    U.S. history unit, grades 6–8, 129–130
Tharp, R., 17
Think-Alouds, for SIOP® lesson plans
    global history unit, grades 9–12
        lesson 1, 149
        lesson 3, 154
        lesson 4, 156
        lesson 5, 159
    social studies, grades K–2
        lesson 1, 101
        lesson 2, 102
        lesson 3, 104
        lesson 4, 106
        lesson 5, 108
        lesson 6, 110

Think-Alouds *(continued)*
  social studies, grades 3–5
    lesson 1, 116
    lesson 2, 118
    lesson 3, 120
    lesson 4, 121
    lesson 5, 123
    lesson 6, 126
  U.S. history, grades 6–8
    lesson 1, 133
    lesson 3, 137–138
    lesson 4, 140
thinking, comments promoting, 19
Tickets Out, Differentiated (activity), 79–80, 146, 185
Todorova, I., 12
tree map example, 108f
Truman Doctrine Speech
  adapted text, 213
  argumentation chart, 218
  original text, 214–217
Turn and Talk (technique), 22
  example, 20–22
turn-taking, in classroom discourse, 18

**U**
unit planning. *see* SIOP® unit planning
U.S. Department of Education, 168
U.S. history
  lesson techniques and activities
    grade K application, 61–62
    grade 4 application, 37
    grade 5 application, 32–33
    grade 7 application, 35–36, 41–42
    grade 8 applications, 31, 56
    grade 11 application, 79–80
  unit planning, grades 6–8, 129–131, 129–140
    lesson plans, 132–140
  word and phrase lists
    grades 3–5, 173–176
    grades 6–8, 177–180
    grades 9-12, 181–184

**V**
Venn diagram, in My Life in the Past and Present lesson plan, 105f
  template, 190

video recordings, 93
Virginia Social Studies Standards of Learning, 98, 113
vocabulary
  academic literacy and, 2
  high frequency, sentence stems and, 9, 10f
  word and definition card templates, 207–210
vocabulary development, social studies/history word and phrase lists
  grades K–2, 171–172
  grades 3–5, 173–176
  grades 6–8, 177–180
  grades 9–12, 181–184
Vocabulary Scan (technique), 38–40
Vogt, M. E., 16, 23, 84, 90, 94, 122, 146, 152, 162, 163, 165

**W**
Walqui, A., 12
*Washington Post, The,* 2
Watson, K., 6
Weiss, A., 2
What's My Hemisphere? blackline masters
  multiple choice, 202
  short answer, 201
What's My Hemisphere? lesson plan, grades 3–5 social studies unit, 118–120
  activity templates, 201–202
What's the Location? lesson plan, grades 3–5 social studies unit, 116–118
  activity template, 200
Where in the World Are You? social studies unit, grades 3–5, 113–116
  lesson plans, 116–127
Whip Around, Pass Option Activity, 76–77, 185
white board(s)
  Group Response with (technique), 65–66, 146, 185
  interactive, 91–92
WIDA (World-class Instructional Design and Assessment), 12, 98, 113
Wiggins, G., 98
word displays, 17
word parts, in SIOP® Model, 16
words. *see also* vocabulary
  comparison, 17
  content, 16

polysemous, 2
Predict Definitions (technique), 36–37, 185
Predicting Definitions (technique), 38f
process/function, 16
signal, 17
in SIOP® Model, 16
world history
  lesson techniques and activities
    grade 7 application, 67–68
    grade 10 application, 39–40, 50–51
    grade 11 application, 66
  unit planning, grades 9–12, 142–144
    lesson plans, 147–159
    lesson topics, 144–146
  word and phrase lists
    grades 3–5, 173–176
    grades 6–8, 177–180
    grades 9–12, 181–184
World-class Instructional Design and Assessment (WIDA), 12, 98, 113
writing
  academic, 7
  analytical, 8
  EL experiences, 7–8
  factual, 7–8
  personal, 8
  self-assessment rubrics, 72–73, 72f, 102, 185

**Y**
You Are There Activity, 56–58, 185
Young, B., 6

**Z**
Zehler, A. M., 168
Zwiers, J., 4, 17, 18, 20, 23

# photo credits

p. 1, iStockPhoto; p. 24, Mary Kate Denny/PhotoEdit; pp. 52, 82, 161, Michael Newman/PhotoEdit; p. 97, Jeff Greenberg/PhotoEdit; p. 112, Tanya Constantine/Getty RF; p. 128, Will Hart/PhotoEdit; p. 141, Will Hart/PhotoEdit